T0304887

Supporting Autistic People with Eating Disorders

Supporting Autistic People with – Eating Disorders –

A GUIDE TO ADAPTING TREATMENT AND SUPPORTING RECOVERY

Edited by Kate Tchanturia

Jessica Kingsley Publishers
London and Philadelphia

First published in Great Britain in 2021 by Jessica Kingsley Publishers
An Hachette Company

6

Copyright © Jessica Kingsley Publishers 2021

A CIP catalogue record for this title is available from the
British Library and the Library of Congress

ISBN 978 1 78775 445 4
eISBN 978 1 78775 446 1

Printed and bound by CPI Group (UK) Ltd, Croydon, CR0 4YY

Jessica Kingsley Publishers' policy is to use papers that are natural,
renewable and recyclable products and made from wood grown in
sustainable forests. The logging and manufacturing processes are expected
to conform to the environmental regulations of the country of origin.

Jessica Kingsley Publishers
Carmelite House
50 Victoria Embankment
London EC4Y 0DZ

www.jkp.com

Contents

Acknowledgements 9

Editor's Note 10

Section 1: Research into Practice   13

1. Translating Research Evidence and Experience to
   Clinical Practice: PEACE Pathway. 15
   Kate Tchanturia

2. Social Anxiety 26
   Jess Kerr-Gaffney and Kate Tchanturia

Section 2: Lived Experience: Stigma, Credit or a Lack of Understanding?   35

3. Anorexia and AutismLessons Learned on the
   Road to Recovery 37
   Pooky Knightsmith

4. A Picture Is Worth a Thousand Words 42
   A. Wadden

Section 3: Clinical Cases: Experience and Learning of a Clinical Team   47

5. Using the Autism Lens: Milly's Story: A Multidisciplinary
   Health Professional Team Approach in Supporting an
   Autistic Female with Anorexia Nervosa. 49
   *Yasemin Dandil, Emma Kinnaird, Jason Maldonado-Page, Danilen
   Nursigadoo, Jessica Gomularz, Claire Baillie and Kate Tchanturia*

6. Adam's Story: Supporting a Male with Anorexia Nervosa
    and Elevated Autistic Features   76
    Katherine Smith, Yasemin Dandil, Claire Baillie,
    Hubertus Himmerich and Kate Tchanturia

Section 4: Supporting the Supporters: Learning How to Understand and Better Support our Loved Ones   87

7. Making the 'Mental Transition' from Clinician to Carer . .
    The Importance of Expressed Emotion   89
    Madeleine Oakley

8. Adapting Carers' Interventions for Families Where Eating
    Disorders and Autism Spectrum Conditions Co-Exist   97
    Amy Harrison

9. Catching 'Sparkling Moments' within Family and Systemic
    Psychotherapy Sessions 108
    Jason Maldonado-Page

Section 5: Food as a Remedy: Advice and Learning from a Dietician   121

10. Understanding the Challenges with Eating 123
    Kate Williams

11. Supporting Recovery of Eating and Nutrition 133
    Kate Williams

Section 6: Sensory Sensitivities: Assessing, Understanding and Adapting   157

12. Assessing Sensory Sensitivities Co-Occurring in Autism
    and Eating Disorders 159
    Emma Kinnaird, Isis McLachlan,
    Katherine Smith and Kate Tchanturia

13. Occupational Therapy Benefits for an Autistic Patient with
    Bulimia Nervosa 171
    Jake Copp-Thomas

Section 7: Skilling Up the Clinical Team and Implementation 179

14. What Can Clinicians Do Differently in Sessions? 181
    Kate Tchanturia, Katherine Smith and Yasemin Dandil

15. Therapy with People on the Autistic Spectrum with Eating
    Disorders: Reflections of an Experienced Therapist 191
    Elaine Smith

16. The Importance of Assessment: Autism Evaluation in
    Healthcare Settings 199
    James Adamson, Jess Kerr-Gaffney,
    Katherine Smith and Kate Tchanturia

17. Can You See Me? How to Build a Business Case in Your
    Team – Clinical Lead Perspective 207
    Danielle Glennon

18. Adopting, Adapting and Improving: Taking a Quality
    Improvement Approach to Cross the Chasm from
    Evidence to Implementation 213
    Anna Burhouse

19. Following the PEACE Pathway in Your Organization:
    Teamwork Makes Dream Work 231
    Kate Tchanturia and Katherine Smith

20. Example of Becoming a More ASD Friendly Inpatient
    Ward on the PEACE Pathway 245
    Pulled together by Claire Baillie

    List of Contributors (in order of appearance in the book) . . . 258

    Subject Index 266

    Author Index 271

Acknowledgements

First of all, I would like to take this opportunity to thank all the co-authors and collaborators who made this book project possible. You all have been amazing!

Many of our team members have not written chapters but worked hard to implement the PEACE project in clinical reality. I do apologize if I missed anyone, but without you:

> Caroline Norton, Caroline Pimblett, Zoe Vazquez-Sanchez, Omara Naseem, Yael Brown, Rafiu Agbalaya, Olayemi Adeniran, Madeleine Love, Catherine Perry, Catherine Clark, Cindy Toloza, Li Zhuo, Emma Connery, Oyenike Oyeleye, Stacey Parker, Anna Carr, Nikolette Thurbin, Amanda Davey,

we could not possibly do it!

I would like to thank the **Maudsley Charity** for their support. Maudsley Charity is an independent NHS mental health charity which works in partnership with patients and families, clinical care teams and researchers at South London and Maudsley NHS Foundation Trust, the Institute of Psychiatry, Psychology and Neuroscience, King's College London, and community organizations, with a common goal of improving mental health, to support innovation, research and service improvement.

Support from the **Health Foundation**, an independent charity committed to bring better healthcare for people in the UK (Ref:AIMS ID): 1115447, was absolutely vital to get us together to make innovation and improvement in the new clinical pathway for ASD and eating disorders which hopefully will evolve in the future.

Editor's Note

Dear Reader,

This book is dedicated to our patients who have eating disorders and autism spectrum conditions, their families and loved ones, the clinical teams and healthcare professionals who are involved in their support and care.

This book is a result of a lot of hard work from many people and each chapter has its own unique focus on different aspects, problems and strengths related to eating disorders and autism spectrum conditions. You will find a list of the book authors and contributors at the end of the book. I was privileged to work with the great team of patients, families, clinicians, academics, and my postgraduate students, allowing us to attempt to make a difference for people who have the co-morbid conditions described in the book.

We have been learning together with our patients and their families how best to support autistic people with eating disorders on the long journey to recovery.

People with lived experience from the Maudsley Eating Disorder National Service clinical team and my research group have put together what we have learned so far for you, dear reader, and we very much hope you will become a member of our community which tries to make a difference for patients and families trying to overcome difficulties with both conditions.

The purpose of our service is to treat eating disorders, but within that what we are aiming to do is to support people both with and without neurodevelopmental conditions as well as we can to help them to recover from the eating disorder.

We are grateful to the Health Foundation and the Maudsley Charity for the generous funding.

This book is the result of the PEACE Pathway which stands for Pathway for Eating disorders and Autism developed from Clinical Experience. This acronym was chosen by our patients and we very much hope that this book will inspire clinical teams and parents to support people with both conditions.

I would like to say a big thank you to all the contributors, funders, families, publisher and illustrators who made this work possible.

Professor Kate Tchanturia

Research into Practice

In the opening section, we discuss translational research and we also discuss social anxiety in autistic people and those with eating disorders.

Chapter 1

Translating Research Evidence and Experience to Clinical Practice

PEACE PATHWAY

Kate Tchanturia

This book is a collaborative effort by healthcare professionals from the South London and Maudsley NHS Foundation Trust, my research team and people with lived experience of having both an eating disorder and autism spectrum condition (ASC – we will use this term because majority of the people I spoke to prefer condition to disorder). We tried our best to include multiple perspectives and involve all key stakeholders to support patients, families and professionals working with these co-existing conditions to make treatment and the recovery process from eating disorders easier. Twenty-one authors worked hard to present in these book chapters their perspectives on how we can improve our understanding and care for people who are on the autistic spectrum and have an eating disorder.

Eating disorders are serious mental illnesses and ASC is a developmental condition with strengths and some significant differences from neurotypical development. For this book, we have gathered information from multiple sources to consider possible ways we can make it easier for neurotypical healthcare workers and families to be more aware of the needs of patients with eating disorders who also have diagnosed or undiagnosed ASC.

It is recognized that ASC is hard to diagnose in women (Gould

& Ashton-Smith, 2011) and, as our understanding and awareness develops, we have seen an increasingly large proportion of females in our eating disorder services who either have a diagnosis of ASC or are potentially on the autism spectrum.

From their early years, autistic girls typically present differently from boys. For example, some might desire to fit in with their peer group and so they start mimicking (copying) their peers' behaviour: the way they interact socially; the way they dress; the way they speak and express themselves. Experts in autism started to notice gender differences and challenges with early diagnosis for women with ASC approximately a couple of decades ago (Lai & Baron-Cohen, 2015).

Figure 1.1. *Camouflaging or mimicking*

Autism is a neurodevelopmental condition, meaning that autistic people experience their environment differently to their neurotypical peers, for example they may be sensitive to specific sensations, and have different ways of processing emotions. Autistic people have lots of strengths and can be very talented in different areas, for example science, art and engineering.

The first take-home message we have identified from our work is that an ASC diagnosis is helpful. If we recognize and 'See it' we can 'Say it' (make patients and families and communities aware of the condition) and 'Sort it' (in other words make adjustments to environment and treatment strategies) to support people with both conditions.

Anorexia nervosa (AN) is a severe eating disorder that tends to affect more girls than boys; in most cases it starts during adolescence.

It has been suggested that that males with AN are often not treated in a timely manner as they tend not to present at the early stages of symptom development (Raisanen & Hunt, 2014). This may be because people are less likely to recognize AN in males, or because of the perceived stigma of it being considered a condition that affects females.

Autism spectrum condition on the other hand is a life-long developmental condition characterized by difficulties with social interaction and restricted, repetitive behaviours and interests. In spite of these demographic differences, these two conditions have a lot in common: similar cognitive/thinking styles, including difficulties with thinking flexibly and bigger-picture thinking; people with both conditions typically have problems with social interaction and emotional processing and while interest in trains, maths and computers spring to mind when most people think of autism, girls with the disorder may have more gender-stereotyped hobbies such as fashion, modelling, make-up, toys or celebrities, or even mimicking other people and try to 'fit in'.

From our extensive research we know that ASC in people with anorexia nervosa and binge eating disorder[1] is particularly common. At the present time, most studies are focusing on the presence of ASC in people with anorexia nervosa. Many examples in this book describe this co-morbidity, but we have also included some stories, case studies and examples about other eating disorder diagnoses.

CASE EXAMPLE

One of our 25-year-old patients with anorexia nervosa told us during her ASC clinical interview that she had two siblings diagnosed with ASC. From her early years she had tried to fit in and tried to learn how girls in her class talked to each other; she was trying to do what they did. She watched make-up tutorials on the internet and mastered tips on how to appear fashionable. When we discussed a possible diagnosis of ASC with her, she was not surprised and said that it might help her to read more and learn how highly functioning individuals with ASC can improve their quality of life and how they deal with their eating disorders.

---

1   Binge eating disorder is characterized by frequent episodes of excessive eating, typically all at once until feeling uncomfortably full (bingeing).

When we interviewed this patient five years ago, we struggled to find relevant literature or resources for her. In terms of developments in treatment not much has changed for people with ASC and eating disorders and we very much hope the work presented in this book will make a difference for people who have similar problems.

Eating difficulties are known to be more common in autistic children than in their typically developing peers, but what is less clear is whether girls with elevated levels of autistic features are more likely to develop eating disorders. We know that when asked, women with anorexia nervosa have more autistic symptoms than their neurotypical counterparts. But is this due to underlying traits or the physical and psychological effects of starvation and a severe eating disorder? It is an important question and we need more research to observe people long term to know the answer.

Starvation or compromised nutrition, even in people without eating disorders, leads to social withdrawal and obsessive behaviour, characteristics commonly associated with autism spectrum conditions. The Minnesota study, conducted in the mid-20th century (during the Second World War), restricted the diet of healthy males for six months, resulting in clear psychological consequences of starvation, amongst which was social withdrawal. These men, who had a very limited diet for several months, gradually became less interested in relationships and social activities and lost sexual interest. There were other significant psychological changes in this group of men, but the social changes were very clear to participants themselves, their families and everyone who was involved in the experiment.

Unpicking the complex relationship between eating disorders and autism spectrum conditions is therefore extremely difficult. Did the girl who was shy at school and wanted to be accepted really have autism or was she socially anxious and lacking confidence? When she became more rigid and withdrawn after developing anorexia nervosa, was this reflecting an underlying developmental disorder or was it a result of compromised nutrition and the all-consuming thought processes that accompany anorexia?

We already know from our clinical audit (in South London and Maudsley NHS Foundation Trust Specialist National Eating Disorder Service) evaluation and PhD work conducted in my group (Westwood PhD thesis 2018 King's College London) that in patients with anorexia nervosa ASC symptoms are overrepresented. The proportion of elevated ASC features in neurotypical women in the community is approximately 2 per cent in comparison with patients' data in our clinical service, which is 35 per cent. When we used a self-report measure of autism symptoms developed by Professor Simon Baron Cohen and his group (www.autismresearchcentre.com/arc_tests) we found that in the inpatient treatment programme 35 per cent of adult women with anorexia nervosa reported very high scores on Autism Quotient (AQ-10); in the outpatient setting where patients with less severe psychopathology are treated 20 per cent report heightened ASC symptoms compared with community, age and socio-demographic matched non-eating disorder control group women.

What we can learn from our data is that patients who had both ASC and AN have higher levels of depression, anxiety and more difficulties with work and social adjustment (measured with the Hospital Anxiety and Depression Scale and the Work and Social Assessment Scale). More research is needed in other eating disorder diagnoses looking at the ASC co-morbidity.

In order to improve our understanding and shape better support for people who have both ASC and anorexia nervosa, we have developed a collaboration between expert academics and clinicians working with eating disorders and ASC including clinical psychologists, dieticians, occupational therapists, family therapists and nurses. We have invited people with lived experience of both conditions and carers to take part in this project, to benefit from hearing their accounts and experiences.

What we do know at this stage is that the cognitive profile that underpins both autism and anorexia nervosa is present in children with eating disorders before the long-term effects of starvation take hold. We also know that women with both anorexia nervosa and elevated levels of autistic features report having difficulties with friendships during childhood. These observations indicate that certain features of autism spectrum are present in girls who go on to develop anorexia nervosa, but can we conclude from this that these individuals have underlying autism?

Exploring the link between ASC and eating disorders is not about labelling people with an additional diagnosis, it is about identifying the people who have a developmental condition. It is about recognizing that not everyone with an eating disorder fits the fear-of-being-fat, perfection-driven stereotyped view of anorexia nervosa. It is about tailoring interventions to fit the needs of every individual with an eating disorder, whatever these may be.

We know that one of the best ways to find out how we can improve care for patients is to ask patients themselves what they think about existing treatments. For this reason, we have done qualitative interviews with people who had both ASC and AN, and published this work in a peer-reviewed scientific journal (see Kinnaird *et al.*, 2019).

From the patient's perspective, it is obvious that they want clarity sooner rather than later on their condition as this helps them to understand and plan their recovery journey. They also need calibration and adjustment on communication, something which we will discuss later (see Chapter 14) along with suggestions for creating a friendly environment. They also want more understanding of their difficulties and diet requirements and more time to complete treatment.

In the current clinical guidelines (see NICE, 2017) short inpatient admissions (4–8 weeks) are recommended for nutritionally compromised, low body mass index (BMI) patients. This does not take into account co-morbidity and our existing data suggests that patients with ASC and AN need a longer admission. Our qualitative interview study also clearly showed this is needed (Tchanturia *et al.*, 2020).

We also assessed experienced clinicians working in the eating disorder national specialist services (Kinnaird, Norton and Tchanturia, 2017). The aim of our qualitative assessment of clinicians' views was to understand how clinicians approach treating co-morbid eating disorders and ASC, and how they adapt their typical therapeutic techniques for these patients. This paper focused on the following questions:

- How do clinicians react if their patient presents with co-morbid ASC or ASC features?

- What specific issues do clinicians face when treating co-morbid ASC and AN?

- What treatment techniques or approaches are effective in treating co-morbid ASC and AN?

From careful analysis and reflection on the study's results we concluded that:

At present, treatment modifications appear to be the result of individual therapist experience and knowledge, rather than representing a standardized method. A more standardized approach could incorporate the suggestions for treatment recommended by clinicians in this study, thus providing support to clinicians who lack experience in treating this challenging patient group. This approach could take the form of specific guidelines, treatment pathways, or staff training.

After exploring the needs of patients and clinicians, we also approached parents who have loved ones with both conditions and found that many overlapping issues and themes emerged between patients', clinicians' and carers' interviews.

Table 1.1. Overlap with patients', clinicians' and carers' interviews

Patients	Clinicians	Carers
AN & autism interlinked	AN & autism interlinked	AN & autism interlinked
Sensory difficulties	Sensory difficulties	Sensory difficulties
Not enough time/clinician rapport	Takes longer to build rapport	Takes longer to build rapport
Flexible & individualized treatment	Adaptations & specific modifications	Flexible & individualized approach
Difficulty getting diagnosis	No clear pathways for assessment	Difficulty getting diagnosis
Clinician education	Clinician education	Clinician education

Parents often commented that they were frustrated with treatment in specialist eating disorder services as they were completely ignoring the whole person. One of the mothers told us:

I said she is such a textbook scenario of a female with autism and he [the healthcare professional] looks at me, just when the two of us were in the room together. He looks at me and he says, 'No, not really, the fact that she was diagnosed at 16 makes her very unusual' and I said, 'No, that is actually not true'. I said, 'The majority of females are either misdiagnosed or not diagnosed, sometimes until their 20s, 30s or 40s' and he said, 'No, most people that have autism are just boys'. And so again you get to a point where as a care-giver, and this is truly where we are at this point, we have given up. In my mind there are no systems, there are no programmes, there is no structured help for my daughter and the only way that I think that my daughter can succeed and succeeding to me really means living because, again, I am fully aware that at some point there is a good chance that her body will just give out.

Figure 1.2. *Rigid thinking and behaviours, a preference for order exactness is common feature we see in girls with ASC as well as boys*

The voice of this frustrated mother represents the voice of many families and loved ones of those with the co-morbidity. I receive emails and telephone calls every week from people in similar situations asking for help. We analysed the themes from the carers' interviews and mapped them to think about the gaps in the support. We are aiming to develop a network for carers; Madeleine Oakley, who is our carer collaborator and author of Chapter 7, will lead this work.

Building on what we learned from patients, experienced clinicians and extensive research evidence from our group and other academic work and with support from The Health Foundation, we have decided to share what we know already and offer some practical recommendations to improve support for people, particularly women, with both diagnoses.

In our conversation with people who have lived experience of eating disorders and ASC we learned that many of them prefer to use the term ASC – autism spectrum condition. In this book we will use ASD and ASC interchangeably with the hope that we have respected both professional diagnostic guidelines and the wishes of our patients. As well as this, we found a preference for identity-first language, as opposed to person-first language, meaning that throughout the book we use 'autistic person' rather than 'person with autism'. Another term I want to clarify: we often refer to people with lived experience as patients (not service users or clients). This is what the patients wanted and we would like to respect their wishes. We have done several focus groups with our patients and we are confident in our choice of terminology.

Treatment

There is no treatment for ASC. It is a neurodevelopmental condition, which means individuals with ASC are different from people with neurotypical development.

Communication and social skills can be problematic even for autistic people with high IQ and the ability to camouflage. Autistic females are prone to 'camouflaging' their social difficulties (Hull, Petrides & Mandy, 2020). We believe therefore that understanding their condition and receiving coaching in social skills might be beneficial for people with ASC who have the desire to fit in and interact with family members, colleagues and other people more effectively.

Regarding eating disorders, the NICE guideline (2017) recommends various treatments for adults with eating disorders such as cognitive behavioural therapy for eating disorders (CBT-ED), the Maudsley Anorexia Treatment for Adults (MANTRA) and specialist supportive clinical management (SSCM), but without considering ASC co-morbidity.

We think that adaptations in treatment environment and communication *can* make a difference for patients with the co-morbidity.

Even late diagnosis of ASC might make a patient who has both conditions less confused and help to focus them, their clinical team and their family on their recovery journey in the most helpful and adaptive way.

Recommendations

For the past couple of years, we have tried to translate our research work into a clinical care pathway specifically for ASC and eating disorders. In addition to some recommendations below, we have provided a detailed checklist, resource packs, references and useful websites to help clinicians and families to support individuals with ASC and eating disorders on our website (www.peacepathway.org).

From our existing knowledge from working with individuals with ASC, we think that the best implementations for improvement might look like this:

- Screening patients to be aware of autism spectrum characteristics.

- Adapting and making the environment friendly for autistic people (we are confident that such changes are also appreciated by the neurotypical community).

- Giving clear information about treatment.

- Giving a choice of alternative menus with consideration of sensory issues.

- Allowing people on the spectrum more time to engage with the treatment team.

- Improving communication, using what we have learned from our observations and needs assessments from patients, carers and healthcare teams.

- Adapting and adjusting adjunct and mainstream psychological therapies in both individual and group format.

In this book you will find more detailed descriptions of the support materials created by our clinical team on how to support people with ASC and eating disorders with sensory sensitivities, nutritional rehabilitation, and psychological treatment in individual and group formats.

References

Gould, J. & Ashton-Smith, J. (2011) 'Missed diagnosis or misdiagnosis? Girls and women on the autism spectrum.' *Good Autism Practice (GAP)*, *12*(1), 34–41.

Hull, L., Petrides, K.V. & Mandy, W. (2020) 'The female autism phenotype and camouflaging: A narrative review.' *Review Journal of Autism and Developmental Disorders*, https://doi.org/10.1007/s40489-020-00197-9.

Kinnaird, E., Norton, C., Stewart, C. & Tchanturia, K. (2019) 'Same behaviours, different reasons: What do patients with co-occurring anorexia and autism want from treatment?' *International Review of Psychiatry*, *31*(4), 308–317.

Kinnaird, E., Norton, C. & Tchanturia, K. (2017) 'Clinicians' views on working with anorexia nervosa and autism spectrum disorder comorbidity: A qualitative study.' *BMC Psychiatry*, *17*, 292.

Lai, M.-C. & Baron-Cohen, S. (2015) 'Identifying the lost generation of adults with autism spectrum conditions.' *The Lancet. Psychiatry*, *2*(11), 1013–1027.

National Institute for Health and Care Excellence (2017) *Eating disorders: Recognition and treatment* (NG69). Retrieved from www.nice.org.uk/guidance/ng69 on 04/07/20.

Raisanen, U. & Hunt, K. (2014) 'The role of gendered constructions of eating disorders in delayed help-seeking in men: A qualitative interview study.' *BMJ Open*, *4*(4), e004342.

Tchanturia, K., Dandil, Y., Li, Z., Smith, K., Leslie, M. & Byford, S. (2020) 'A novel approach for autism spectrum condition patients with eating disorders: Analysis of treatment cost-savings.' *European Eating Disorders Review*, doi: 10.1002/erv.2760.

Chapter 2

Social Anxiety

—— *Jess Kerr-Gaffney and Kate Tchanturia* ——

Social anxiety disorder (SAD; also known as social phobia) is characterized by marked fear or anxiety caused by social situations, resulting in significant distress or impairment in functioning (APA, 2013). Individuals with SAD fear that they will show their anxiety symptoms (e.g. blushing, trembling), or act in a way that will be negatively evaluated by others. Although everyone feels anxiety around social situations on occasion, feared social situations almost always provoke some degree of fear or anxiety in those with SAD. Between 3 and 12 per cent of individuals in the general population are estimated to experience SAD at some point in their lives (Grant *et al.*, 2005; Kessler *et al.*, 2005). Many different environmental, genetic and psychological factors are implicated in the development of SAD. These include behavioural inhibition (a shy and inhibited temperamental style), fear of negative evaluation, and aversive social experiences such as childhood maltreatment and bullying or rejection from peers (Spence & Rapee, 2016). In this chapter we review research findings relating to social anxiety in those with eating disorders, and provide resources and tips from research in autism spectrum disorder that may help people with these difficulties. We hope that overcoming social anxiety will aid in building relationships and social networks, a key part of recovery from an eating disorder.

Social anxiety in eating disorders

Social anxiety disorder (SAD) is one of the most common co-morbid anxiety disorders in those with eating disorders, with prevalence rates ranging from 16 to 88.2 per cent in anorexia nervosa (AN) and 17–67.8

per cent in bulimia nervosa (BN) (Godart *et al.*, 2000; Swinbourne *et al.*, 2012;) and their age of onset relative to that of eating disorders (ED). In addition, a significant proportion of individuals with eating disorders show clinically significant social anxiety symptomatology on self-report questionnaires but do not necessarily meet full criteria for the disorder (Kerr-Gaffney, Harrison & Tchanturia, 2018). There is some evidence to suggest that social anxiety is associated with a more severe eating disorder presentation. For example, high social anxiety is associated with older age and a longer duration of illness, as well as more admissions to hospital (Goddard & Treasure, 2013; Mattar, Huas & Godart, 2012). Altered attention for social stimuli and poor recognition of emotions were examined as putative intermediate phenotypes of EDs. Further, high social anxiety is associated with more severe eating disorder symptoms across different forms of eating disorders (Buchholz *et al.*, 2007; Hinrichsen, Sheffield & Waller, 2007; Hinrichsen *et al.*, 2003; Hinrichsen, Waller & Emanuelli, 2004; Hinrichsen, Waller & van Gerko, 2004; Ostrovsky *et al.*, 2013; Sawaoka *et al.*, 2012).

Social anxiety in individuals with eating disorders does not appear to be a result of starvation or low body weight. In a review of the literature, we found that social anxiety was not related to body mass index (BMI) across the eating disorder spectrum (Kerr-Gaffney *et al.*, 2018). Further, in those with both SAD and an eating disorder, it is reported that SAD often develops before the eating disorder (Bulik *et al.*, 1997; Godart *et al.*, 2000; Kaye *et al.*, 2004; Swinbourne *et al.*, 2012). This suggests SAD might be a risk factor for the development of an eating disorder, or that both disorders share common vulnerability factors. Indeed, some of the risk factors for SAD are also implicated in the development of EDs, such as early social difficulties and a shy and inhibited temperamental style (Cardi, Tchanturia & Treasure, 2018).

Social anxiety in autism spectrum disorder (ASD)

Between 12 and 56 per cent of individuals with ASD also meet diagnostic criteria for SAD (Spain *et al.*, 2016). However, because there is substantial overlap in symptoms between ASD and SAD, the process of diagnosing SAD in individuals with ASD can be difficult. For example, difficulties in reciprocal communication, avoidance of social situations, and difficulties with non-verbal communication (such as eye contact, expressive body language, and facial expressions) are often seen in both disorders. In someone with SAD, avoidance of a social situation is often due to intense anxiety in anticipation of the event. However, in ASD, this behaviour might be driven by, for example, difficulties with tolerating the unpredictable and uncertain nature of social events. Delineating which symptoms arise from ASD and which might arise from a possible co-morbid anxiety disorder is highly important not only in reaching an accurate diagnosis, but also in treating or managing symptoms.

It has been hypothesized that some of the core symptoms of ASD may increase risk of developing SAD (Halim, Richdale & Uljarević, 2018; Spain *et al.*, 2016). For example, poorer social skills, repetitive body movements, or a preference for discussing circumscribed interests may lead to peer rejection and negative social experiences during formative years, factors which are implicated in the development of SAD. Similarly, difficulties in recognizing emotions and mental states in others may also result in social misunderstandings and negative experiences. These experiences can, in turn, lead to individuals with ASD developing negative core beliefs about their abilities, and feelings of inadequacy and inferiority. The resulting increased withdrawal from social activities can then limit the amount of opportunities to practise social skills and observe social norms. Indeed, in individuals with ASD, high social anxiety is associated with poorer social skills and social competence, as well as less social motivation (Spain *et al.*, 2018).

Clinical considerations and treatment

Although there is little research exploring the impact of social anxiety on treatment in eating disorders, several recommendations have been put forward for those with ASD and SAD (Maddox, Miyazaki & White, 2017; Spain, Rumball *et al.*, 2017; Spain, Sin *et al.*, 2017). These may be helpful in adapting treatment for those with an eating disorder as well as ASD and/or high levels of social anxiety:

- The core symptoms of ASD or SAD (e.g. lack of social overtures) may mean that individuals do not seek help for their social anxiety symptoms. Clinicians can be proactive in asking about thoughts and behaviours that might be indicative of social anxiety.

- Given the overlap in symptoms between SAD and ASD, assessment of co-morbid psychopathology in those with ASD will likely benefit from a multifaceted approach, incorporating informant ratings from parents or significant others where appropriate. Such observations can be useful in understanding subtle changes in behaviour that might not be picked up on by the individual themselves.

- Assessment and therapy sessions may be longer in both duration and frequency for those with social anxiety. For example, pre-therapy interventions to develop trust and a sense of safety have been identified as important in those with ASD and SAD. In those with eating disorders, this could take the form of psychoeducation about the condition, cognitive remediation therapy, or emotion processing coaching. Booster sessions may also be useful for those with social anxiety in order to sustain improvements made during therapy.

- Modifications to facilitate communication and engagement during therapy have also been suggested. These will be highly dependent on the individual's unique needs, but some suggestions include: offering appointments at a time that suits the patient (for example, avoiding timings which would involve using public transport at rush hour or interfere with meal times), offering appointments at their home initially, using alternative methods of communication (for example, letter writing if the patient has difficulty in verbalizing their difficulties), and providing clear information in appointment letters regarding where to go on arrival, where facilities (e.g. toilets) are located, and what will happen at the appointment.

Regarding the content of therapy offered, clinical guidelines in the UK recommend cognitive behavioural therapy (CBT) for the treatment of SAD (NICE, 2013). Preliminary evidence suggests this might be useful for individuals with ASD who also have high levels of social anxiety. Trials in those with ASD have often incorporated social skills training into CBT (which isn't the case in treatment for those with SAD only). For example, a CBT-based group social skills intervention was found to significantly decrease levels of social anxiety in a small group of adults with ASD (Spain, Blainey & Vaillancourt, 2017). Participants of the group also reported feeling more confident and having improved social understanding. In a randomized controlled trial adolescents with ASD and an anxiety disorder either received CBT or were allocated to a wait-list control condition (Maddox *et al.*, 2017). Although those with higher social anxiety had greater pre-treatment social impairment, they showed steeper improvements in social skills during treatment than those with lower social anxiety. However, three months after the intervention, social skills had worsened in those with high social anxiety compared with those with low social anxiety. This suggests that further modifications may be required for those with high social anxiety in order to sustain improvements gained during therapy, such as the inclusion of booster sessions. Other modifications include:

- extra sessions of psychoeducation
- detailed information about abstract concepts (e.g. anxiety)
- positive self-talk and coping statements
- opportunities for skills rehearsal
- modelling of social skills by therapists
- use of visual aids.

Treatment of SAD in individuals with eating disorders has received far less research attention. Lázaro *et al.* (2011) reported on a social skills and self-esteem group programme in adolescents with AN or BN which found significant improvements in social withdrawal, leadership, and social anxiety at the end of treatment. Future studies in those with eating disorders could examine the following research questions in order to gain a better understanding of the interaction between social anxiety, ASD and treatment response:

- Does social anxiety moderate treatment response in those with eating disorders? If so, for which treatments?
- Are modifications to recommended treatments (e.g. CBT) required in those with eating disorders and co-morbid SAD? Can recommendations from ASD literature work for those with eating disorders?

- What are clinicians' views on recognizing and treating SAD in those with eating disorders?

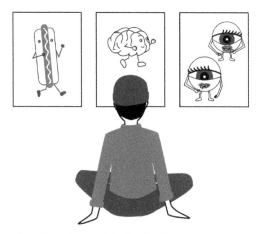

Figure 2.1. *Knowing each individual's communication style is essential – do they get the message you are giving them?*

If you or your loved ones or patients you work with have problems with social anxiety, the National Autistic Society anxiety resources could be helpful:

www.autism.org.uk/about/behaviour/anxiety.aspx.

We also recommend this resource by Pooky Knightsmith, who wrote the next chapter of this book and has produced many helpful materials like this: Knightsmith, P. (2020). *Cards Against Anxiety: A Guidebook and Cards to Help You Stress Less.* Quarto Publishing.

Please also see www.peacepathway.org for additional resources.

References

American Psychiatric Association (2013) *Diagnostic and Statistical Manual of Mental Disorders* (5th edition). Arlington, VA: American Psychiatric Publishing.

Buchholz, A., Henderson, K., Hounsell, A., Wagner, A., Norris, M. & Spettigue, W. (2007) 'Self-silencing in a clinical sample of female adolescents with eating disorders.' *Journal of the Canadian Academy of Child and Adolescent Psychiatry, 16*(4), 158–163.

Bulik, C.M., Sullivan, P.F., Fear, J.L. & Joyce, P.R. (1997) 'Eating disorders and antecedent anxiety disorders: A controlled study.' *Acta Psychiatrica Scandinavica, 96*(1), 101–107.

Cardi, V., Tchanturia, K. & Treasure, J. (2018) 'Premorbid and illness-related social difficulties in eating disorders: An overview of the literature and treatment developments.' *Current Neuropharmacology, 16*(8), 1122–1130.

Godart, N.T., Flament, M.F., Lecrubier, Y. & Jeammet, P. (2000) 'Anxiety disorders in anorexia nervosa and bulimia nervosa: Co-morbidity and chronology of appearance.' *European Psychiatry*, 15(1), 38–45.

Goddard, E. & Treasure, J. (2013) 'Anxiety and social-emotional processing in eating disorders: Examination of family trios.' *Cognitive Therapy and Research*, 37(5), 890–904.

Grant, B.F., Hasin, D.S., Blanco, C., Stinson, F.S. *et al.* (2005) 'The epidemiology of social anxiety disorder in the United States.' *The Journal of Clinical Psychiatry*, 66(11), 1351–1361.

Halim, A.T., Richdale, A.L. & Uljarević, M. (2018) 'Exploring the nature of anxiety in young adults on the autism spectrum: A qualitative study.' *Research in Autism Spectrum Disorders*, 55, 25–37.

Hinrichsen, H., Sheffield, A. & Waller, G. (2007) 'The role of parenting experiences in the development of social anxiety and agoraphobia in the eating disorders.' *Eating Behaviors*, 8(3), 285–290.

Hinrichsen, H., Waller, G. & Emanuelli, F. (2004) 'Social anxiety and agoraphobia in the eating disorders: Associations with core beliefs.' *The Journal of Nervous and Mental Disease*, 192(11), 784–787.

Hinrichsen, H., Waller, G. & van Gerko, K. (2004) 'Social anxiety and agoraphobia in the eating disorders: Associations with eating attitudes and behaviours.' *Eating Behaviors*, 5(4), 285–290.

Hinrichsen, H., Wright, F., Waller, G. & Meyer, C. (2003) 'Social anxiety and coping strategies in the eating disorders.' *Eating Behaviors*, 4(2), 117–126.

Kaye, W.H., Bulik, C.M., Thornton, L., Barbarich, N. & Masters, K. (2004) 'Comorbidity of anxiety disorders with anorexia and bulimia nervosa.' *American Journal of Psychiatry*, 161(12), 2215–2221.

Kerr-Gaffney, J., Harrison, A. & Tchanturia, K. (2018) 'Social anxiety in the eating disorders: A systematic review and meta-analysis.' *Psychological Medicine*, 48(15), 2477–2491.

Kessler, R.C., Berglund, P., Demler, O., Jin, R., Merikangas, K.R. & Walters, E.E. (2005) 'Lifetime prevalence and age-of-onset distributions of DSM-IV disorders in the National Comorbidity Survey Replication.' *Archives of General Psychiatry*, 62(6), 593.

Lázaro, L., Font, E., Moreno, E., Calvo, R. *et al.* (2011) 'Effectiveness of self-esteem and social skills group therapy in adolescent eating disorder patients attending a day hospital treatment programme.' *European Eating Disorders Review*, 19(5), 398–406.

Maddox, B.B., Miyazaki, Y. & White, S.W. (2017) 'Long-term effects of CBT on social impairment in adolescents with ASD.' *Journal of Autism and Developmental Disorders*, 47(12), 3872–3882.

Maddox, B.B. & White, S.W. (2015) 'Comorbid social anxiety disorder in adults with autism spectrum disorder.' *Journal of Autism and Developmental Disorders*, 45(12), 3949–3960.

Mattar, L., Huas, C. & Godart, N. (2012) 'Relationship between affective symptoms and malnutrition severity in severe anorexia nervosa.' *PLoS ONE*, 7(11), 3–8.

National Institute for Health and Care Excellence (2013) *Social anxiety disorder: Recognition, assessment and treatment* (CG1590). Retrieved from www.nice.org.uk/guidance/cg159 on 04/07/20.

Ostrovsky, N.W., Swencionis, C., Wylie-Rosett, J. & Isasi, C.R. (2013) 'Social anxiety and disordered overeating: An association among overweight and obese individuals.' *Eating Behaviors*, 14(2), 145–148.

Sawaoka, T., Barnes, R.D., Blomquist, K.K., Masheb, R.M. & Grilo, C.M. (2012) 'Social anxiety and self-consciousness in binge eating disorder: Associations with eating disorder psychopathology.' *Comprehensive Psychiatry*, 53(6), 740–745.

Spain, D., Blainey, S.H. & Vaillancourt, K. (2017) 'Group cognitive behaviour therapy (CBT) for social interaction anxiety in adults with autism spectrum disorders (ASD).' *Research in Autism Spectrum Disorders*, 41–42, 20–30.

Spain, D., Happé, F., Johnston, P., Campbell, M. *et al.* (2016) 'Social anxiety in adult males with autism spectrum disorders.' *Research in Autism Spectrum Disorders*, 32, 13–23.

Spain, D., Rumball, F., O'Neill, L., Sin, J., Prunty, J. & Happé, F. (2017) 'Conceptualizing and treating social anxiety in autism spectrum disorder: A focus group study with multidisciplinary professionals.' *Journal of Applied Research in Intellectual Disabilities*, 30, 10–21.

Spain, D., Sin, J., Harwood, L., Mendez, M.A. & Happé, F. (2017) 'Cognitive behaviour therapy for social anxiety in autism spectrum disorder: A systematic review.' *Advances in Autism*, 3(1), 34–46.

Spain, D., Sin, J., Linder, K.B., McMahon, J. & Happé, F. (2018) 'Social anxiety in autism spectrum disorder: A systematic review.' *Research in Autism Spectrum Disorders, 52*, 51–68.

Spence, S.H. & Rapee, R.M. (2016) 'The etiology of social anxiety disorder: An evidence-based model.' *Behaviour Research and Therapy, 86*, 50–67.

Swinbourne, J., Hunt, C., Abbott, M., Russell, J., St Clare, T. & Touyz, S. (2012) 'The comorbidity between eating disorders and anxiety disorders: Prevalence in an eating disorder sample and anxiety disorder sample.' *Australian & New Zealand Journal of Psychiatry, 46*(2), 118–131.

Swinbourne, J. & Touyz, S. (2007) 'The co-morbidity of eating disorders and anxiety disorders: A review.' *European Eating Disorders Review, 15*, 215–221.

Lived Experience

STIGMA, CREDIT OR A LACK OF UNDERSTANDING?

In this section we hear from two people with lived experience. It is important to learn from people with lived experiences and to use this learning to inform our practice. Pooky describes the lessons she has learned on the road to recovery whilst A. Wadden uses powerful imagery to demonstrate her experience with an eating disorder.

Chapter 3

Anorexia and Autism

LESSONS LEARNED ON THE ROAD TO RECOVERY

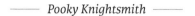

Pooky Knightsmith

I have a long history of anorexia and I have spent years walking through a constantly revolving door of illness and recovery. I was hospitalized in 2017 and at first I got rapidly more unwell until I was given a diagnosis of autism and my treatment was radically revised. Here are some of the lessons I've learned (or am learning) now that things are finally beginning to settle…

Lesson 1 – I'm more than a label, but a label helps

Being labelled as autistic led to an overnight overhaul of my treatment and I went from getting rapidly more unwell to being given the right support to take positive steps in my treatment. The label gave my treatment team permission to revise the way they treated me and to realize that sometimes we had to turn the typical approach on its head in order to make progress with me. The label also helped me to begin to understand myself and helped me to make sense of a lot of the difficulties I've faced day to day my whole life. Being able to view myself through this new lens was incredibly helpful and allowed me to be a little kinder to myself and to begin to rethink my approach to many things. The label also gave me a community I could identify with and an avenue into learning how best to support myself day to day as there is quite a lot of advice out there that I'd never thought of applying to myself.

Lesson 2 – Traditional treatment can do more harm than good

For example, before diagnosis I was being forced to engage with a wide range of food types; after diagnosis I was allowed to be very selective at first and create a plan with my treatment team for very slowly increasing my range. This has taken an incredibly long time and, having been a healthy weight for more than 18 months, I am still slowly introducing food groups, but this very slow and stepped approach has enabled me to make consistent progress. The traditional approach resulted in me completely shutting down, disengaging and rapidly losing weight even when in treatment.

Another example is that the ward I was on relied heavily on group therapy. For me this was actively harmful. Working as part of a group is very complicated for me even when I'm in good health and I was entirely unable to engage with the content and would sit mute, but highly distressed. Following my diagnosis I was withdrawn from group therapy and given entirely one-to-one support which allowed me to engage with the same content (which was largely skills based/ dialectical behaviour therapy (DBT))[1] in a way that was helpful rather than harmful.

Lesson 3 – Little things can make a big difference

Once I became a little more confident in my new label and had gained more understanding about which parts of my daily experience were likely linked to my autism, I found I was able to ask for adaptations to be made which seemed minor but which made a big difference. For example, the room in which I had therapy had a clock in it. For the first few sessions I was considered not to be engaging in the sessions but the truth was that I couldn't focus on anything other than the sound of the clock. Once I understood that this was simply because I'm very sensitive to sensory stimuli and it was reasonable to ask for the clock to be removed, things got quickly better. Other minor adjustments that made big differences included:

---

1   Dialectical behaviour therapy (DBT) is a talking therapy that aims to support people to understand and accept difficult feelings, learn skills to manage the feelings and be able to make positive changes in their lives (Linehan, 1998).

- Timekeeping wasn't always good on my ward. I found it very hard if things didn't happen when I was told they would, so this was addressed.

- Minor substitutions would be routinely made in meals – for me this would mean I wasn't presented with what I was expecting and couldn't eat it at all so efforts were made to avoid substitutions and to warn me ahead if they were made.

- I was allowed to wear headphones with calming music whenever I wanted to drown out background noise.

Lesson 4 – The combination of autism and starvation is like autism on steroids

When my brain was very starved, the symptoms of my autism went into overdrive. When I am healthier I am very high functioning and able to largely mask my symptoms (hence not getting a diagnosis until my 30s, I guess) but when I was very underweight, I presented far more typically and didn't have the ability to mask and manage. This meant that weight gain was arguably even more important for me than for many of my peers because it became hugely important to break the cycle as every day my world was shrinking and my anxiety and distress was increasing.

This meant that any way we could find of me taking on calories was fair game. At first I lived off a single flavour of Ensure and the introduction to solid food was far slower than usual treatment pathways would have recommended; but we did whatever we could to halt the weight loss and help me to re-feed my body and brain.

Lesson 5 – Adjustment to life outside the unit required significant support

The great things about life on the ward were that there was a very rigid routine and very carefully planned meals and everything was made very predictable. This was great and hugely supported my progress whilst I was there and was an ideal fit with my autistic traits, but it meant that the transition back to the real world needed very careful management. We tried to take what had worked well on the unit (planned meals, fixed timings etc.) and replicate this at home. We did find though that I was very motivated to eat well and function well with my children, so we built this into my treatment plan and whilst I was on the intensive day patient programme at the Bethlem Royal Hospital I was allowed to eat breakfast and dinner at home with my family whenever I felt able to do so. When I wasn't able to do this I could eat at the unit – having the safety net in place allowed me to be braver in my steps to recovery; but everything had to be carefully planned and well supported.

Lesson 6 – I've had to adjust my expectations of recovery

I always thought that when I got better I'd suddenly fit – that I'd enjoy all the things my friends enjoy and I'd become some sort of social butterfly and find life much easier than I had in the past. I've had to realize that this is not the case and that recovery looks a little different than I thought it might and that being and staying well will always be an active process for me.

Lesson 7 – I have to work hard to stay well, being honest with those around me helps

Now that I understand more about myself in the context of my autism diagnosis, I can trace back many of my historic relapses and realize that autistic burnout was a recurring theme. Now, I am much more careful to be aware of my day-to-day needs and to build in adequate down time and time for self-care to help me reset. I've revised my working patterns and also how, when and with whom I socialize. I'm also aware of flashpoints, like the school holidays when routines change and I get less time alone. As a family we've made adjustments to help me manage and I'm also much better now at realizing that to stay well I must step back sometimes. I've also worked hard to re-educate those I work with and my friends too. Having masked my autism so well for so long, people can sometimes be dismissive, which is hard, but when I take time to truly explain, I find that on the whole people are supportive and will make the accommodations that might feel small to them but feel huge for me – that might mean if I'm speaking at a conference that I'm not expected to network at lunchtime but am given a room to take time out; or if I'm meeting with a friend that I meet one-to-one instead of in a group and that we meet somewhere quiet rather than in a busy bar. There are a whole host of little things – but added together they make a big difference to me and I think will mean me finally being able to stay well instead of constantly nose-diving back into anorexia.

Reference

Linehan, M.M. (1998) 'An illustration of dialectical behavior therapy.' *In Session: Psychotherapy in Practice,* 4(2), 21–44.

Chapter 4

A Picture Is Worth a Thousand Words

—— A. Wadden ——

A note from the editor:

I am very grateful to A. Wadden (A.W), whom I met with a while ago in our eating disorder service. A.W kindly contributed this image to our book and explained it in her own words. She gave me permission to refer to her lived experience as 'complex mental health challenges alongside severe eating disorders/eating difficulties'.

Many thanks to A.W for sharing her thoughts and feelings with us using this powerful image and its accompanying explanation.

You were very helpful to all of our team in thinking about the PEACE Pathway when we were working with the National Autistic Society experts and the multidisciplinary team.

We wish you all the best and we are all very grateful.

Left side image 'Painful Progression'

A gravestone contained within the mind of a dark-haired girl (left side of image) symbolizes a constant wish for peace, for all of it to end. For what is the point of painfully progressing when progression leads to treatment ending before recovery is sufficient to manage autonomously? Or when the environment required to take that path does not understand enough and leaves compound triggers in its wake rather than calmly, slowly supporting growth?

Her face highlights the torture of being denied treatment due to case complexity (usually in this instance the severity of Obsessive-compulsive disorder coupled with other labels). Instead of the individual being considered worth working with, such obstacles are seen as barriers which teams do not realize mask desire and potential.

Thus these symptoms are left (as is she), to become sadly set into her world and then in turn, most likely, embedded into her memorial stone.

She wants to recover.

She is not permitted, facilitated or welcomed in that process. The system is as tired and hopeless as her soul.

A collective of people inside this figure symbolize voices once misunderstood as demons to be removed or medicated. Decades later they are given time and she is at last encouraged to hear their messages, understand their idiosyncratic fears, beliefs, separate symptoms, coping patterns and concerns. These 'parts' of her are beginning to calm a little as appropriate guidance is won for what was undetected (and too often misrepresented) dissociative identity disorder. The almost lifelong battle for such an accurate approach (exceeding 23 years) takes its toll on all involved at a huge avoidable physical, mental and practical cost. An unnecessary war leaving embers to dampen down, long after that battle is won.

A flood surrounds the house (for she is considered too complex once diagnosis is secured) further preventing escape from her confined universe. As terror intensifies the flood outside extinguishes the fire in her external and internal world. This equally stands for the way she is 'treated' when placed in settings that eventually accepted her but not her confusing symptoms.

Barbed wire entering at a flower above the girl's head leads into her mouth, knotting up, extending further, cutting deeper, preventing her consuming any fluid, any food without terror or pain. As confusion, isolation and fear exacerbates, this torturous wire extends into and encircles the house that is no longer her own, imprisoning, for fear of what may occur.

As months stretched to years, the 'helpers' remove piece by piece every positive element of life she fought so hard to achieve until...she is deemed too unwell to continue with a role and training that gives life meaning, yet not unwell enough for the intensive input required to thrive. Now she cannot remember how her functional self operated prior to it all being taken.

And they leave her until... So unstable she no longer even exists to those who may assist her. Therefore the wire grates deeper, scars concealed and visible.

Ultimately the 'wire' is forced into her nose and hands without consideration, despite her pleading for help months sooner. It is too painful a memory to include in pictorial form.

Treatment of her 'disordered eating', though desperately needed, always feels threatening once inside. The bees represent such elements of treatment and the wasp how she has to defend her corner in fear and anger, ultimately acting far removed from the kind, calm, collected, peaceful dragonfly she wishes to embody.

Everyone in the places she finds herself has different presentations too, frequently as unseen or unheard as hers. When elements of her care are finally adapted and theirs not attended to, she is rendered again the subject of ridicule, guilt or envy. A painful, double-edged sword. She seeks equality for them too, alongside acceptance and peer support. It is not her fault, nor theirs. She is lucky enough to twice experience unconditional peer acceptance.

Now let us progress to the more hopeful (right) side of the picture 'Spectrum Sightings'

Here we find the same girl. Yet she appears different. The bees are guiding upward instead of threatening or defending. They provide sufficient support to allow eating of the nectar – or cherry muffin in her cheek. The (same) girl forever adored such delicacies even though parts of her do not or perhaps won't allow tasting.

With eventual consistent structure and flexibility, the flowers (her goals and values) are released from the painfully constraining barbed wire.

They are finally allowed to bloom with the girl's now nourished body, mind and soul.

She moves into a much longed for home of her own, with love and gratitude welcoming her and all that enter (see a heart replacing the once blacked-out door). This bright-haired girl has secured a healing place where her next journey can begin and uses this transformative journey to prevent others experiencing what she had to for almost her entire existence.

A spectrum represents living (not existing) alongside all of her 'parts' integrating into every cell, exhibited in hair.

Ebbing and flowing at first (as recovery does) the flood resolves, allowing her to embrace life outside with all its spectrum colours. The fire leaves embers which instead of killing hope ignite a positive determination.

Her once black hair remains, seen as outline shadows helping guide her and those who seek her support to find their own path. Neither they (nor she now) are alone. This 'collected' individual is finally safe 'enough', service free. She is accepting, forgiving of herself and others. Grateful to those who saw, believed and (most critically) acted as was needed.

The sky is no longer sad. The beauty of life beyond treatment is unveiled and it is so much appreciated.

The right image therefore depicts the difference it can make once provided with accurate diagnosis and when adapted care plans are allowed. It demonstrates the potential efficacy of a slow, gentle, progressive approach rather than (in effect) trapping someone into a 'one size fits all' method with no room for breathers. The opposite was required from sudden rule alterations, a constantly fast pace and rigid boundaries. Instead, slowly, creatively, collaboratively working at a pace tailored to these so-called 'too complex' challenges. The others then who once discarded her as 'never to recover' are able to be forgiven then forgotten as her new teams allow for astonishing transformation.

Yet still the transition to the next phase lacks eating disorder or other essential input and so the cycle returns to revisit her barbed wire cage. She saw it coming, though she fought so hard to evade it. An unnecessary torturous postcode lottery of housing and treatment gaps too frequently experienced and witnessed (not only in her own narrative). With full spectrum hair thanks to all she is learning, the girl continues venturing forth for resolution.

Clinical Cases

EXPERIENCE AND LEARNING
OF A CLINICAL TEAM

This section focuses on case studies from an eating disorder clinical team's perspective. The section covers two, in-depth, cases. We hope these cases will give insight into how our clinical team works on a multidisciplinary level. We also hope that there is some useful learning and adaptations that can be taken from each unique case.

Chapter 5

Using the Autism Lens: Milly's Story

A MULTIDISCIPLINARY HEALTH PROFESSIONAL TEAM APPROACH IN SUPPORTING AN AUTISTIC FEMALE WITH ANOREXIA NERVOSA

Yasemin Dandil, Emma Kinnaird, Jason Maldonado-Page, Danilen Nursigadoo, Jessica Gomularz, Claire Baillie and Kate Tchanturia

Milly's story describes the work from a multidisciplinary specialist eating disorder (ED) team with a complex case with autism spectrum disorder (ASD) co-morbidity. Clinical and self-report data collected before and after psychological treatment are presented. This case study provides a reflection on the therapy and possible ways to adapt and calibrate treatment to individual needs. Reflections on what we can learn to mind the gap in clinical work are also discussed.

Theoretical framework

Current treatments for anorexia nervosa (AN) do not meet the unique needs of people with an eating disorder (ED) and co-morbid autism spectrum disorder (ASD). Our research among this population identified that both patients and families experience significant barriers to treatment and there is a failure to adapt to the specific needs of patients with co-morbid AN and ASD (Kinnaird *et al.*, 2019; Tchanturia *et al.*, 2019). Also, clinicians report needs for confidence and skills to treat ED/ASD co-morbidity (Kinnaird *et al.*, 2017). Research evidence has shown that the lack of adaptation for ASD needs amongst ED services is associated with poorer patient experiences and treatment outcomes (Kinnaird *et al.*, 2019a).

An important strategy towards generating treatment advances for AN involves targeting the core maintaining factors of the illness. The cognitive-interpersonal model (Treasure & Schmidt, 2013) proposed focuses on four maintaining factors: emotion avoidance, cognitive rigidity, pro-anorexic beliefs, and the response of close others. The maintaining factors such as cognitive rigidity and social difficulties can be exacerbated when patients have both ASD and AN (Tchanturia *et al.*, 2017).

This case study evaluates the inpatient work with a young lady with a complex presentation. Several members of the multidisciplinary team provided therapeutic support. The chapter authors discussed the case in the joint meetings with attempts to communicate their input and develop an ASD/AN clinical pathway for this patient and to learn how to make the inpatient programme ASD co-morbidity friendly.

Eighteen sessions of individual cognitive remediation therapy (CRT) were offered to engage the patient in the treatment programme and to address cognitive features of AN; namely cognitive inflexibility, extreme attention to detailed thinking and perfectionism (Tchanturia *et al.*, 2010). The sessions then went on to use other modalities such as cognitive behavioural therapy (CBT) to address unhelpful thinking patterns (Beck, 1993). The patient also had input from family systemic therapists, an occupational health therapist, a counselling psychologist facilitating the groups, a dietician and researchers helping the clinical team to assess clinical features and sensory difficulties. There is the potential to develop a better-integrated case formulation and well-adapted clinical treatment pathway for those who have ASD and AN (see www.youtube.com/watch?v=aN17vc8_d08&t=30s). The multidisciplinary team worked hard to communicate a shared formulation and a clear understanding of multiple forms of the support which was provided.

CASE PRESENTATION

A 21-year-old woman (referred to as Milly for anonymity) met the diagnostic criteria for AN (restricting type). Milly was also diagnosed with ASD at age 11. Milly's eating problems were first associated with weight gain as a result of chemotherapy (at age 12, Milly was diagnosed with Hodgkin's Lymphoma, from which she is currently in remission). Milly had previously had three inpatient admissions, of between three and four months' duration, within the past 16 months. Upon each discharge, she had struggled to maintain her weight which led to the multiple re-admissions, including being admitted to the inpatient treatment programme with low weight. Furthermore, Milly reported being with others as difficult and struggled to make friends. On the ward she was often observed sitting on her own covered with a blanket.

PERSONAL HISTORY

Milly described a challenging childhood; as described above she was diagnosed with ASD at age 11 and had a serious physical illness. She had lived a socially isolated adolescence; she reported her ASD made it hard for her to make friends as she was a shy teenager. Milly described how her ASD meant that she would get nervous talking to people she did not know. Milly recalled that in addition to her weight gain from chemotherapy, she had begun comfort eating to manage the feelings of abandonment and sadness she experienced after her father left the family home. Following her recovery, she was supported by her mother to use a personal trainer to become fitter, stronger and healthier. However, she then recalls being 'obsessed' with being healthy and relates this to her ASD traits for 'driving me the wrong way' to over-exercising and abusing laxatives. Milly reports, 'I never had a target weight. I just wanted my weight to get lower and lower'. She also stated that she holds her ASD accountable for her fixation on restricting her food intake and rigidity about doing specific exercises.

FAMILY HISTORY

Milly is the middle child of three siblings. She lived with her mother, Sally, and younger brother age 18. Milly described having a close relationship with her mother and recalled that she witnessed the arguments between her parents and denied that they were physical. She reported feeling 'distressed' at the time her parents divorced. Milly's father left the family home when she was 17. Milly reported that this was a particularly challenging time for her. Milly has had no contact with her father since he left the family home and, at present, she does not want to be in contact with him as she reported she will find this 'too stressful'.

Milly reports that she has an 'okay' relationship with her brother. However, she alleged that he finds it difficult to adjust to Milly being at home and hospital and she only speaks to him when she is at home. Milly then disclosed that she thinks her brother has traits of ASD 'as he doesn't like change and finds it difficult to adjust'. She reported having a 'better' relationship with her older sister who is age 23 and lives with her boyfriend.

Milly had a close relationship with her maternal grandfather who passed away a few months after her father left the family home. Milly reported that her grandfather was like a father figure to her when her father left. She has happy memories of playing football with her brother and grandfather. Her grandfather's death was a difficult time for Milly as she had longed to have a father figure in her life. However, later on, her mother's partner of a year decided to adopt Milly which she reported being 'delighted' about.

WHAT WE LEARNED FROM THE ASSESSMENT

Milly was assessed by a consultant psychiatrist on admission to the inpatient ward and met DSM-5 criteria for AN restricting type. The symptoms include a BMI of <17.5, and behaviours such as restriction of food. Milly also completed the Autism Diagnostic Observation Schedule, Second Edition (ADOS-2) with a trained researcher to confirm her previous autism diagnosis from the specialist clinical team. Using the recently updated algorithm, a score of 8 or above indicates potentially clinically significant levels of autistic traits (Hus & Lord, 2014). Milly scored 11 according to the new scoring system which is more sensitive to female ASD features (Sedgewick et al., 2019). In our research, we found that applying new the algorithm to the ADOS-2 identifies more females with ASD in our clinical population with eating disorders.

With newly admitted patients we typically offer remedial therapies (CRT or CREST) before we offer more complex psychological treatments.

Cognitive remediation and emotion skills training (CREST) aims to help patients identify their thinking styles and also uses exercises and discussions to support individuals in learning about identifying, expressing and managing emotions (Tchanturia, 2015b).

The assessments described below were administered as outcome measures for cognitive remediation therapy (CRT), which addresses thinking styles and strategies (for a systematic review of the literature see Tchanturia, Lounes & Holttum, 2014, Tchanturia *et al.*, 2017 and Tchanturia, 2015a). The assessment before the therapy included clinical questionnaires relating to eating pathology and mood, and calculation of BMI over the course of treatment. Although eating pathology, mood and weight were not being directly targeted in CRT, it was important to see if these clinical symptoms changed after CRT. The main focus of CRT is targeting thinking processes by using cognitive exercises.

The following self-report measures were administered before and after individual CRT:

- *The Rey-Osterrieth Complex Figure* (ROCF; Osterrieth, 1944) is a neuropsychological assessment that measures whether a person is adopting a detailed information processing style or a global information processing style when copying a complex figure (see Lang *et al.*, 2016 for more details).

- *The Brixton Spatial Anticipation Test* (Burgess & Shallice, 1997) is a visuospatial sequencing task with rule changes. The test assesses executive function and the ability to detect rules in sequences of stimuli by switching between mental representations (Tchanturia *et al.*, 2011 for more details).

- *The Detail and Flexibility Questionnaire* (DFlex; Roberts *et al.*, 2011) is a 24-item self-report scale measuring two aspects of neurocognitive functioning: cognitive rigidity (difficulty with set-shifting/flexibility) and attention to detail (weak coherence).

Other self-report measures included:

- *The Eating Disorder Examination Questionnaire* (EDE-Q; Fairburn & Beglin, 1994): This is a measure of psychopathological and behavioural indicators of disordered eating. The EDE-Q provides a global score and has four subscales measuring dietary restraint, eating concern, weight concern and shape concern. Higher scores represent greater pathology. For this assessment, we report only the global score, which is calculated as the mean of the four subscales.

- *The motivational ruler.* This tool comprises a visual analogue scale with scores from 1–10. The motivational ruler explores beliefs about the importance to change and perceived ability to change.

Milly also completed a sensory assessment during the course of her treatment to evaluate her taste and smell sensitivity. Taste Strips were used to measure her taste (Mueller *et al.*, 2003) and sniffing sticks were used to measure her smell sensitivity (Hummel *et al.*, 1997). Lower scores indicate poorer sensitivity, and the measures provide cut-offs that classify individuals as having reduced sensitivity. She also completed a self-report measure (Sensory Perception Quotient, Tavassoli, Hoekstra & Baron-Cohen, 2014) assessing how she perceives her overall sensory sensitivity.

Milly's scores on both taste and smell measures indicate that she has reduced sensitivity in these areas. On the smell test, an overall score of ≤30 indicates reduced sensitivity; Milly scored 28.25. On the taste test, an overall score of <9 suggests reduced sensitivity; Milly scored only 1. Milly was able to identify tastes from the strips but identified these wrongly, suggesting that she has reduced taste sensitivity, rather than no ability to taste. By contrast, on the self-report measure, Milly rated herself as highly sensitive. These findings suggest that while Milly self-rates as highly sensitive, in the areas of taste and smell she in fact has reduced physical sensory sensitivity. Although the sensory assessment principally focused on taste and smell, an interview with Milly's mum suggested that Milly also experiences auditory sensitivity. We have also observed this in the ward environment.

DIETETIC FEEDBACK

Milly does not seem to show a sensory aversion to complex textures, taste or smells in foods. She has a preference for nuts, hummus or peanut butter with crackers and oranges. She has stated an aversion to hard cheese and oral nutrition supplements without stating a reason. In the dining room, she is observed to have mixed varied texture items such as yoghurt with nuts or fruit. However, we previously have restricted Milly's access to oranges for a time when she was eating them by sucking the juice out and not eating the fibrous component.

She rarely chose the alternative menu items which contain ASD-friendly options that are low in smell, taste and complex textures.

Her interest during dietetic sessions seems to be mostly around calories with a preoccupation with having 'too much' and 'getting fat'. When she is able to see past her eating disorder and remain motivated for change she is able to accept the recommended calorie increase; however, when her eating disorder is apparent she becomes very strong-willed and determined and can at times demand calorie decreases and states a distrust for the recommendations made to support weight restoration at a safe and manageable speed according to the ward weekly weight targets.

CASE FORMULATION

The following formulation was developed collaboratively with Milly using her assessment data and is followed by a diagrammatic snapshot (see Figure 5.1). The predisposing factors associated with Milly's eating problems began following her diagnosis of Hodgkin's Lymphoma at age 12. Milly gained weight with the steroids associated with chemotherapy. Milly's eating disorder problems were further exacerbated by her father leaving the family home when she was 17. This was a particularly difficult time for Milly. She reported that soon after she was diagnosed with cancer, her father seemed to become depressed and began drinking (alcohol) frequently. Milly reported that her father attributed his depression to Milly's cancer and the eventual end of his marriage to Milly's mother.

At age 11 Milly was diagnosed with ASD. Milly struggled with this diagnosis as she reported, 'I did not feel normal and I found it hard to make friends and connect to people'. These social interactions and social relationship difficulties were underpinned by a theory of mind deficit. Milly reported problems processing information about herself and others. Furthermore, neuropsychology inefficiencies in Milly's executive function and central coherence could have potentially heightened her vulnerability. At age 13 Milly was also diagnosed with anxiety and depression.

These early experiences were consequently stressors for Milly and impacted on her beliefs and values about herself, relationships and her future. Subsequently, Milly's core beliefs were characterized by overarching low self-worth that manifested as an over-focus on eating, shape and weight as signifiers of personal worth and happiness.

Precipitating factors to the onset of Milly's AN were the weight gain following chemotherapy, her 'abandonment' by her father and the death of her grandfather a few months later. In the context of these stressors, Milly reported comfort eating, which led to a high BMI. Following her weight gain, Milly stated that she tried to lose weight by exercising and eating a healthy diet. Milly reported that her ASD traits (i.e. fixation and rigidity) were then accountable for her being preoccupied with continuously restricting her diet, abusing laxatives and her specific exercise regime. Milly also reported her anxiety around the fear of her cancer reoccurring.

A significant maintaining factor for Milly's eating disorder was identified as 'a sense of achievement and safety' where she reported she feared change and feeling unhappy if her weight increased. Milly held pro-anorexia beliefs and values, a detailed focus and inflexible thinking style; she had difficulties tolerating uncertainty and unrelenting standards of perfectionism. It appeared that Milly's eating disorder also held a function of managing and controlling her emotional experience by avoiding the negative emotions she feels such as being 'sad and hurt'. Milly reported that her family life felt 'out of control' and the eating disorder was the only factor that she could control. Milly viewed her ASD and AN as interlinked. She then processed this information with her cognitive and behavioural rigidity, with her insistence on sameness and ritualized patterns of behaviour impacted by starvation. This same inflexible thinking style associated with her ASD made it challenging for Milly to change her AN behaviours.

Milly's protective factors include her stepfather wanting to adopt her and the positive emotions this evoked in Milly. She has longed to have a father figure in her life and associated this with feelings of 'happiness, safety and motivation'. Milly's supportive family is a significant protective factor for her. Further protective factors were Milly's motivation to engage meaningfully with psychological therapy and challenge unhelpful thinking styles around her AN and her detail-focused thinking style. Milly also stated that she was able to build friendships in the hospital and enjoyed occupational therapy activities. Milly's long-term goals were to complete a childcare course, have her own family and write her own books.

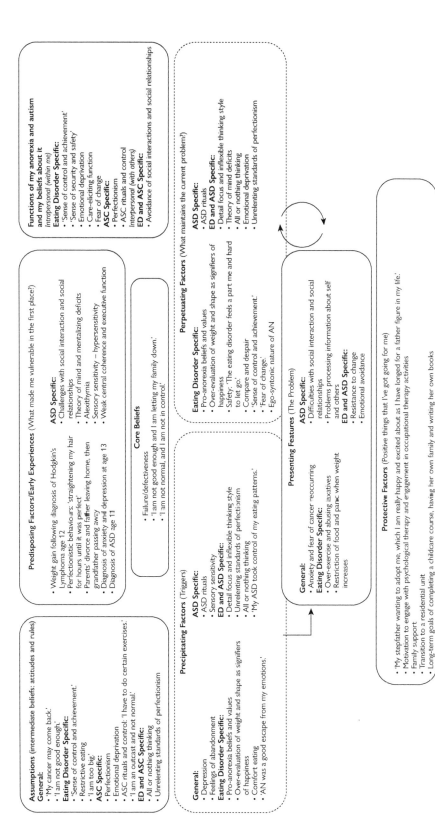

Figure 5.1. *Case formulation (diagrammatic snapshot)*

SECOND ASSESSMENT EVALUATING PROGRESS

Cognitive remediation therapy (CRT)

From the first of the individual CRT 20 sessions Milly was often tearful during initial check-ins; however, when she was given the space to openly express herself, she was able to compose herself and move on with the CRT session content. The therapeutic safe space also helped with building rapport and Milly appeared to be more open in sessions when expressing her thoughts and feelings. Milly reported that her usual thinking style was 'detailed and focused' and the increasing weight was difficult for her. Milly reflected that she likes being detailed; however, being flexible will be 'less stressful'. Furthermore, as sessions progressed, she was able to view her weight gain in terms of the 'bigger picture' and aiming to go to a residential unit.

CRT usually consists of eight or ten sessions, but Milly requested more sessions as she reported she needed further help with thinking and behaving more flexibly. Therefore, Milly was offered a total of 18 CRT sessions (30 minutes each) often twice a week. Table 5.1 outlines the tasks and aims of the CRT sessions. It also includes further examples from Milly's CRT sessions.

Milly appeared to find the tasks easier when she was given concrete examples. She also benefited from frequent repetitions and inquiring about her understanding of the directions during tasks. Milly was continually prompted throughout the sessions to reflect on her thinking styles and to relate these styles to her daily life. Her confidence in her cognitive abilities increased, and she responded well to praise and encouragement. Once Milly appeared to reflect more on her thinking styles, the idea of Specific Measurable Achievable Realistic Timely (SMART) goals was introduced. The aim was to enhance Milly's flexibility by implementing small behavioural changes in her daily life to reinforce strategies that had been discussed during exercises. Milly and her therapist collaboratively identified goals which included Milly wearing her hair differently every other day, walking her dog slowly as an alternative to walking at a fast pace, and explaining CRT to her mother and coming up with another goal together.

A particular theme that was identified in the sessions was Milly's distress over her rigid walking patterns – she would walk for a specific time, at a specific pace and on a specific route. She related her rigid walks to her ASD and reported the anxiety she experienced if routines are removed. Therefore, one of the goals collaboratively identified was for Milly to take a different route during her walks to help with flexibility and, therefore, to start with going on a mindfulness walk with her therapist (Yasemin). The walk was a difficult and challenging experience for Milly as she talked about her difficulties with change. After the walk, Milly appeared upset and reported, 'That was the slowest walk ever and I never want to do a mindfulness walk again'.

However, in subsequent sessions, Milly completed a mindfulness walk on her own where she changed her route slightly. She then later disclosed that she has changed her walking patterns and is also going on walks with her peers, which keep her distracted and are helping her to build friendships. It was clear that undertaking these small behavioural tasks gave Milly a sense of achievement and helped to mentalize and internalize different cognitive styles.

By the completion of CRT, Milly was able to demonstrate bigger picture thinking and flexibility, and stated, 'I need to view my weight in terms of moving on and going to the residential unit'. Please also refer to Milly's CRT ending letter in Figure 5.2.

Table 5.1. CRT session outline and examples from Milly's sessions

Session	Content and CRT tasks	Aims	Examples from Milly's CRT sessions
Session 1	Introduction to CRT and exploration of thinking styles using a continuum (big picture vs. detailed thinking and flexible vs. focused); 'complex picture task'	Familiarization with concepts and approach of CRT. To highlight and promote switching between the bigger picture alongside smaller details.	Milly described a detailed focused thinking style and rigid behaviours, particularly around walking patterns. During the 'complex picture task', Milly demonstrated detailed thinking by focusing on the components of the pictures as separate entities instead of in terms of the bigger picture. Milly appeared to find the task easier when she was given concrete examples.
Session 2	'Main idea task'. Synthesize detail to a summative main point	To encourage bigger picture thinking rather than detailed focused thinking. Targeting central coherence.	Milly was competent in the 'main idea task'. She reported being drawn to the main points and summarized the letter in bullet points then into a short paragraph. Milly reported, 'I need to think about the whole day instead of small routines'.

Session	Content and CRT tasks	Aims	Examples from Milly's CRT sessions
Session 3	'Illusions and Stroop task'	Practising cognitive flexibility, or 'switching'.	Milly identified, 'that there is more than one view-point and there is more to something than it seems'. Milly reflected, 'I can see the big picture sometimes and I am also quite detailed'.
Session 4	'Switching attention and embedded words task'	Practise switching between two different pieces of information (going through the alphabet and switching between male and female names).	Milly found the 'switching task' challenging. She recognized that when she has many things to keep track of it is easier to follow one than others. We discussed what Milly learned about this task and she reported, 'My thinking style is focused'. She related this to real-life by citing that she is focused when she goes on her walks.
Session 5	'Word search and estimating task'	To focus on relevant information amongst irrelevant information. Encourages estimating and considers things as being 'good enough' rather than perfect.	Milly reported that she does not like guessing during the 'estimating task' and likes to be 'accurate'. The advantages and disadvantages of guessing were explored in the session. She identified that 'The task showed me I was detailed, and I am also detailed with my walking patterns and if I am not, I will get anxious.'
Session 6	Goal setting using Specific Measurable Achievable Realistic Timely (SMART) goals	To introduce small behavioural changes outside of sessions to reinforce strategies that have been discussed during exercises.	Milly was particularly good in identifying goals to enhance her flexibility. One of the goals identified by Milly was to take a different route during her walks to help with flexibility. A further goal was for Milly to explain CRT to her mother and come up with a shared goal.
Session 7	Review goals	To introduce small behavioural changes outside of sessions to reinforce strategies that have been discussed during exercises.	Longer check-in due to Milly's distressed presentation as a result of changes in her ASD rituals and changes in her medication. The session then reviewed Milly's goals and provided her with encouragement and support.

Session 8	Review goals and big picture discussions	To introduce small behavioural changes outside of sessions to reinforce strategies that have been discussed during exercises.	Continued to review Milly's goals and agreed to go on a mindfulness walk together.
Session 9	Mindfulness walk/-flexibility. 'Arm folding task' and 'mind map task'	To reinforce strategies that have been discussed in sessions and to enhance flexibility.	Milly was very brave to go on a mindfulness walk with her therapist which included a different route from her usual walking pattern. Milly was initially distressed. Nevertheless, in subsequent sessions she was able to change her walking patterns on her own and this helped her build friendships with her peers on the ward.
Session 10	'Arm folding task' and 'maps task'	Multitasking and encouragement to think in different ways. Requires thinking in terms of the bigger picture and thinking flexibly.	Milly was printed a map of the hospital grounds so she could map out her walks and then map out alternative routes she could take, which she engaged well in.
Session 11	The 'Professor's Lesson'	Prioritizing the meaningful things in life.	Milly identified 'family, friends, Izzy (dog), cooking and baking' as the most important things in her life. She also reported that she enjoyed baking in the past and her future aspirations of studying childcare and working with children. Milly was able to demonstrate bigger picture thinking and flexibility and stated, 'I need to view my weight in terms of moving on and going to a residential unit'.
Session 12	Draw a mind map putting the central phrase of 'flexibility' in the bigger picture of individual recovery	To summarize and consolidate what has been covered in the previous sessions.	Milly was encouraged to think about how flexibility is related to her general plan for recovery, and how it helps to take the next steps in treatment and to the future in general. Milly reported she would use bigger picture thinking and flexibility in her day-to-day life.

Session	Content and CRT tasks	Aims	Examples from Milly's CRT sessions
Session 13	Joint session with the dietician	To link in the bigger picture thinking with eating.	Due to Milly's struggles with completing her meals, a joint session was conducted with the dietician to encourage Milly to apply the CRT strategies she has learned to meal completion. For example, applying bigger picture thinking during her meals instead of focusing on the components as separate entities.
Session 14	'How to…plant a sunflower task'	To practise expressing herself in a succinct way.	Milly preferred to use the task of 'how to bake a cake' as it was something, she had the experience of and she was able to think and explain the instructions in a succinct way. Milly found it helpful to focus on the main points and use bullet points.
Session 15	Bigger picture thinking	Linking bigger picture thinking to individual recovery journey of discovery.	Discussions around linking eating into the bigger picture and her recovery. Milly found it useful to use bigger picture thinking to reflect on her long-term goals.
Session 16	'Illusions task'	Practising cognitive flexibility.	Milly reported that from the task she learned that she needs to try to see other people's opinions and point of view.
Session 17	Bigger picture thinking	To encourage bigger picture thinking rather than detailed, focused thinking	We linked in big picture thinking with Milly's recovery by Milly mapping on a ladder the steps she needs to take to reach her big picture goals, which she reported was helpful having a visual representation.
Session 18	CRT ending letters	The ending letter helps to reflect and summarize what was learned.	Milly reported in her ending letter, 'The sessions have helped me open up which I normally have trouble doing. I am now able to be detailed when needed but also able to switch up my thinking skills when needed. I found CRT really helpful and I would recommend it to others.'

Dear Yasemin,

Thank you for working with me over the last couple of months. Our sessions have helped a great lot but I also felt like I could open up to you and bond with you which I normally have trouble doing, so it was nice to find someone I could trust and be vulnerable with.

These are the things I found useful about our sessions, firstly thinking about the bigger picture in life. I was always stuck in a very rigid routine when I first met you and even though I still am in certain ways I have definitely found ways to apply your techniques to my everyday life. It helped a lot with timings of things I had to do in a certain way. I'm now able to move things around a little bit easier, its still hard but it has become a bit easier.

I'm able to be detailed when needed but also be able to switch up my thinking skills when its needed. The mindfulness work was hard but a big achievement for me even though it was hard I still did it and I did it with your help so thank you.

Some sessions were hard for example if I was feeling low but you helped me carry on with the sessions.

I would recommend this to others because of how helpful it was to me.

The one thing I think I would / could be improved is if I was able to put our strategies into practice a bit more and also if I was less tired during our sessions but overall I have found this therapy useful and helpful and im going to try and carry on putting the strategies into practice even after we finish with our sessions.

Thank you for all to your help and advice, they have really helped me a lot and im sad our sessions are finishing but I know I can still use the advice in the future so thank you alot,

Figure 5.2. *Milly's CRT ending letter to therapist (Yasemin)*

COGNITIVE BEHAVIOURAL THERAPY (CBT)

Following Milly's engagement in CRT and her collaborative formulation, Milly reported feeling motivated to continue with therapy. Therefore, it was agreed to start more complex individual work, such as CBT. This was to identify unhelpful patterns of thinking and behaviours using different strategies and techniques (Beck, 1993) and to help us explore the accuracy of the beliefs of weight gain as signifiers of happiness with the aim to change these thoughts and behaviours. It was significant to develop a shared understanding of the problem and the potential solution.

Milly engaged well in the CBT work and reported that her goal for this work was 'to change my mindset and view weight gain as a good thing and look at food as nourishment for my body instead of something that will make me gain weight and be unhappy. I will continue to use my thought record sheet to help me with alternative thinking and I will also categorize my unhelpful thoughts in terms of fact or the opinion.'

Milly found keeping the 'thought record sheet' (Figure 5.3) particularly helpful, where she would challenge her unhelpful thoughts around her body image with alternative thoughts and implement defusing techniques. Additionally, she was able to complete this as inter-session work and we would reflect on her thoughts in individual sessions. Milly was also able to implement the thought record sheet during other distressing times, such as changes in her routines and to address self-harming behaviour. Milly reported that she found this piece of work most effective in her recovery journey of self-discovery because it enabled her to view the alternatives as it was laid out clearly on a worksheet and she liked the layout of the columns on the sheet as she prefers visual handouts. Milly reported that focusing on the alternatives stopped her over-thinking and enabled her to stop and think of a solution. Milly also completed a mind map of all her alternative thoughts (Figure 5.4).

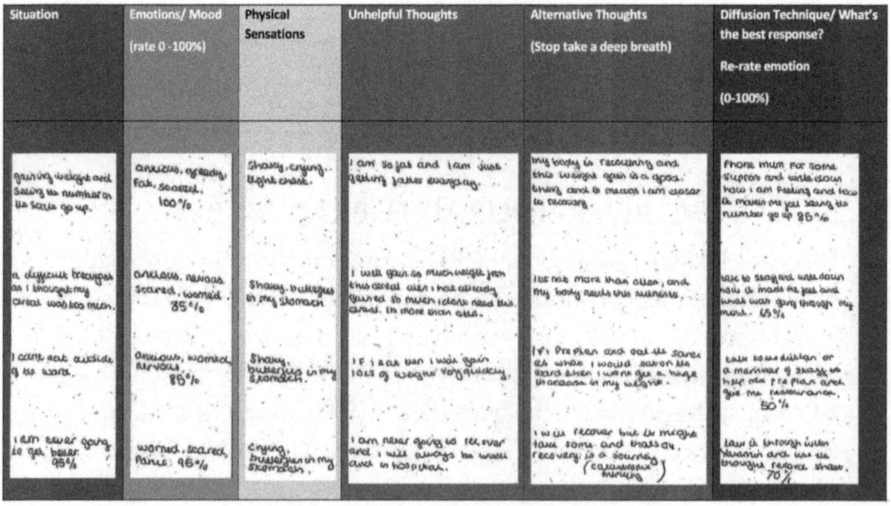

Figure 5.3. *My thought record sheet*

I have gained weight recently and I am happier.

Fact or opinion?

I am not greedy I just need to focus on myself

weight gain means I am moving forward.

Your body is getting stronger and healthier, you are closer to reaching your goals so weight gain is a good thing and not a negative thing.

change is a good thing and it will help me reach my goals.

Alternative thoughts

write all of my feelings down into my journal and thought record diary and look at the bigger picture.

Don't jump to conclusions and see what happens before I start to panic about anything.

get support from mum or stay when I am worried.

Be rational with the situation.

I was unhappy at a low weight. gaining weight wont make me that unhappy.

Figure 5.4. *Milly's mind map of her alternative thoughts*

Using a visual exercise, we then looked at the evidence against the thought of: 'If I put on weight, I will be unhappy.' Milly stated, 'I have gained weight recently and I am not that unhappy because I have positive things happening from the outcome of gaining weight. I am at a better weight and I am the happiest I have been in a long time and when I was at a lower weight, I was very unhappy so gaining weight won't always make me unhappy.' Milly was then able to reflect that she also had other events going on in her life, which would have affected her mood. Milly reported that she could not think rationally or properly when she was at a lower BMI and now she thinks more clearly about her goals and enjoys the things she likes. She reported, 'I am now figuring out who I am, and I want to be someone who writes and helps others'.

During Milly's last session we completed a 'communication passport' (created by Yasemin) for Milly's next therapist that will assist Milly with her communication, sensory needs and coping with distress (see Figure 5.5). Milly reported that the main message that she will be taking with her is: 'Recovery is possible and gaining weight won't make me unhappy because I will start to find out who I am and who I want to be.' A clear smile conveying positive regard was a helpful indication for Milly that the therapeutic sessions were going well. We agreed that we would like her next therapist to continue embedding the work she has completed in the CBT sessions particularly with regards to her thought record diary.

Table 5.2. CBT session outline and examples from Milly's sessions

Session	Content	Aims	Examples from Milly's CBT sessions
Session 1	Introduction to CBT	Familiarization with concepts and approach of CBT.	When the concept of 'unhelpful thinking patterns' was introduced, Milly reported she was prone to 'compare and despair, critical thoughts, should and musts and catastrophizing'.
Session 2	Facts or opinions and introduction of simple thought record sheet	To be able to differentiate whether thoughts were facts or opinions.	Milly identified facts had to be 'evidence-based' and 'an opinion is what you believe to be true and it's not always true'. Milly then related this task to her real life by stating, 'I relate it to my beliefs about my weight gain and it's my opinion and not actually the truth'.
Session 3	Theory A versus Theory B	Work through the different possible outcomes of a situation.	On reflection on the task, Milly reported that she learned that she needs to use strategies instead of jumping to the worst-case scenario.
Session 4	Thought record sheet	To teach the interaction between thoughts, feelings and behaviours and generate alternative thoughts to negative automatic thoughts.	Milly reported that she liked the idea of a 'thought record sheet'. The concept of a more detailed thought record sheet was, therefore, introduced, which Milly was keen on. She reported, 'It is good to look at other columns like more balanced perspectives instead of just the unhelpful thoughts' and requested more copies.
Session 5	Defusion techniques/ Positive affirmations	To develop a new attitude towards self and situations.	Milly identified positive self-talk phrases and repeated these in the session and was encouraged to repeat these daily.
Session 6	Thought record sheet	Repetition of the strategies in the thought record sheet.	Milly was able to be more reflective when we frequently went through her thought record sheet together.
Session 7	Thought record sheet and assertiveness	Repetition of learned ideas/ to effectively communicate.	Milly was able to identify alternative thoughts to comments of others and practised being assertive.
Session 8	Thought record sheet	Repetition of learned ideas.	Space to reflect on Milly's thought record sheet.

Session 9	Visual exercise of 'Facts or opinions'	To identify evidence for and against thoughts.	Milly was able to identify that the thoughts around her weight were opinions and not facts.
Session 10	Mind map of alternative thoughts and reflection of endings	To summarize and consolidate the alternative thoughts.	Milly enjoyed the visual task and the idea of focusing on only the alternatives. We then linked the alternative thoughts to her general plan of recovery and future.
Session 11	Communication Passport for next therapist and managing endings	To provide a space to reflect on the therapeutic relationship and manage endings.	Milly reflected that CRT helped her with her flexibility, but she most enjoyed the CBT work. Milly then reported, 'Realizing that gaining weight won't make me unhappy was a significant moment for me'. Milly completed a communication passport to provide a handover and assist with communication, sensory needs and coping with distress. She liked that it was one page, simple and visual.

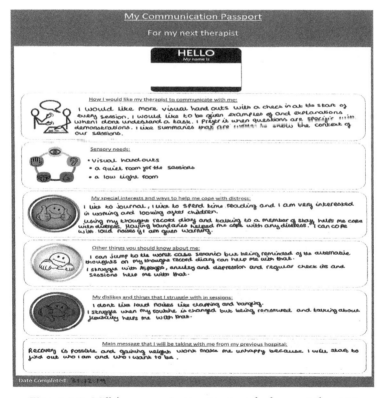

Figure 5.5. *Milly's communication passport for her next therapist*

COMPLICATING FACTORS

One of the challenges with maximizing family support was that Milly's mother was working in several places and consequently finding it difficult to attend family therapy sessions.

Following individual CRT, Milly was admitted to hospital with *Clostridium* infection. Unfortunately, during this period, she lost weight and had great difficulty eating. Over this time Milly also noticed some swelling of lymph nodes in her groin and neck. This led to heightened anxiety for Milly as she reported, 'I am scared my cancer may come back'.

Furthermore, on Milly's return to the ward, some new patients were self-harming, her mother was on holiday and there were uncertainties around her transition to a residential placement. Milly's mental state deteriorated, and this was demonstrated by significant stress and self-harming behaviour. Milly reported that part of this presentation was related to her ASD rituals and she counted the number of times that she was harming herself.

FOLLOW-UP

Following CRT, Milly remained on the ward and engaged in further individual psychological work with her therapist. Themes included working on a collaborative formulation in order to come up with a shared understanding of the AN. We then agreed to start more complex individual psychological work, such as cognitive behavioural therapy. This was to identify unhelpful patterns of thinking and behaviours using different strategies and techniques and where we can explore the accuracy of the beliefs of weight gain as signifiers of happiness with the aim to change these thoughts and behaviours.

Furthermore, individual CRT assisted with Milly's confidence in attending psychology groups and she attended the flexibility group (group version of CRT) and the self-esteem group. Milly seems more likely to attend groups and to stay longer in the sessions when she is partially familiar with the materials and has a therapeutic relationship with a facilitator, for instance if her individual therapist is present. In groups, Milly seemed to work well in pairs with a peer and will reflect on tasks but struggles more with group discussions.

Milly also engaged in systemic family therapy with her mother where themes of the ongoing therapeutic work included externalizing (White, 1988) *ASD, OCD, ED*, and *routine*, as well as exploring 'loss', 'missing out' and being on an inpatient ED ward. Other themes included the interplay of guilt, both Milly's and her mother's, with *ASD, OCD, ED*, and *routine*.

The family had engaged in four sessions of systemic family therapy at an irregular interval due to scheduling conflicts. Prior to this, four individual systemic sessions were offered to Milly to build rapport and to prepare for the therapeutic context with other family members and another systemic clinician. The decision to engage systemically with Milly individually was made in collaboration with her and her mother, and was useful in helping the systemic clinicians agree the most suitable therapeutic space for the joint sessions. The systemic interventions were provided by a family and systemic psychotherapy trainee and a senior family and systemic psychotherapist using a reflecting team model (Andersen, 1987). At Milly's request, she and her mother were the only family members to attend the sessions despite there being an open invitation for others to join. Nevertheless, a genogram (McGoldrick & Gerson, 1985) was used to bring the unheard voices of other family members into the therapy room. Milly and her mother had previous experience of family therapy during a different admission at another institution and had some reservations about family therapy. They were clear they wanted sessions to be purposeful and not 'airy fairy', so time was taken to explore how the systemic clinicians would know when the process was useful or not or if they had entered into the 'airy fairy' zone.

Early individual systemic sessions focused on loss, and particularly the death of Milly's grandfather, and the estrangement with her father through parental separation. Those sessions also provided Milly with a space to think about her father's depression and alcohol misuse, and she disclosed how her father had blamed his own personal challenges on her cancer diagnosis and treatment. This had an understandable impact on Milly's relationship with her father and she expressed certainty that she did not want him to engage in the systemic family sessions or with any other aspect of her treatment. Although expressing certainty about not wanting a relationship with her father, Milly also showed ambivalence due to wanting a 'father figure' in her life, but she knew that her father's past attempts at communication often resulted in emotional difficulties and other challenges for her and her mother.

Exploring and making meaning from their individual lived experiences and relationships with *ASD, OCD, ED,* and *routine* were an important part of the systemic interventions. The various externalized terms were put onto colourful signs which were placed in the therapeutic room with Milly, her mother and the systemic clinicians, along with their evolving genogram. The use of these signs allowed a dialogue between and with the various components, and provided a fertile space for exploration of their individual lived experiences and subjective meanings, and also allowed a safe therapeutic space to challenge some of Milly's black or white thinking. The systemic clinicians regularly engaged with the various signs in the room which will be explored in more detail in Chapter 9.

The Structural (Minuchin, 1974), Milan (Selivini, *et al.,* 1980) and Narrative (White & Epston, 1990) models amongst a range of approaches informed the systemic individual and family interventions with Milly and her mother. The systemic clinicians also used visual charts and diagrams to contextualize 'healthy' weight and to engage with those conversations Milly's mother believed their previous family therapy had skirted around. The systemic family therapy focused on creating a thinking space which provided consistency in terms of the room layout, the session plan and conditions. These were, however, checked throughout sessions to ensure Milly could fully engage in the process. There was a continual balancing act between being consistent and also flexible enough to meet the needs of Milly and her mother, often against a background of challenges from an ever-changing ward life. Despite trying to be consistent, it was challenging to arrange sessions at the same time and during times that did not conflict with Milly's routines. Some sessions were scheduled when Milly had hoped to be on her walk and so she struggled with remaining emotionally and cognitively present in the room. This posed a dilemma for the systemic clinicians where on the one hand this offered an opportunity for Milly to be more flexible and to challenge her routines, whilst on the other hand scheduling around routines ensured that she could be as present as possible within the therapeutic space. Nevertheless, this challenge was often openly shared by the systemic clinicians with Milly and her mother, and whilst they had differing opinions, they were able to engage in a constructive dialogue that prioritized the sessions over routine. Throughout all of the systemic interventions offered one thing that became clear to the systemic clinicians is that both Milly and her mother responded well to creativity, humour and most importantly, transparency.

TREATMENT STRATEGIES: WHAT WE
LEARNED FROM WORKING WITH MILLY

The clinical team engaged Milly collaboratively in her care planning. For example, we explored what was most challenging for Milly in terms of the inpatient environment. Milly reported that her rigidity was making the inpatient environment most difficult for her. Subsequently, Milly was first offered CRT (Tchanturia et al., 2010) from the psychological therapies team. Our work with Milly taught us the following:

- Acutely ill AN inpatients are difficult to engage in psychological work. CRT aimed to offer a collaborative adjunct treatment that would motivate further psychological engagement later on in treatment. Milly engaged well during her individual CRT sessions with Yasemin, which helped her during the treatment journey on the ward. She needed twice as many sessions as usual, though.

- From Milly we learned useful adaptations that can be applied to psychological therapy and can enhance engagement. For example, more sessions, and developing a communication passport to give her an easy way to communicate and engage with her new therapist.

- Milly's work with the occupational therapist and other members of the psychological therapy team allowed us to be reflective on her sensory styles. For example, we supported Milly with headphones to minimize noise and help her to concentrate on food.

- After meals, we noticed that Milly was often covered with a blanket and after discussing this with her, we were clear that this was Milly's way to reduce her anxiety and isolate herself. Gradually we introduced a weighted shoulder massager, which Milly found useful and meant it was easier for the team and other patients in the ward to be with her. We changed the lighting as well, which made the environment more comfortable for Milly.

- Milly was finding groups extremely difficult, but groups (community meetings, meal times, psychological groups) are a core treatment element for the inpatient treatment programme. Engagement with the CRT therapist and trusting her made it possible for Milly to attend the group programme fully (instead of leaving groups after 10 minutes as she had done previously).

TREATMENT IMPLICATIONS OF THE CASE

Clinical outcomes show that, following CRT, Milly's body mass index (BMI) increased. Table 5.3 illustrates Milly's scores on the self-report measures described above pre- and post-CRT. It also provides the healthy control normative scores for each of these measures to put Milly's scores into context. Clinical outcomes also demonstrated an improvement in the global score of the EDE-Q, decreasing from 5.1 to 4.8. To put this into context, the global score from a community sample of women is 1.5 (Fairburn & Beglin, 1994). Furthermore, Milly's scores on the DFlex suggest that her cognitive rigidity and attention to detail have improved. However, interestingly, Milly's scores on the neuropsychological tests Rey-Osterrieth Complex Figure and The Brixton Spatial Anticipation Test demonstrated that her central coherence scores had marginally decreased and set-shifting skills had slightly decreased. This may be because of her being more aware and insightful of her thinking styles following weight restoration and her honest nature.

Table 5.3. Changes after CRT

Outcome measures	Time 1 Before CRT	Time 2 After CRT	Healthy control norms	+ improved = no change - worse
BMI	-	-	19–25	+
Eating Disorder Examination-Questionnaire (Global Score)	5.1		1.5	+
Detail Flexibility Questionnaire: Cognitive rigidity	63	55	31	+
Attention to detail	53	42	31	+
The Rey-Osterrieth Complex Figure (ROCF)	0.7	0.4	1.6	-
The Brixton Spatial Anticipation Test	10	11	9.8	-
Motivational Ruler: Importance to change	10	10	n/a	=
Ability	6	9	n/a	+

Summary

This case study provides support for the acceptability and effectiveness of the inpatient eating disorder treatment programme, when co-morbidity with ASD is taken into account, and an integrated formulation and treatment work with good communication amongst the multidisciplinary team is the main focus. Considering patients with AN are often difficult to engage and retain in treatment and ASD makes it more difficult, CRT has enabled Milly to engage in a collaborative and reflective psychoeducational and cognitive training intervention (see Tchanturia *et al.*, 2014, 2017 for systematic reviews).

Recognition of ASD in females is very challenging. Milly's mother explained:

> I pressed and pressed and pressed and we got a formal diagnosis of Asperger's when she was 13. However, we were going to be referred to whoever, I don't know and then very soon after it all got sort of swallowed up…

Milly's mother voiced the thoughts of other families who are frustrated with the existing care pathway:

> No one listens to me. …if they listened maybe the help is not there, I do not know, but she is not getting it. She is now getting some form of therapy in the ward and the OT department I think is fantastic, but that just occupies her, It is not solving the issue, it is not dealing with the issue, it is a distraction.

After completing CRT, patients may be more aware of their thinking style and how this impacts on their daily functioning. It is possible that after receiving this intervention patients will be more equipped with strategies to adapt to the environment and make better use of treatment if they choose to. One of the strengths highlighted in the literature is the average to high IQ in AN population (Lopez Stahl & Tchanturia, 2010).

CRT also provides an opportunity to establish a therapeutic relationship in the acute stage of AN/ASD, which may positively influence engagement in further comprehensive psychological therapy. For example, in Milly's case, she was able to continue with individual psychological work and she was also able to attend the group treatment programme, where patients have a safe space and support to be with the other people and develop social skills.

Undoubtedly further work needs to be carried out to assess the therapeutic value of CRT and diagnostic tools for sensory sensitivities and female ASD diagnostic tools (Sedgewick *et al.*, 2019). Ideally, large-scale studies would be conducted across multiple sites to evaluate the intervention and its generalizability.

In summary, this case study highlights support for the acceptability of a multidisciplinary team approach. Good communication is vital in the initial treatment calibration exercise to facilitate engagement and address thinking styles and cognitive features before moving onto more in-depth and complex psychological work.

References

American Psychiatric Association (2013) *Diagnostic and Statistical Manual of Mental Disorders* (5th edition). Arlington, VA: American Psychiatric Publishing.

Andersen, T. (1987) 'The reflecting team: Dialogue and meta-dialogue in clinical work.' *Family Process, 26,* 415–428.

Beck, A. (1993) 'Cognitive therapy: Past, present, and future.' *Journal of Consulting and Clinical Psychology, 61*(2), 194–198.

Burgess, P.W. & Shallice, T. (1997) *The Hayling and Brixton tests* [Test manual]. Thames Valley Test Company Limited.

Fairburn, C.G. & Beglin, S.J. (1994) 'Assessment of eating disorders: Interview or Self-report Questionnaire?' *The International Journal of Eating Disorders, 16*(4), 363–370.

Hummel, T., Sekinger, B., Wolf, S.R., Pauli, E. & Kobal, G. (1997) '"Sniffin'sticks": Olfactory performance assessed by the combined testing of odor identification, odor discrimination and olfactory threshold.' *Chemical Senses, 22*(1), 39–52.

Hus, V. & Lord, C. (2014) 'The autism diagnostic observation schedule, module 4: Revised algorithm and standardized severity scores.' *Journal of Autism and Developmental Disorders, 44*(8), 1996–2012.

Kinnaird, E., Norton, C. & Tchanturia, K. (2017) 'Clinicians' views on working with anorexia nervosa and autism spectrum disorder comorbidity: A qualitative study.' *BMC Psychiatry, 17,* 292.

Kinnaird, E., Norton, C., Pimblett, C., Stewart, C. & Tchanturia, K. (2019a) 'Eating as an autistic adult: An exploratory qualitative study.' *PlosOne, 29, 14*(8), e0221937.

Kinnaird, E., Norton, C., Stewart, C. & Tchanturia, K. (2019b) 'Same behaviours, different reasons: What do patients with co-occurring anorexia and autism want from treatment?' *International Review of Psychiatry, 31*(4), 308–317.

Lang, K., Roberts, M., Harrison, A., Lopez, C., Goddard, E., Khondoker, M. & Tchanturia, K. (2016) 'Central coherence in eating disorders: A synthesis of studies using the Rey Osterrieth Complex Figure test.' *PlosOne, 11*(11), e0165467.

Lopez, C., Stahl, D. & Tchanturia, K. (2010) 'Estimated intelligence quotient in anorexia nervosa: A systematic review and meta-analysis of the literature.' *Annals of General Psychiatry, 9,* doi: 10.1186/1744-859X-9-40.

McGoldrick, M. & Gerson, R. (1985) *Genograms in Family Assessment.* New York: W. W. Norton & Company.

Minuchin, S. (1974) *Families and Family Therapy.* Cambridge, MA: Harvard University Press.

Mueller, C., Kallert, S., Renner, B., Stiassny, K., Temmel, A.F., Hummel, T. & Kobal, G. (2003) 'Quantitative assessment of gustatory function in a clinical context using impregnated "taste strips".' *Rhinology, 41*(1), 2.

Osterrieth, P.A. (1944) 'Filetest de copie d'une figure complex: Contribution à l'étude de la perception et de la mémoire [The test of copying a complex figure: A contribution to the study of perception and memory].' *Archives de Psychologie, 30*, 286–356.

Roberts, M.E., Barthel, F.M.S., Lopez, C., Tchanturia, K. & Treasure, J.L. (2011) 'Development and validation of the Detail and Flexibility Questionnaire (DFlex) in eating disorders.' *Eating Behaviors, 12*, 168–174.

Sedgewick, F., Kerr-Gaffney, J., Leppanen, J. & Tchanturia, K. (2019) 'Anorexia nervosa, autism, and the ADOS: How appropriate is the new algorithm in identifying cases? *Frontiers in Psychiatry, 10*, 507.

Selvini, M.P., Boscolo, L., Cecchin, G. & Prata, G. (1980) 'Hypothesizing-Circularity-Neutrality: Three guidelines for the conductor of the session.' *Family Process, 19*, 3–12.

Tavassoli, T., Hoekstra, R. & Baron-Cohen, S. (2014) 'The Sensory Perception Quotient (SPQ): Development and validation of a new sensory questionnaire for adults with and without autism.' *Molecular Autism, 5*(1), 29.

Tchanturia, K. (2015a) *Cognitive Remediation Therapy (CRT) for Eating and Weight Disorders.* London and New York: Routledge, Taylor & Francis Group.

Tchanturia, K. (2015b) 'Cognitive Remediation and Emotion Skills Training.' London: King's College London. Retrieved from https://131e99a4-b06b-135c-641a-44c0c057bded.filesusr.com/ugd/2e1018_6471824d0240489e8bef9781064bd023.pdf on 11/08/20.

Tchanturia, K., Adamson, J., Leppanen, J. & Westwood, H. (2019) 'Characteristics of autism spectrum disorder in anorexia nervosa: A naturalistic study in an inpatient treatment programme.' *Autism, 23*(1), 123–130.

Tchanturia, K., Davies, H., Reeder, C. & Wykes, T. (2010) 'Cognitive remediation therapy for anorexia nervosa.' London: King's College London, University of London. Retrieved from. https://docs.wixstatic.com/ugd/2e1018_f71866481f9f44e5a342fb068b891a8c.pdf on 06/07/20.

Tchanturia, K., Giombini, L., Leppanen, J. & Kinnaird, E. (2017) 'Evidence for cognitive remediation therapy in young people with anorexia nervosa: Systematic review and meta-analysis of the literature.' *European Eating Disorders Review, 25*(4), 227–236.

Tchanturia, K., Harrison, A., Davies, H., Roberts, M., Oldershaw, A., Nakazato, M., Morris, R., Schmidt, U. & Treasure, J. (2011) 'Cognitive flexibility and clinical severity in Eating Disorders.' *Plos one* 6(6): e20462.

Tchanturia, K., Lounes, N. & Holttum, S. (2014) 'Cognitive remediation in anorexia nervosa and related conditions: A systematic review.' *European Eating Disorders Review, 22*, 454–462.

Treasure, J. & Schmidt, U. (2013) 'The cognitive-interpersonal maintenance model of anorexia nervosa revisited: A summary of the evidence for cognitive, socio-emotional and interpersonal predisposing and perpetuating factors.' *Journal of Eating Disorders, 1*(1), 13.

White, M. (1988) 'The externalizing of the problem and the re-authoring of lives and relationships.' *Dulwich Centre Newsletter*, Summer, 3–21.

White, M. & Epston, D. (1990) *Narrative Means to Therapeutic Ends.* New York: W. W. Norton & Company.

Chapter 6

Adam's Story

SUPPORTING A MALE WITH ANOREXIA NERVOSA AND ELEVATED AUTISTIC FEATURES

Katherine Smith, Yasemin Dandil, Claire Baillie,
———— *Hubertus Himmerich and Kate Tchanturia* ————

Adam's story describes the work from a multidisciplinary specialist eating disorder team in supporting a male with anorexia nervosa and elevated autistic features. We also reflect on what we learned as a health professional team from Adam.

PATIENT HISTORY

Adam was a 24-year-old man with a diagnosis of anorexia nervosa (AN). Adam had been in varying levels of treatment intensity for over two years before his current admission, during which time he had made little improvement and had struggled to restore his weight. He had been at an intensive day care programme for five months before his inpatient stay and previous to that he had been in an outpatient programme for a year and a half. Adam had a fear of 'fatness' and his body becoming 'soft'. He also had obsessive-compulsive disorder (OCD) pre-eating disorder (ED) onset.

Adam was diagnosed with AN when he was 17 after losing his appetite following a trauma of being mugged, which intensified his OCD rituals. Adam reported that he wanted to be strong to be able to protect himself and others. He liked his new physique and wanted to lose more weight and he started to exercise. At this stage he believed his OCD took over, making his exercise obsessive and compulsive. Adam wanted to restore his weight, but his fear of fatness prevented that.

PERSONAL AND FAMILY HISTORY

Adam grew up in the city with his parents and reported being a 'tight unit'. He was the only child and described his childhood as happy. Adam reported that his family are proud perfectionists with a sense of superiority over others. Adam's father has a diagnosis of paranoid schizophrenia and his mother had a diagnosis of bulimia when she was a teenager. Adam reported wanting to 'be in charge' and an 'authority figure' at school and consequently there were disciplinary issues throughout school. Adam reported having no friends and never having had a romantic relationship. Adam usually worked in information technology (IT) but was currently off work due to his illness.

PHYSICAL HEALTH

When Adam presented to our clinic, his body mass index (BMI) was in the severe to extreme range of AN. In the physical examination, he was clearly underweight, and the left medial aspect of his thumb was caved in due to multiple skin picking.

He showed markers of malnutrition in his laboratory parameters, e.g. a low white blood cell count of 3.62x109 cells/litre (normal limits: 4x109–11x109 cells/litre), a low red blood cell count of 3.81x1012/litre (normal limits: 4.5x1012–5.8x1012), a low globulin concentration of 16 grams/litre (normal limits: 25–35) and a low albumin concentration of 54 grams/litre (normal limits: 35–50). Additionally, his urea levels were raised to 8.5 mmol/litre (normal limits: 3.3–6.7) which is a sign of not having enough fluid intake.

Some hormones were also out of range. His testosterone level was extremely low <0.4 nmol/litre (normal limits: 8.6–29.0) and his prolactin level was significantly raised to 1287 mIU/litre (normal limits: 86–324). Those disturbances were most probably consequences of self-starvation.

PRESENTATION

Adam presented atypically in the inpatient ward environment. It is important to note, for context, that Adam was the first male patient admitted to a previously female-only inpatient ward. Reports have described Adam as 'an old person in a young person's body'. He was always overly appreciative and respectful to both staff and patients. Staff reported that Adam appeared 'uncomfortable' in the patient 'role', often using generic 'scripted' language to describe his thoughts, feelings and needs. He often seemed unable to read the level of formality in an interaction, for example being unsure if a handshake or a hug was appropriate. Adam would also often seem distracted – scanning the room looking for switches; he reported that one of his OCD rituals is to ensure all switches that are not in use are turned off.

Adam presented with limited facial expressions which often would not coincide with his body language and what he was saying. However, Adam was also humorous and had a quick wit.

Adam asked for support with his exercise compulsions, such as leaving his bedroom door open so he does not exercise in his bedroom. Furthermore, seemingly related to his ideals of being strong, Adam had an intense interest in 'macho' figures, such as Mark Wahlberg and characters from 'Dragon Ball Z'. Adam had a strong preference for non-sweet foods and was fairly rigid regarding his meal choices (e.g. only eating the same amount of nuts each day).

ASSESSMENTS

Adam completed several ASD screening assessments such as the Autism Diagnostic Observation Schedule, Second Edition (ADOS-2) and Autism Spectrum Quotient (AQ-10). In both of them he scored under the threshold for an ASD diagnosis. More details of each assessment:

- ADOS-2 Module 4: Adam scored 7 according to the new algorithm (Hus & Lord, 2014). The cut-off for suspected ASD is set at 8. Adam's scores suggested he had complete lack of empathetic or emotional gestures and slightly formalized use of language integrated with otherwise flexible speech. However, Adam scored as having no problems in conversational and social abilities.

- AQ-50 & AQ-10: For the longer version of this self-report measure of ASD, Adam scored 25; the cut-off is 32. For the shorter version, completed on admission, Adam scored 5. The cut-off for ASD is 6, meaning he scored below the threshold for both.

- Adam completed a sensory study (experiment and self-report) which indicated that his sense of taste and smell were within the range similar to healthy control participants of the study.

- Adam completed a second sensory extended assessment in Occupational Therapy. He scored more than most people on sensory sensitivity and sensory avoiding. He also scored lower than most on sensory seeking.

- Intelligence quotient (IQ) test: Adam scored 85 on this test and the average IQ is 100.

EVALUATING TREATMENT PROGRESS

Adam reported that his thinking style was detailed and focused which can be a 'burden' on him. Adam and his therapist, therefore, agreed that cognitive remediation therapy (CRT; Tchanturia et al., 2010) can be a potentially helpful intervention in exploring and working towards managing Adam's flexibility and perfectionism. Individual CRT sessions were completed in 10 twice-weekly sessions (30 minutes each). With regard to exploring the work of CRT with Adam, this case study will take a 'bigger picture' perspective and summarize the content of the sessions. Adam reported that by the end of his admission he would like to be able to see the bigger picture and be flexible. Adam also wished his therapist to be able to see the bigger picture and be flexible to instil hope in him by reminding him of his goals.

CRT tasks

Adam was particularly good at the 'complex picture task' (Figure 6.1), which encourages bigger picture thinking and involved him being asked to describe a picture for his therapist to draw. In subsequent sessions, this was related to applying bigger picture thinking during his meals instead of focusing on the components as separate entities.

Adam was also good at identifying small behavioural changes using the concept of Specific Measurable Achievable Realistic Timely (SMART) goals, to enhance his flexibility. One of the goals identified was to 'keep changing my walks when taking 15-minute walks once a week for flexibility'. Adam was then courageous enough to use one of these walks to go on a mindfulness walk with his therapist, which he appeared to engage well in. On reflection Adam reported that it was an uncomfortable experience for him; however, he was then able to reflect, 'The walk taught me I take things for granted and I should be grateful for my surroundings around me. The walk was very relaxing, and I enjoyed it.' Further goals Adam identified included choosing other options during his meals and 'on home leave, I will offer to help my parents more instead of isolating myself in my room (watch football with father or help mother in the kitchen)'.

Figure 6.1. *Example of CRT 'complex picture task'*

Towards the end of the sessions, Adam created a mind map (Figure 6.2) which aimed to summarize and consolidate what had been covered in the CRT sessions. We also had discussions around how flexibility is related to his general plan for recovery, and how it helps to take the next steps in treatment and to the future in general. Adam related the quotes in the mind map to his recovery by reporting he would view his meal plan in terms of holding on to the bigger picture. He also reported, 'I need to take a step back and not have such rigid routines as I miss out on things and my motivation helps me see things from different angles'.

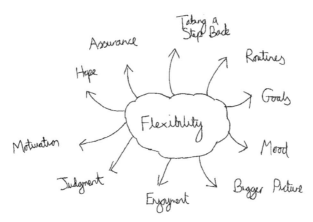

Figure 6.2. *Adam's mind map summarizing his work in individual CRT*

Cognitive remediation and emotion skills training (CREST)

Following individual CRT Adam was offered Cognitive Remediation and Emotion Skills Training (CREST; Tchanturia, 2015) which primarily aimed to target emotion recognition and management, expression of emotions and positive communication. CREST usually consists of 10 sessions. However, Adam did not engage in all sessions on offer due to requesting self-discharge after session five. Therefore, this section will summarize the sessions offered.

Adam recognized that he is prone to negative biases and wanted to use the sessions 'to gain a balanced perspective and focus more on the positives'. He also reported, 'I want to embrace my emotions more instead of hiding away and bottling them up'. To address Adam's negative bias, it was agreed that Adam would identify three good things in his day which included what he appreciated, what he valued and what he felt positive about. In subsequent sessions, Adam reported that he found the exercise made it easier for him to focus on the positives and made him feel more 'grateful'. Therefore, Adam was encouraged to continue with this exercise every day and reported that he has seen an improvement in his negative bias. Adam also engaged in the 'Optimal positive to negative emotions ratio task', which encouraged him to look for a balance of three positive emotions/experiences to one negative emotion/experience. Additionally, Adam reported that he would just smile more often to improve the experience of positive emotions.

During a task in which we explored an emotion words list which aimed to recognize specific emotions and to provide Adam with a broader emotion vocabulary, Adam reported that he would most like to be peaceful and he felt this emotion when he was praised and recognized at work by his colleagues for doing a good job. He described feeling satisfied and content and, in his body, he felt blushed/ hot in the face with a smile on his face too, light in the chest and no intrusive thoughts going on in his mind or second-guessing. He reported that this moment helped him see the glass as 'half full and not half empty' and strengthened his beliefs in himself.

Sessions also explored how emotions are transient and tell us something about our environment at the time rather than being permanent. Adam was able to reflect that he realized that it is not just the eating disorder dictating his thoughts, there are positive thoughts as well. Adam reported that he managed difficult  emotions by bottling them up and the difficult emotions included 'sadness, disappointment, hurt, embarrassment, being impressed, stressed or worthless'. Adam reported that his father also tended to bottle up feelings; however, his mother tended to express hers. We then looked at the advantages of bottling up feelings in which Adam identified that 'You can then keep feelings to yourself and can be private and professional at work and not let emotions get in the way, you are more independent and people think you are all right and good to talk too'. He identified the negative effect of bottling up emotions to be 'People are unaware of how you are really feeling, isolated in the community and the emotions can then overflow'. Adam reported that he deals with difficult emotions and anxiety by exercising. However, he was then able to identify alternative ways he can try to help himself deal with his emotions; these included talking to others, such as family, friends and health professionals; drawing, art, colouring; and embracing emotions and expressing them and focusing on the good things when having a bad day.

On reflection, in terms of what he learned about himself from the therapy, he stated, 'I have learned that emotions are not fixed, and they tend to come and go.' Aspects of therapy that Adam identified as especially helpful included 'looking at the brighter side of seemingly negative emotions by using the optimal positive to negative ratio and three good things'. He felt that the fact that some of the strategies offered temporary relief but some issues remained ongoing was not helpful. Adam then reported that he learned strategies that he could use in the future which include the three positives to one negative method, learning to smile more and the three good things per day. He also reported that he has learned to 'put his oxygen mask on first'.

Adam and his therapist then agreed to a joint meeting with his key worker when he was discharged to the other treatment department: a day residential programme. Adam reported that he wanted his key worker to continue to encourage him to identify three good things, be flexible by trying new things, help him with his motivation and give him hope by reminding him of his goals.

Psychological therapy groups

Adam attended the body image group and reported that he sometimes gets overwhelmed in group settings and apologized in advance to other participants if he walked out, which he never did. However, Adam appeared more vocal and confident in groups since being an inpatient and being more familiar with his peers. He was thoughtful and insightful in groups, contributing to discussions and adding real depth.

CHALLENGES FACED IN TREATMENT

Adam struggled with excessive exercise during his admission, with his weight remaining stagnant for the four months of his inpatient admission before requesting to be self-discharged back to a residential day care unit. His request for self-discharge also meant he was unable to complete all the CREST sessions on offer.

Due to Adam perceiving that it is hard for him to change his mind about things and see other people's perspectives due to his rigidity, there were times that Adam appeared to struggle with implementing the skills from the sessions in real-life situations. Although Adam seemed willing to challenge this rigidity, he found change difficult and was often guarded to suggestions and resistant to therapy.

USEFUL ADAPTATIONS APPLIED

Adam demonstrated detailed thinking and found it challenging to summarize information in CRT sessions. Adam then found it helpful when he went through the task and identified strategies with his therapist. He consequently found it helpful to use bullet points and then found it even easier to provide a verbal summary. In some situations, in CRT, Adam found it easier to provide verbal responses. This is important for adaptation of interventions such as CRT where written responses are often required. Adaptations also included being able to embrace the positives in Adam's detailed thinking and relating it to his job which he was particularly fond of. We discussed that in areas in his job, detail focused thinking can be beneficial. Adam was then able to relate this task to real life. He reported that bigger picture thinking can help him 'speed things up' on certain tasks at work. Further useful adaptations to his CRT included frequent repetitions of the content of the sessions.

When the sessions progressed and with the rapport Adam was able to build with his therapist, he appeared to start to let his guard down and was able to be more open in his sessions and expressed his thoughts and feelings. He would often report the stressors he faced with his father being unwell and supporting fellow peers on the ward. We therefore spoke about the importance of Adam looking after himself first and the analogy of 'putting on your oxygen mask first'. A useful adaption was to ensure that the materials in sessions were covered at a slower pace and that Adam was provided with a therapeutic space where he felt comfortable to open up his feelings.

Adam found structured assessments useful. Using questionnaires, images and giving Adam written information to take away also proved effective. Adam also seemed to appreciate working together with the healthcare team who encouraged him to generate his manageable suggestions.

What we learned as a health professional team from Adam

Although Adam did not formally score above the threshold on ASD measures, he did have elevated ASD features such as complete lack of empathetic or emotional gestures and formalized use of language. Adam needed additional support, especially when clinicians were flagging up his atypical behaviour. From Adam, we learned the importance of a wider understanding of AN and ASD. Just because a patient's behaviour is atypical does not mean they have ASD. We have to be careful about additional labels. Through Adam taking part in a research study, he had to complete an IQ test. Having the additional information of an IQ test proved significant in Adam's case as this is what flagged up that he may possibly have a learning disability, which we would then be able to support and manage appropriately. We also found it is useful to work with the patient at their pace and adapting our communication style; the rate of change in behaviour with Adam was slower but significant.

References

Hus, V. & Lord, C. (2014) 'The autism diagnostic observation schedule, module 4: Revised algorithm and standardized severity scores.' *Journal of Autism and Developmental Disorders*, 44(8), 1996–2012.

Tchanturia, K. (2015) 'Cognitive Remediation and Emotion Skills Training.' London: King's College London. Retrieved from. https://131e99a4-b06b-135c-641a-44c0c057bded.filesusr.com/ugd/2e1018_6471824d0240489e8bef9781064bd023.pdf on 06/07/20.

Tchanturia, K., Davies, H., Reeder, C. & Wykes, T. (2010) 'Cognitive remediation therapy for anorexia nervosa.' London: King's College London, University of London. Retrieved from https://docs.wixstatic.com/ugd/2e1018_f71866481f9f44e5a342fb068b891a8c.pdf on 06/07/20.

Supporting the Supporters

LEARNING HOW TO UNDERSTAND AND BETTER SUPPORT OUR LOVED ONES

In this section, we hear from a carer with an autistic son, who is also a psychotherapist. We also hear from two family therapists who have been actively involved in developing the PEACE Pathway. This section demonstrates struggles carers often face, whilst putting a psychological 'hat' on them. I hope it shows how the PEACE Pathway can be implemented in the context of carers in a clinical setting.

Chapter 7

Making the 'Mental Transition' from Clinician to Carer

THE IMPORTANCE OF EXPRESSED EMOTION

 *Madeleine Oakley*

My now grown-up son was diagnosed with autism at the age of two and also has an intellectual disability. Following his diagnosis, which came as a shock, I struggled with the idea of having a dual identity – I worked as a mental health clinician and now, suddenly, as a parent of a child with a disability, I was referred to as a 'carer'. I needed to make a mental transition from being one of the professionals, who had treated other people and families in need, to being a patient – a parent struggling with her own toddler son, who had not met the milestones of typically developing children and did not seem to be developing language. I was myself now totally dependent on professionals for getting any help for my son.

On a family holiday when my son was around five years of age, the reluctance he had shown towards eating different and varied types of food came to a head. We were stuck in the middle of rural France and, aware that none of his usual preferred foods or comforts were available, he suddenly refused to eat anything except for things that were chocolate-based. I was in a panic: would he starve to death? 'As long as he was eating something…'

The holiday was intrinsically stressful because three family generations were present and the accommodation was basic and less comfortable than expected. As a result, my son witnessed his parents arguing, which made him cry uncontrollably. This continued for some hours and up until bedtime, I tried to soothe him in every empathic way I could think of, but then, worn down myself by facing all the disruption to the routines which I had carefully developed over the past few years to make him feel secure, I gave up in despair myself and cried alongside him helplessly.

At that moment, Alara, the professional carer who usually looked after my son after school so that I could work, came into my mind. I couldn't imagine her crying in despair over not being able to soothe him. In fact, he never cried in this way at all when she cared for him. I then remembered the research in Expressed Emotion (known as EE), which I had learnt about while training to be a systemic family therapist.

Expressed Emotion

This research had come about in the 1970s when Vaughn & Leff (1976), using the Camberwell Family Interview, recognized that patients who had schizophrenia had better outcomes when they were looked after by professional carers compared with when they were looked after by family members or 'family carers'. This was because family carers were more likely to be critical, hostile and emotionally over-involved with their cared-for family member.

The idea of Expressed Emotion involved measuring the emotional environment in families where a member had schizophrenia (Leff & Vaughn, 1985). Expressed Emotion consisted of the following four qualities in family carers:

- critical comments

- hostility

- emotional over-involvement

- warmth.

If there was a high number of the first three of these qualities in family interactions, the family member with schizophrenia was more likely to relapse. If these first three qualities were less intense, then the family member with schizophrenia was more likely to recover. It all made a lot of sense, apart from the idea that if the family carer was emotionally over-involved with the cared-for family member, it would be detrimental to their recovery and general emotional equilibrium. This was counter-intuitive. Surely being emotionally over-involved could be seen as a sign of love from the carer towards the cared-for family member? How could the parent and carer of a son or daughter with special needs – a full-time job – not be emotionally over-involved?

What became apparent to me through my own experience was that these research findings had not found their way to parent-carers of autistic children such as myself. 'Autism parents' were a difficult group to engage. Their lives were chaotic and often dominated by their children having unpredictable meltdowns, however much they tried to avoid situations which might act as a trigger. 'Autism parents' generally felt unsupported and misunderstood. They had little time or respect for Child and Adolescent Mental Health Services (CAMHS). Many had tried to get help from CAMHS, as we discovered in our research with carers in the PEACE project (Adamson *et al.*, 2020), and were met with a hostile reception: 'trying to get a child with autism to go to CAMHS when everything about CAMHS is a sensory overload and the people leave a lot to be desired. They might have the qualifications but they don't have the ability to communicate to an autistic child' (parent interview).

Very little was offered to parents in my situation 20 years ago, beyond the Early Bird Programme (1998), where, among other things, parents were advised to throw away their autistic children's videos and VCR machines. Any autism parent then knew that these machines and their 'Thomas the Tank Engine' videos were absolute lifelines for autistic children and their families, providing the child with hours of engagement and fascination with the different train engines and the parents with respite.

Just as it became clear to me that if I were to interact with my son in a low Expressed Emotion way (by not crying alongside him but stepping back and behaving more calmly), I might find it easier to de-escalate his distressed behaviour, substantial research over the past three decades has now demonstrated the benefits of low EE in families and carers in their behaviour towards people they care for (Amaresha & Venkatasubramanian, 2012).

Carers of family members who have concurrent autism and anorexia nervosa

In looking at tools that could be developed to help carers of family members with mental health disorders, we became aware that there has not yet been research into the needs of carers of family members who have concurrent eating disorders and autism. A preliminary analysis of carers' interviews by our team (Adamson *et al.,* 2020) in the 'Pathway for Eating disorders and Autism developed from Clinical Experience' (the PEACE project) demonstrated the difficulties these carers have in accessing services and getting diagnoses for their loved ones. For example, one carer said, 'It wasn't an early diagnosis, it was a really late diagnosis…she [her daughter] was just over 13'.

We found in the PEACE project that, consequently, carers needed to involve themselves intensely in the practical affairs of the family members they were caring for; they were 'case managing' their own children:

> You wouldn't be allowed to type the word I would like to say. It was absolutely appalling. I mean even now I have other mums sitting at my kitchen table and I am doing their EHCPs (Education, Health and Care Plans) with them because most…of the places… they don't have the funding, they don't have the staff and they don't have the interest.

The interviews also revealed that the carers were suffering greatly themselves, feeling that they were isolated:

> It is really hard. You want sympathy, you want empathy, but you just don't want…people going, 'God, what an awful nightmare', which is why I think I have cut myself off from a lot of people because I just don't want that kind of, 'Oh, how devastating for you', I don't want that kind of thing.

One commented about a health professional whom she spoke to about her daughter's condition:

> She didn't provide the right support for me at all. I mean she just kept saying to look after yourself and have massages and that kind of stuff… I can't be bothered to have a massage, you know you are lying there having a massage and you just kind of start worrying about everything, it is kind of pointless.

PEACE Pathway carers reported having nowhere to turn other than to their own groups on social media sites such as Facebook, and that they would really welcome more input from professionals aimed at supporting carers:

> I mean it is incredibly complex [their child having anorexia and autism], so it is really stressful and actually…now I am just dealing with it on my own with my husband and my daughter.

We found mapping the themes that emerged from the qualitative interviews we have conducted with carers very useful (Figure 7.1).

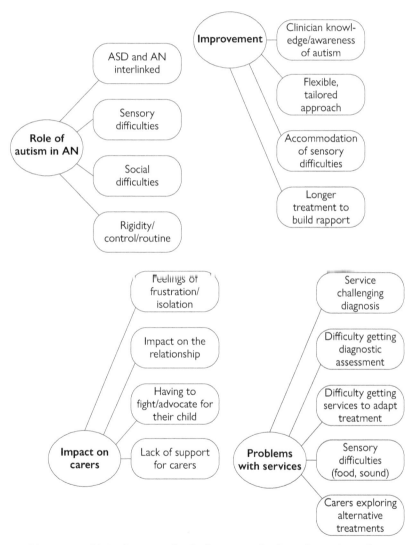

Figure 7.1. *Main themes and sub-themes results from thematic analysis*

The paradox of Expressed Emotions in complex cases

There is a paradox which became apparent from the initial interviews done by Adamson *et al.* (2020). If low emotional over-involvement is desirable in family carers, how can this be achieved when the very complexity of the cared-for family members' problems requires the carers to be highly emotionally involved? Resources for autistic people with anorexia nervosa are scarce and often need to be paid for privately by the carers themselves (diagnoses, reports and treatments). Dual diagnoses are often denied by the professionals, or one is prioritized over the other: 'You have to leave the autism at the door', said one of the clinicians from an eating disorder service to the carer we interviewed for the carers' needs assessment (we used this quote for the title of our paper (Adamson *et al.*, 2020) because it is a common shared experience amongst carers for ASD and eating disorders), so it is up to carers themselves to become advocates for appropriate treatment of their family members. They often need to resort to the use of expensive solicitors and sometimes even court proceedings in order to get important legal documents such as Education, Health and Care Plans (EHCPs) for their loved ones under the age of 25. How can you tell the parent of a dual diagnosis young person who is fighting for their loved one's right to an EHCP, a diagnosis, or specialist treatment to give up the struggles because they are emotionally over-involved? Often, the quest for these things can become the carers' very reason for existence. How can they step back?

How Expressed Emotion works in family systems

How Expressed Emotion works in families, or more specifically, between carers and cared-for family members, has been described by Kuipers, Leff & Lam (2002). When family carers look after other family members with enduring or life-long mental health problems, they will inevitably experience carer fatigue, particularly if they are emotionally over-involved with their cared-for family member. They will consequently respond in more negative ways to the cared-for family member. This becomes a negative cycle.

Family questionnaire

In 2002, Wiedemann and colleagues developed a self-reporting instrument to enable family carers to measure Expressed Emotion in their relationships with their cared-for family members. Family carers can answer their questionnaire to measure their levels of Expressed Emotion in their relationships with their loved ones who have an eating disorder and autism. The answer options are on a continuum: Never, Very Rarely, Rarely, Often and Very Often. If you answer 'Very Often' to the questions, this would indicate that you are emotionally over-involved with your cared-for/loved one. If you answer 'Never' or 'Very Rarely' to the questions then you are less likely to be emotionally over-involved.

Examples of the questions include: 'I tend to neglect myself because of him/her', 'I have given up important things in order to be able to help him/her', 'When something about him/her bothers me, I keep it to myself'.

Further steps

The following strategies are being developed as part of the PEACE project to help carers who have identified that they may be emotionally over-involved with their cared-for loved ones:

- Psychoeducation aimed at lowering carers' emotional over-involvement. This would be delivered by clinicians who are also carers and would emphasize the importance of self-care and self-focus for carers, using stories about their own lived experiences. It would also give simple information aimed at explaining how family systems work and can impact negatively on carers and their cared-for family members where carers are emotionally over-involved.

- PEACE carers' forum – a closed online forum which carers would access at any time to share things about themselves: stories, photos, struggles, successes, jokes, tips. The forum would be a shared online space for PEACE carers which they could access via their phones or other devices, with the idea that there's always someone there, even when they're not there. Carers would post stories about themselves and tips to support and inspire others.

Positive stories would be shared, but the forum would also be a place where people could share difficulties and ask for advice. There could be a resources section which could incorporate contact details of professionals whom other carers have found helpful, benefits advice for carers, legal advice, details about how carers can access fitness facilities, subsidized holidays for carers, any practical self-care tips which carers would like to share with other carers, and details of how carers can access massages and wellbeing treatments for themselves. On this forum, it might be the individual stories from other carers which are motivational and helpful. Carers would be encouraged to share tips on self-care with others and anything else that has brought them joy.

- The creation of Carer Champions who would run regular connecting and networking events for carers who are using the PEACE carers' forum. Local meetings would be held where carers would be able to meet each other for coffee mornings and other events.

I very much hope that, within the PEACE Pathway project, I will be able use my experience both as a professional and as a carer to develop this forum for carers to support them on their journeys.

References

Adamson, J., Kinnaird, E., Glennon, D., Oakley, M. & Tchanturia, K. (2020) *Carers' views on autism and eating disorders co-morbidity: A qualitative study.* BJPsych Open doi: https://doi.org/10.1192/bjo.2020.

Amaresha, A.C. & Venkatasubramanian, G. (2012) 'Expressed emotion in schizophrenia: An overview.' *Indian Journal of Psychological Medicine, 34*(1), 12–20.

Kuipers, E., Leff, J. & Lam, D. (2002) *Family Work for Schizophrenia: A Practical Guide* (2nd edition). London: Gaskell.

Leff, J.P. & Vaughn, C. (1985) *Expressed Emotion in Families: Its Significance for Mental Illness.* London/New York: Guilford Press.

Vaughn, C.E. & Leff, J.P. (1976) 'The influence of family and social factors on the course of psychiatric illness: A comparison of schizophrenia and depressed neurotic patients.' *British Journal of Psychiatry, 129*, 125–137.

Wiedemann, G., Rayki, O., Feinstein, E. & Hahlweg, K. (2002) 'The Family Questionnaire: Development and validation of a new self-report scale for assessing expressed emotion.' *Psychiatry Research, 109*(3), 265–279.

Chapter 8

Adapting Carers' Interventions for Families Where Eating Disorders and Autism Spectrum Conditions Co-Exist

—— *Amy Harrison* ——

This chapter will examine some of the considerations we have discussed in our multidisciplinary team around the experience of looking after a loved one with both an eating disorder (ED) and autism spectrum disorder (ASD). After, the chapter will explore how we have adapted our provision for carers in our services whose loved ones have both an ED and ASD. This will be achieved through discussing how carers' workshops have been delivered at the South London and Maudsley NHS Foundation Trust, Bethlem Royal Hospital adult ED service to better meet the needs of carers whose loved ones have EDs and ASD, and the adaptations made to the Carers' Pathway across our service.

A brief definition of a 'carer'

In our treatment context, we refer to a carer as anyone supporting our patients in their recovery, or anyone involved in their care. This can include professional, paid carers, such as staff working on the inpatient unit or in supported accommodation where some of our patients might return to or transition to after they have accessed our services. It can include the biological and non-biological family members of our patients, as well as their friends, colleagues and neighbours. We openly invite patients to include carers in their care and treatment; to bring them to their admission assessment, ward rounds, care planning meetings and discharge planning meetings. We encourage regular visits to retain and build social connections which are a vital component of our model of care and recovery.

The needs of carers of people with eating disorders and autism spectrum disorders

It is well established that carers of people with EDs report high levels of psychological distress and poor quality of life (e.g. Kyriacou, Treasure & Schmidt, 2008) and parents of people with ASD are also significantly more likely to experience their own psychological difficulties compared with parents of non-disabled children (Bromley *et al.*, 2004). Previous work has shown that caregiver distress is higher where their adult child with ASD has unmet needs (Hare *et al.*, 2004) and this is a topic discussed in depth in Chapter 7 of this book. Therefore, looking after a loved one with both an ED and ASD is likely to present an even greater challenge to the health and wellbeing of the carer.

Another important aspect to consider when thinking about how to meet the needs of carers of people with EDs and ASD is the high heritability of ASD. For example, in a meta-analysis of heritability studies of 6,413 twin pairs, Tick *et al.* (2016) found substantial heritability estimates of 64–91 per cent. This suggests that ASD runs in families and that where our patients with EDs present with co-morbid ASD, there would be a greater likelihood of their other family members involved in their care and treatment also having ASD, or with significant traits of ASD. This knowledge is important for our work because it helps us to better understand the carers we seek to support, and the adaptations made for patients on the ward discussed elsewhere in this book may also be needed and useful for the biologically related carers of our patients with EDs and ASD.

Adaptations to the carers' workshop

The carers' workshop is a one-day skills-based training workshop which is delivered approximately every two months in the education room at our inpatient service. The workshop involves sharing 1) psychoeducation on EDs and 2) professional communication skills (motivational interviewing) to better equip carers to support their loved ones with an ED based on the New Maudsley Method (Treasure, Schmidt & Macdonald, 2009). It is provided to all carers whose loved ones are accessing any of the South London and Maudsley NHS Foundation Trust ED services and can also be attended by staff as part of their induction and ongoing continued professional development. Participants can attend the workshop as many times as they wish and the workshop is provided free of charge to carers whose loved ones are accessing our national ED treatment programmes. We also open up places to staff in services to which our patients are discharged outside of our Trust. The workshop is typically delivered by three members of clinical team from different disciplines within the multidisciplinary team (for example, a clinical psychologist, social worker and family therapist). We typically have around 25 participants in attendance at each workshop.

Addressing autism spectrum disorders as a co-morbidity in eating disorders

Within the psychoeducation section of the workshop, we explore the common co-morbid psychiatric challenges that people with EDs experience and discuss these with the workshop participants. One key adaptation we have made as part of the PEACE Pathway has been to include a section on the co-morbidity with ASD and ASD traits. This has opened up discussions around what ASDs are and how they can affect people with EDs and allowed a space for carers of people with EDs and ASD to discuss and receive support around some of the additional challenges they face.

Introduction of metaphors to understand interpersonal responses to eating disorders in the context of autism spectrum disorders or autism spectrum disorder traits

The New Maudsley Method (Treasure *et al.*, 2009) explores the interpersonal responses evoked by the ED and describes these through the use of animal metaphors. For example, this model suggests describing interpersonal responses associated with anger, hostility and confrontation through the metaphor of a rhinoceros. An anxious, frightened response is represented by the jellyfish. A nagging, frustrated reaction is characterized by a terrier dog. An avoidant, confused and overwhelmed response is represented by an ostrich, with its head in the sand in denial. An overprotective, over-involved interpersonal style is reflected through the kangaroo figure with the person with an ED in the pouch. Carers are supported to develop communication skills to provide 'dolphin care' and to draw on the St Bernard dog as a metaphor for good enough support, because these animals represent emotional intelligence and the idea of gently nudging the person towards recovery (in the case of the dolphin) and going out to the depths of despair and providing comfort and rescue, supported by something for the carer's own needs in the barrel around the dog's neck (in the case of the St Bernard dog). We discuss these metaphors during the workshops and carers are invited to explore how the animals might represent their own responses to their loved one's ED. We have found that these metaphors are helpful to carers whose loved ones have an ED as well as ASD.

Through this work, we have begun to explore an animal metaphor with carers whose loved one has an ED in the context of their ASD. One idea was that of a hedgehog which, rather than reflecting the interpersonal responses of the carers, might reflect the interpersonal responses of the autistic person with an ED. The spines of this mammal might represent the prickly response of the individual when their routine is disrupted or an expected change occurs. Hedgehogs roll into a ball in self-defence and this reflects the 'freeze' response that we have seen in autistic patients with EDs when faced with a challenging decision or situation. Hedgehogs also have rare traits, such as being immune to snake venom, and this perhaps represents the unique strengths of autistic people with EDs which might evoke awe and wonder in others.

Thinking about how to use metaphor to characterize the interpersonal responses of carers of people with ASD and EDs, with carers, we thought about a pink flamingo. Pink flamingos are very striking and distinctive, and stand out in their habitats. These characteristic reflects the difference that people supporting loved ones with ASD can experience. These elegant birds live in large social groups, reflecting the social support a carer will need to draw on to manage the challenges of caring for a loved one with an ED and ASD. This social group may also provide scaffolding for the social life of their loved one, as building their own social network may be more challenging for an autistic person with an ED. Pink flamingos are known to be very vocal birds and this characteristic reflects the feedback that carers have shared around having to speak up for their loved one, and in many cases, having to shout very loudly to get the understanding, help and support that their loved one needs and deserves. Pink flamingos are also described as 'skittish', meaning they run away easily and hide from potential threats, and this trait reflects the stress and anxiety experienced by carers of an individual with an ED and ASD. Further, pink flamingos move location when resources are lacking, and this nicely reflects the difficulties that many families have experienced around getting care locally, as many have had to travel to services in other parts of the country, have not found good resources locally, and some have had to wait a long time for a specialist appointment and diagnosis. We will be trialling this new animal metaphor to help carers of people with ASD and EDs to talk about their responses to their loved one's difficulties in future workshops.

CARERS' WORKSHOP CASE EXAMPLE

A case example from a workshop which took place in 2019 involves two mothers who attended the workshop and through this section were able to disclose their experiences of support, in one case, the mother of a daughter with anorexia nervosa (AN) and ASD referred to here as Elle, and in the other case, the mother of a son with binge eating disorder (BED) and ASD referred to here as Bryan. These parents were able to reflect on the additional challenges faced by their loved ones around food. These included sensory differences in relation to food (for example, Elle was only able to consume soft, bland foods) and the additional costs incurred as a result of having to purchase from particular outlets (takeaways were preferred by Bryan). Anxiety was a theme common to eating with both a loved one with an ED and a loved one with an ED and ASD, and these are shared experiences discussed by carers of people with both neurotypical development and ASD. Whereas Bryan's and Elle's parents had experienced life-long challenges with their loved ones' food choices and eating, many of the other carers noted that eating had become more selective and challenging when the ED had first developed. The workshop leaders reflected on how this section of the workshop could be adapted to explore what might need to be challenged in terms of ED behaviours (e.g. increasing variety and quantity) during recovery from an ED and how it could be adapted to support carers whose loved ones have both an ED and an ASD.

Useful adaptations to the Carers' Pathway
Carers' Pathway handbook

Across the South London and Maudsley NHS Foundation Trust ED treatment programmes, which include outpatient, day care, inpatient and a recovery model/approach-based step down day service called Step Up, we have developed a Carers' Pathway to ensure carers of our patients are well supported throughout each stage of their loved one's recovery. To communicate the different sources of support across the service available to carers, we have produced a Carers' Pathway handbook which is a brief leaflet that provides information about the monthly carers' support group held in our outpatient service, our carers' workshops held every two months at the Bethlem Royal Hospital site which hosts our inpatient unit, details of national charities such as Beat who provide excellent sources of information and support for carers, and details of local support groups, Trust-wide carers' support and workshops run by external providers for carers. We also inform carers about how to access a Carers' Assessment through this leaflet. We update the leaflet every six months with new dates and information and the leaflet is available in our outpatient, day care, inpatient and Step Up services.

As part of the PEACE Pathway, representatives of the Carers' Pathway from the outpatient, day care and inpatient teams met to discuss how we might adapt the leaflet to be more ASD-friendly. We were informed by research evidence of hyper- and hypo-sensory stimulation (Kinnaird, Stewart & Tchanturia, 2018; Kinnaird *et al.*, 2019), by reviewing how information is presented and shared on the National Autistic Society website, by feedback provided to us by users of the leaflet and by discussions we had attended as part of the PEACE

Pathway. The adapted leaflet was also informed by the six fundamental principles of design. These are:

- Balance – distributing weight around the design of the leaflet by the placement of elements within it.

- Proximity – the consideration of the relationship and visual connection between elements within the leaflet.

- Alignment – aligning elements to create clear order and organization.

- Repetition – strengthening the design by tying together individual elements to create association and consistency and a sense of organized movement through the leaflet.

- Contrast – juxtaposing opposing elements to highlight key elements within the leaflet.

- Space – considering the distance between, around, above, below and within elements that make up the leaflet.

We removed the colourful background that we had used on the original leaflet design, which was distracting, and also made the leaflet into an A4 size, which could be flipped back to back, rather than presenting it as a smaller handheld leaflet which opened in a concertina fashion, because we thought an A4 document might be a more familiar format for readers as well as being easier to handle. We ensured that all headings were clearly presented in bold and any pictures used clearly related to the content of the leaflet. This meant removing any superfluous illustrations and eliminating illustrations that may require additional information processing to infer their meaning and distracting borders. We standardized the font used and the font size and colour. We also added the details of the National Autistic Society, which we felt would be of interest to carers of people with both EDs and ASD. Before implementing the leaflet in our Carers' Pathway, we showed it to two carers of patients with an ED and diagnosed ASD and asked for feedback. The review accessibility option was also utilized in word-processing software to further explore ways that we might make the leaflet more readable. Many of these changes improved the design and accessibility of the leaflet more generally and this was an interesting task which enabled us to think more about the visual formats we use in order to convey information to our services users.

Figure 8.1 provides an illustration of our original Carers' Pathway leaflet and Figure 8.2 subsequently shows the adapted PEACE Pathway leaflet for carers.

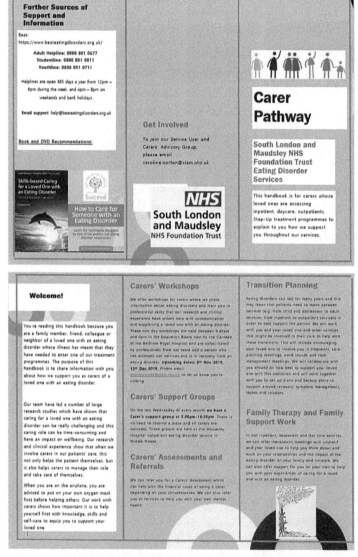

Figure 8.1. *Original Carers' Pathway leaflet*

Transition Planning

We can also refer you to services to help you with your own mental health. Eating disorders can last for many years and this may mean that patients need to move between services (e.g. from child and adolescent to adult services, from inpatient to outpatient services) in order to best support the person. We will work with you and your loved one and other services that might be involved in their care to help with these transitions. This will include encouraging your loved one to involve you in treatment, care planning meetings, ward rounds and case management meetings. We will collaborate with you around on how best to support your loved one with this transition and will work together with you to set up plans and backup plans to support around recovery, symptom management, lapses and relapses.

Family Therapy and Family Support Work

In our inpatient, outpatient and day care services, we can offer therapeutic meetings with yourself and your loved one to help you think about and work on your relationships and the impact of the eating disorder on your family and network. We can also offer support for you on your own to help you with your experiences of caring for a loved one with an eating disorder.

Carers' Assessments and Referrals Further Sources of Support and Information

We can refer you for a Carers' Assessment which can help with the financial costs of being a carer, depending on your circumstances. We can also refer you to services to help you with your own mental health.

Get Involved

To join our Service User and Carers' Advisory Group, email caroline.norton@slam.nhs.uk

Further Sources of Support and Information

Beat: https://www.beateatingdisorders.org.uk/ Adult Helpline: 0808 801 0677, Studentline: 0808 801 0811, Youthline: 0808 801 0711. Email support: help@beateatingdisorders.org.uk

National Autistic Society: www.autism.org.uk

Book and DVD Recommendations

Figure 8.2. *Adapted Carers' Pathway leaflet after implementation of the PEACE Pathway*

Referrals across the Pathway

Within the South London and Maudsley NHS Foundation Trust ED services, carers are able to access family therapy both at the inpatient and at the outpatient/day care services. This family support is delivered by two family therapists on the inpatient unit and through a family therapy clinic at the outpatient and day care service and therefore when a patient moves between these services, a referral is made to enable them to access these family-based interventions. One adaptation we have made to this referral pathway as part of the PEACE project is to clearly state where there is a known or suspected diagnosis of ASD which is being investigated, or where there are significant ASD traits which help to inform the formulation. In this section of our referral, we would also detail any particular adaptations that have been helpful for the patient and their family when accessing family therapy. Some examples have involved adaptations to the set-up of the room, such as holding the session in a quieter room, with lower light or less echo; having the appointment at the same time weekly, or at a particular time of day; booking additional time for the appointment slot; giving written information at the end of the session; looking for opportunities to provide time out during the session to allow people to manage arousal from the social interaction of therapy and to process the information discussed with greater ease; and, offering a debrief to the patient themselves, in the absence of any family members or other carers after the session so that they have a chance to clarify any misunderstandings and to provide them support to better manage any emotional arousal experienced during the session.

This has enabled us to provide more consistent care across the Carers' Pathway designed to suit families where there is an ED and ASD so that we better meet their needs as they engage in the family support on offer. It also provides an opportunity to share good practice with colleagues across the service and to develop a toolbox of possible adaptations that we can offer to patients and their family members and other carers so that they are more able to access family interventions within our service.

What I learnt from this Pathway as a professional

There are three key areas of learning that I have taken away from my continued involvement in the PEACE Pathway. The first is that adaptations that might be helpful for those with EDs and ASD may also be useful for the wider population of people with EDs. For example, the design changes made to the Carers' Pathway handbook contributed to making this document more readable, attractive and accessible for all readers. Similarly, sharing information on key ASD co-morbidity with carers was highly relevant for carers whose loved ones did not have a known diagnosis of ASD because the inflexibility and detail focus present in both disorders was of interest to a wide range of carers.

Second, I learnt about the additional challenges that carers of people with EDs and ASD face. As ASD is a neurodevelopmental disorder, it was important to work with carers a little differently and in the context of ASD, rather than supporting them to challenge symptoms and help their loved ones make small changes to their behaviours, the work with carers focused more on helping the family to manage and live with the challenges (and strengths) inherent to ASD.

Third and finally, helping carers whose loved ones have ASD and autism to understand the challenges their loved one and the wider family face was very rewarding because for many, the diagnosis itself was a useful explanation of why it had been so difficult to recover from the ED and armed with this knowledge it became more possible for carers to think of different ways to relate to their loved one. This really highlights the importance of screening and good diagnostic assessments in clinical work. Conversely, because there is a paucity of support for adult women with ASD, for some families it was frustrating to have a diagnosis in the absence of good community aftercare, and this is something that we could collaborate with carers to improve in future work.

References

Bromley, J., Hare, D.J., Davison, K. & Emerson, E. (2004) 'Mothers supporting children with autistic spectrum disorders: Social support, mental health status and satisfaction with services.' *Autism*, 8(4), 409–423.

Hare, D., Pratt, C., Burton, M., Bromley, J. & Emerson, E. (2004) 'The health and social care needs of family carers supporting adults with autistic spectrum disorders.' *Autism*, 8(4), 425–444.

Kinnaird, E., Norton, C., Stewart, C. & Tchanturia, K. (2019) 'Same behaviours, different reasons: What do patients with co-occurring anorexia and autism want from treatment?' *International Review of Psychiatry*, 31(4), 308–317.

Kinnaird, E., Stewart, C. & Tchanturia, K. (2018) 'Taste sensitivity in anorexia nervosa: A systematic review.' *International Journal of Eating Disorders*, 51(8), 771–784.

Kyriacou, O., Treasure, J. & Schmidt, U. (2008) 'Understanding how parents cope with living with someone with anorexia nervosa: Modelling the factors that are associated with carer distress.' *International Journal of Eating Disorders*, 41(3), 233–242.

Tick, B., Bolton, P., Happé, F., Rutter, M. & Rijsdijk, F. (2016) 'Heritability of autism spectrum disorders: A meta-analysis of twin studies.' *Journal of Child Psychology and Psychiatry*, 57(5), 5.

Treasure, J., Schmidt, U. & Macdonald, P. (eds) (2009) *The Clinician's Guide to Collaborative Caring in Eating Disorders: The New Maudsley Method*. London: Routledge.

Chapter 9

Catching 'Sparkling Moments' within Family and Systemic Psychotherapy Sessions

—— *Jason Maldonado-Page* ——

Welcome To Holland

by Emily Perl Kingsley

I am often asked to describe the experience of raising a child with a disability – to try to help people who have not shared that unique experience to understand it, to imagine how it would feel. It's like this......

When you're going to have a baby, it's like planning a fabulous vacation trip – to Italy. You buy a bunch of guide books and make your wonderful plans. The Coliseum. The Michelangelo David. The gondolas in Venice. You may learn some handy phrases in Italian. It's all very exciting.

After months of eager anticipation, the day finally arrives. You pack your bags and off you go. Several hours later, the plane lands. The flight attendant comes in and says, "Welcome to Holland."

"Holland?!?" you say. "What do you mean Holland?? I signed up for Italy! I'm supposed to be in Italy. All my life I've dreamed of going to Italy."

But there's been a change in the flight plan. They've landed in Holland and there you must stay.

The important thing is that they haven't taken you to a horrible, disgusting, filthy place, full of pestilence, famine and disease. It's just a different place.

So you must go out and buy new guide books. And you must learn a whole new language. And you will meet a whole new group of people you would never have met.

It's just a different place. It's slower-paced than Italy, less flashy than Italy. But after you've been there for a while and you catch your breath, you look around.... and you begin to notice that Holland has windmills....and Holland has tulips. Holland even has Rembrandts.

But everyone you know is busy coming and going from Italy... and they're all bragging about what a wonderful time they had there. And for the rest of your life, you will say "Yes, that's where I was supposed to go. That's what I had planned."

And the pain of that will never, ever, ever, ever go away... because the loss of that dream is a very very significant loss.

But... if you spend your life mourning the fact that you didn't get to Italy, you may never be free to enjoy the very special, the very lovely things ... about Holland.

⋆ ⋆ ⋆

This chapter aims to be self-reflexive and written from my perspective of family and systemic psychotherapy with family and patients with a co-morbid diagnosis of eating disorders (EDs) and autistic spectrum disorders (ASDs). I will be drawing from my varied experiences of working with ASD throughout my career, as well as paediatric oncology which is relevant to my contact with Milly and her mother Sally who were discussed in detail in Chapter 5, as well as my experiences of working in a specialist national adult inpatient eating disorders service. I am writing from a social constructionist perspective (Burr, 2003), where there is a multiverse of truths, each one as valid as another. This chapter is one version of my truth which I hope will offer some insight into my clinical work with families in an inpatient setting. My focus is on the family members present and I will try to understand and appreciate their lived experiences. The above poem by Emily Kingsley shows the unexpected yet eventful life ahead, when having a child with a disability. However, that unexpected adventure can be exhausting and frightening for some. I will explore that within my work with Sally where ASD, childhood cancer and now ED has truly challenged her hopes for parenthood.

Language is important to me as a clinician. I agree with Wittgenstein (1953) that 'there is an ocean of meaning in a drop of grammar'. This is evident in an adult ED context where words such as 'carers' and 'patients' are routinely used. Within this chapter I will substitute the word 'family' for the word 'carer', with 'family' meaning anyone of significance who can be a resource and where the relationship can with time hopefully become reciprocal where caring is a mutual responsibility. I have found that the word 'carer' can denote a power imbalance with the carer ultimately providing or needing to provide care to someone who may otherwise live independently outside of the ward context. The word 'family' for me does not always mean biological relationships such as parents, grandparents and siblings; it could be husbands, wives, partners, children, friends, neighbours, keyworkers or other significant professionals. I invite anyone and everyone into the therapeutic room who can help to make a difference. ED is both a mental and physical health condition and the inpatient ward attends to both, so I will use the word 'patients'.

Family and systemic psychotherapy has played a key role in the treatment and understanding of child and adolescent ED (Eisler, Lock & Le Grange, 2010), with significant clinical research and randomized control trials which have culminated in a manualized evidence-based approach which recognizes families as strengths and recourses in the treatment of the illness, rather than the cause of it as earlier literature (Minuchin, Rosman & Baker, 1978) has implied. The Maudsley model integrates several systemic models such as Structural (Minuchin, 1974; Minuchin & Fishman, 1981), Strategic (Hayley, 1976; Madanes, 1981) and Narrative (White & Epston, 1990) to give families the tools to help their loved ones. Working with families is a significant part of the treatment of ED with adults as well, but it often focuses on skilling up carers (Treasure, Smith & Crane, 2007). Whilst the recognized manualized treatment is within child and adolescent services, the range of systemic models used are just as useful in exploring the illness within the context of family life for adult patients. Similarly, over the past decade family and systemic psychotherapy has increasingly thought of engaging those with intellectual disabilities and ASD (Baum &

Lynggaard, 2006; Helps, 2016b) into systemic family therapy, as well as how ASD may present differently in woman resulting in numerous psychiatric diagnoses (Helps, 2016a). Clinically we have shifted the approach from people with ASD needing to fit into our neurotypical world, to instead clinicians and families understanding theirs.

Systemic psychotherapy is a relational rather than intrapsychic therapeutic approach which in recent years has allowed clinicians to recognize, validate and scaffold the expertise people hold in their own lives (Anderson & Goolishian, 1992). The systemic clinician becomes the expert in the therapeutic process and people remain the experts in their own lives, with the clinician skilfully providing a therapeutic space to explore and deconstruct the various challenges of family life.

Catching those 'sparkling moments' in therapy

Setting the scene for systemic family therapy is always important and it is particularly so when working with people with ASD. Prior to each session I look around the room for anything that may distract from the therapeutic process. This could be any potential sensory stimulus: fans whirring, noises from the outside or adjoining rooms, and room temperature, for example. I may even move chairs around if there are brightly coloured walls and remove distractions such as noisy clocks. Despite careful attention to the therapeutic environment, I do not always get it right and so I always start the session off with checking with the patient about these things and sometimes I am asked to open a window, turn on the lights and even the fan, which I had initially thought would be distractions. Not everyone with ASD is sensorially sensitive to stimulus in the environment, so it is a continuous process to ensure that whoever sits in front of me is comfortable enough to focus. It is sometimes the things that one does not think of that become a barrier to this process. For example, with Milly (see Chapter 5) the time that best suited everyone to meet for sessions corresponded with her walking routine. We cannot always get it right for everyone all the time, but not making any adjustments means that we unintentionally put barriers in the way. Whilst I am always more mindful of the therapeutic environment when working with people with an ASD diagnosis, this is something which would be useful for everyone that comes to therapy, as they too may be easily distracted by sensory stimulation in the environment or a scheduling conflict that may take their focus elsewhere. PEACE Pathway development work helped us to integrate clinical experience, research evidence and good clinical practice and it became pretty much team philosophy.

I am an animated person who brings a lot of energy into the therapeutic room. I would think nothing of spontaneously standing up and making everyone line up in the room in some exercise that I thought of on the spot. I also love the use of metaphor and I at times get myself muddled up in what I was hoping to say, and even though I can be clunky at times, it is usually in that humorous episode that we can nicely segue to a theme we may really need to go to. I have had to learn over the years to adapt my style, but this was always most pertinent when working with patients with ASD. In those sessions I work hard at tempering my energy and clinical spontaneity. I am more tentative and avoid speaking in broad metaphors.

Exploring one's experiences of family and systemic psychotherapy is always an important starting place, and I have been surprised by the number of families over the years who have spoken of feeling blamed in therapy. Many families have been clear that they want the therapeutic work to be useful and directive, but not directive where we focus on one incident as the cause of the ED. Sally was clear that she did not want my systemic family therapy trainee colleague and me to be 'airy fairy' during sessions. She had too many years of people like us skirting around things and getting them nowhere. There is always an invitation to clinicians to bring forth solutions, but this is a simplistic approach which makes the assumptions that we already have the answers. Sadly, like my medical and individual therapeutic clinician colleagues, I do not have a magic wand and not having one can be frustrating for all.

What I do have though is a genogram (McGoldrick & Gerson, 1985; Hardy & Laszloffy, 1995) which I have found useful within my clinical work. 'The genogram is a road map of your family. It will show where you came from and where you are going. If you study the road map, you'll get to know the "territory" – the people, places and events that make up your history' (Marlin, 1989, p.13). A genogram (McGoldrick & Gerson, 1985; Hardy & Laszloffy, 1995) is a dynamic clinical tool that has been regularly used in systemic family therapy for nearly half a century as a way of illustrating and recording information about families over three or more generations, and offering space for therapists to explore and understand family relationships, histories and beliefs (see a genogram example in Figure 9.1). If used sensitively, a genogram can be an effective tool to connect with individuals and families at all stages of the therapeutic process. If integrated into all sessions at various points, and done with patience and care, it can easily become a useful representation of the family – it is never the family itself.

According to Minuchin, 'Change is seen as occurring through the process of the therapist's affiliation with the family and his restructuring of the family in a carefully planned way' (1974, p.91). An important part of achieving change is the therapist joining the family (Minuchin, 1974; Minuchin & Fishman, 1981), which entails using their language and communication style. A genogram can be an important tool to demonstrate to the family that the therapist has joined them, by the therapist commenting on the genogram and actively showing that they have understood the family of origin being presented.

The genogram can also provide therapists with a neutral perspective for working with families and an opportunity for genuine therapeutic curiosity. McGoldrick, Gerson & Petry saw the genogram as 'primarily an interpretive tool that enables clinicians to generate tentative hypotheses for further evaluation' (2008, p.4). However, the genogram can be a clinical tool that can be useful for families themselves to generate their own hypotheses; it invites their curiosity and can connect to their own personal theories for change. Most importantly on an adult inpatient ED unit, especially a national one where not everyone can attend sessions, the genogram can be used as a tool to invite the voices of those family members not physically present into the therapeutic relationship as a way of nudging towards change, and it can help us in slowing down and not understanding too quickly what is going on in a simplistic and reductive way. I have found that for those with neurodevelopmental needs, having a genogram which depicts family, friends and professional networks makes it slightly easier to mentalize and elicit the perspectives of others.

An important part of my clinical practice is always being attentive to language and the meanings people attribute to the words and the stories attached. When working with Milly and Sally, words which kept being repeated included *ASD*, *OCD* (obsessive compulsive disorder), *ED*, *routine* and *guilt*. I thought it would be a good thing for us to start externalizing these words to give them more depth and to create a shared understanding of what they each mean to both Milly and Sally, and to a certain extent us as clinicians.

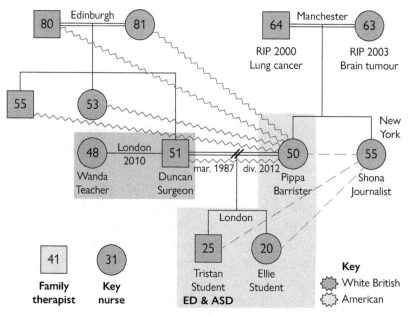

Figure 9.1. *Genogram example*

Externalizing the problem within narrative therapy 'is an approach to therapy that encourages persons to objectify and, at times, to personify the problems that they experience as oppressive' (White & Epston, 1990, p.38). Integral to this approach is helping the person separate themselves and their relationships from the problem, so 'The problem becomes the problem, and then the person's relationship with the problem becomes the problem' (White & Epston, 1990, p.40). This is not done quickly, as with all therapeutic techniques, care, attention and a slower, thoughtful pace is essential. We may spend time giving the problems a name, focusing on the times when they are most and least present, whether they have friends that may accompany them and what they might whisper or yell at any given moment. It is the telling and retelling of their stories that help to illustrate aspects of their lived experiences which may have contributed to the presenting problem. The therapist's goal is to help the person identify unique outcomes or sparkling moments (White & Epston, 1990), which are occasions when the problem did not occur although the likelihood was high that it should have.

For Milly and Sally, the words were put on signs which joined us for each session alongside their growing genogram. The signs were placed on the large green sofa in the therapy room where they joined the therapeutic interplay (see Figure 9.2). Milly and Sally would each be invited to engage with the different signs, and to expand on how the different elements interact and perhaps support each other, and how they may be barriers to change. The sparkling moments in this were having conversations they were often too scared of having, such as Sally stating that she needed a break and was going on holiday to look after her own mental health needs. The session then focused on Sally's guilt about leaving Milly on the ward and, when questioned whether her guilt could stay whilst she left the country, Sally spoke of how impossible that may be. Milly was upset and spoke of being left behind and that ED was stopping her from holidaying with her family. Sally spoke of how Milly being upset just made her guilt stronger. So, as an intervention I stood up, walked up to Sally's guilt sign and tore it up. I then encouraged Sally to throw away her guilt in the nearby bin, which she found difficult to do, opting to put it in her handbag. That was quite a direct approach and the moment I tore it up I became slightly worried that was perhaps too direct, but there was noticeable relief within the room, and a conversation could then be had about what needed to be put in place for Milly whilst Sally was away. That was not an 'airy fairy' thing to do and I have found that sometimes doing something as dramatic as that can shift the conversation in a more productive direction. Sally did go away on holiday and the pieces of her sign stayed at home; she found it too difficult to throw the pieces away and this was then explored in our next session upon her return.

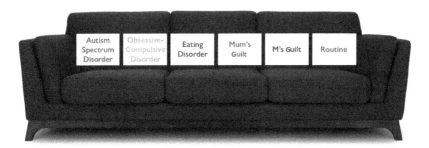

Figure 9.2. *Family therapy with Milly and her mum*

For neurotypical patients I may just verbally externalize, but the signs offer a more concrete and useful way of doing so, which can lead, as with Milly and Sally, to a nice sparkling moment in the systemic family therapy. I love the words 'sparkling moments' and I invite families and patients to keep an eye out for those sparkling moments at home, and even encourage them to play a game where they catch and announce those sparkling moments when they do occur. With an ED and ASD co-morbidity, life on and off the ward gets serious so quickly that the sparkling moments game offers a lovely way of slowly shifting those problem-focused narratives and hopefully leads to more satisfying interactions between families and patients.

In this area of work, the word 'change' is a funny one for me, and I recognize the desired outcome when change is discussed with families and patients is recovery. Even then when recovery is explored with patients and family, recovery is described as a fixed place, a nirvana where the illness no longer exits and has never existed. The word 'recovery', I believe, puts pressure on patients to achieve this monumental task, and it stops them and their families attending to those small and significant changes which snowball into much bigger and more sustainable change. Recovery for me would be a tentative approach to change and so care and attention is required to question the meanings everyone has for change. For those with ASD, the concept of change/recovery may be too abstract and the expectations to get there too vague, so breaking it down into small, realistic and achievable goals may provide the starting blocks for moving forward.

Welcome to Holland... I mean welcome to the eating disorders unit

Throughout my career with parents of children with ASD, and then latterly in my career in childhood cancer, a theme throughout, as well as fear, has been exhaustion. Sally advocated for her daughter to get an ASD diagnosis and then to receive the appropriate educational and social support. Then Milly was diagnosed with childhood cancer and with that comes relentless emotional and physical care during the uncertainty of treatment. I have seen ASD and childhood cancer singularly bring parents to breaking point, but Sally has impressively navigated both whilst attending to a divorce as well as working full-time in multiple jobs and parenting her other children. ED also brings emotional and physical health uncertainties which take an emotional toll on families, ultimately leading to exhaustion.

Understandably, Sally was exhausted when she came to systemic family therapy and I am not quite sure if any of us professionals on the ward truly understood or appreciated the level of exhaustion; she was clearly good at masking. A thread throughout our work with Sally was around self-care and *her guilt* was a real barrier to that. We would often speak about how when a plane is taking off and the safety briefing is being announced, they say if the oxygen mask comes down to place it on yourself first before helping others, implying you would be useless to others if you do not look after yourself. This was hard for Sally to do as I am sure it is for most parents, especially for those with children with an ASD and ED co-morbidity. When patients hear families saying that they are exhausted, what they hear is that they are being a burden. What I hear is the opposite, that they are loved and cared for, and that those closest to them want life to be different for them – free from whatever known and unknown barriers are keeping them from making those small changes towards recovery. If there is one thing I want families to get from reading this, it is that we professionals care and it is okay to be exhausted; we do not judge you for needing to look after yourself, we encourage it, well at least I do. What I want professionals to take away is the need to try to put yourself in the shoes of family members who, whatever the reason, feel blamed, feel guilty, feel judged and perhaps even ashamed. They too need us to find their sparkling moments.

Clinician fatigue and conclusion

Despite the dominant discourse by patients on the ward that they are not supported enough, they are well supported, unlike their families who get relatively little in comparison. ASD and ED on their own are complex diagnoses which are different for each person. As a child I once played with the mercury from a broken thermometer (please don't try this at home) – when you touch it, it moves away or breaks up into smaller blobs. I have found ED to be similar. Despite what we know, to me it acts like mercury. My experience is that when we get our finger on something that we think can help shift things towards recovery, it breaks up into smaller blobs which then each need their own attention and understanding. The work is slow and at times frustrating and can lead to clinician fatigue, which I believe is different to compassion fatigue, as we continue to remain compassionate, sympathetic, empathic, and hopeful. However, the slow pace of the work means that it is also sometimes hard for us to see those smaller nuggets of change ourselves. Ultimately, we want our patients, and their families, to thrive without the complexity and challenges the co-morbidity presents. I wish that I could do more to take away the pain and fear from everyone who sits in front of me, but ultimately what I can bring is hope that things can be different, even when others may feel hopeless.

This chapter has been my personal experience of catching sparkling moments in my therapeutic work on the adult inpatient ED unit with those with a co-morbid ASD and ED diagnosis. I have shared and elaborated on some of my clinical work as well as my thinking around the experiences of patients and their families, whilst weaving in my own lived experiences. It is with hope and dedication, patience, transparency and honesty, and let's not forget compassionate humour, that we can be a useful resource to families and patients.

References

Anderson, H. & Goolishian, H. (1992) 'The Client is the Expert: A Not-Knowing Approach to Therapy.' In S. McNamee and K. Gergen (eds) *Social Construction and the Therapeutic Process*. London: Sage.

Baum, S. & Lynggaard, H. (2006) *Intellectual Disabilities: A Systemic Approach*. London: Karnac.

Burr, V. (2003) 'What Is Discourse?' In V. Burr *Social Constructionism*. London: Routledge.

Eisler, I., Lock, J. & Le Grange, D. (2010) 'Family-Based Treatments for Adolescent Anorexia Nervosa.' In C.M. Grilo & J.E. Mitchell (eds) *The Treatment of Eating Disorders*. New York: Guilford Press.

Hardy, K.V. & Laszloffy, T.A. (1995) 'The cultural genogram: Key to training culturally competent family therapists.' *Journal of Marital and Family Therapy, 21*(3), 227–237.

Hayley, J. (1976) *Problem Solving Therapy: New Strategies for Effective Family Therapy*. New York: Harper and Row.

Helps, S. (2016a) 'How some systemic practices might help young women with autistic spectrum conditions, and their families.' *Context, 144*, 24–26.

Helps, S. (2016b) 'Systemic psychotherapy with families where someone has an autism spectrum condition.' *NeuroRehabilitation, 38*(3), 223–230.

Madanes, C. (1981) *Strategic Family Therapy*. San Francisco, CA: Jossey-Bass Inc.

Marlin, E. (1989) *Genograms: The New Tool for Exploring the Personality, Career, and Love Patterns You Inherit*. Chicago, IL: Contemporary Books.

McGoldrick, M. & Gerson, R. (1985) *Genograms in Family Assessment*. New York: W. W. Norton & Company.

McGoldrick, M., Gerson, R. & Petry, S. (2008) *Genograms Assessment and Intervention* (3rd edition). New York: W. W. Norton & Company.

Minuchin, S. (1974) *Families and Family Therapy*. Cambridge, MA: Harvard University Press.

Minuchin, S. & Fishman, H.C. (1981) *Family Therapy Techniques*. London: Harvard University Press.

Minuchin, S., Rosman, B.L. & Baker, L. (1978) *Psychosomatic Families: Anorexia Nervosa in Context*. Cambridge, MA: Harvard University Press.

Treasure, J., Smith, G. & Crane, A. (2007) *Skills-Based Learning for Caring for a Loved One with an Eating Disorder: The New Maudsley Method*. London: Routledge.

White, M. & Epston, D. (1990) *Narrative Means to Therapeutic Ends*. New York: W. W. Norton & Company.

Wittgenstein, L. (1953) *Philosophical Investigations*. Oxford: Basil Blackwell Ltd.

Food as a Remedy

ADVICE AND LEARNING FROM A DIETICIAN

In this section, we talk about the additional challenges an autistic person living with an eating disorder might have with eating. We also look at how we can best support change towards eating disorder recovery with some helpful ideas around goal setting.

Chapter 10

Understanding the Challenges with Eating

—— *Kate Williams* ——

All of us have experience of anxiety, and are familiar with the loss of appetite that is integral to it. We recognize this as normal, and usually it is temporary, so does not interfere significantly with normal eating or nutrition.

Anxiety is a major driver of the restriction of food intake in anorexia nervosa (AN) and in autism spectrum disorders (ASD). People with ASD may have physical and sensory difficulties with processing food, leading to distressing experiences with eating, and the food refusal and selectivity, and rigid, limited and repetitive eating patterns that are characteristic of ASD from an early age. These difficulties, and the associated anxiety with eating, may contribute to the risk of developing an eating disorder. Such eating difficulties persist into adulthood (Tavassoli *et al.*, 2013; Horder *et al.*, 2014), perhaps especially in women (Spek *et al.*, 2019), though other studies have found equal gender distribution. So, when anorexia nervosa occurs in a person with autistic features, the vicious cycle of anxiety and restriction of eating develops and becomes entrenched more quickly, and is more difficult to reverse, as there are more driving and maintaining factors. An understanding of the interplay of the eating disorder and the autistic features can be integrated at every stage of the recovery process, to make it more achievable and sustainable.

In anorexia nervosa, and often also in ASD, anxiety is specifically provoked by eating, or even talking or thinking about food or eating, so that trying to eat worsens the anxiety, making eating more difficult. This generates an escalating and paralysing vicious cycle of restricting and avoiding eating, and sometimes also purging food that has been eaten, resulting in weight loss and malnutrition (Johnson *et al.*, 2014). This has a damaging impact on every part of the body, including the brain. The normal effects of starvation on the brain include raised anxiety and agitation, intrusive thoughts about food, and increased rigidity of thinking. These are a necessary survival mechanism, which should drive the person to active food-seeking, but in anorexia nervosa the increasing anxiety and rigidity entrench and intensify the problem further, making it increasingly difficult and distressing to make the changes in eating that are needed to reverse the malnutrition. The anxiety and distress naturally build, for the person experiencing the disorder, and for those around them, adding further misery and suffering to the situation, and tightening the cycle. In attempting to control the anxiety, individuals work creatively to develop ways of trying to think about and use food to minimize the distress, for example stereotyped eating behaviour, and constructing rules to achieve a feeling of control, safety or rightness. The characteristic need for familiar and repetitive behaviour in ASD serves to entrench damaging eating habits more severely.

An essential element in loosening the grip of this cycle is work to find a shared understanding of the individual's experience, thinking and feeling about food and eating, and the links with disordered eating behaviour, so that recovery can address the specific maintaining factors that are operating.

Identifying and exploring behaviour, experience, thoughts and feelings that maintain disordered eating

A usual aim in supporting recovery from eating disorders is a return to socially normal eating, with increasing confidence and flexibility, alongside restoring healthy eating routines, variety and amounts of food. People with autistic traits may have had idiosyncrasies or difficulties with eating from an early age (Rogers, Magill-Evans & Rempel, 2012; Nadon *et al.*, 2010), which are unlikely to change, so efforts to increase flexibility with eating may be counter-productive, serving only to increase anxiety and so entrench the disorder. There may also be very longstanding eating habits which have developed to manage life-long eating difficulties and may be very resistant to change.

Some adults with autistic traits, especially perhaps women, learn to behave in a socially acceptable way when necessary, although it may be difficult and exhausting for them to behave in ways that are not congruent with their thinking and emotional style. Because of the masking effect this has, it may take time and skill to reveal and work with the underlying thoughts and feelings. It can help to support improved eating behaviour to explore with the individual the specific drivers of the anxiety, and experiment with strategies to reduce their negative impact on eating (see Chapter 1 for further information).

The thinking that drives disordered eating behaviour may feel very private, and even shameful, so it may be difficult to talk about openly. Some people may find it difficult to bring these entrenched thinking habits into their own awareness, so it may be difficult to articulate them. Because of this, it is important to approach the topic with sensitivity, and allow enough time (Kinnaird, Norton & Tchanturia 2017). Some individuals may find it easier to complete a questionnaire in their own time to help identify thoughts and experiences that make eating difficult, before discussing and planning for changes. The Swedish Eating Assessment for Autism Spectrum Disorders (Karlsson, Råstam & Wentz, 2013) is an example that may be useful. Some may find it helpful to invite a friend or family member to take part in the discussion, others may feel more free to talk to a professional without other familiar people present. Offering choices can help the person feel more comfortable to talk.

Areas of concern to consider
Attempts to control body weight and shape
Intense anxiety about weight and shape, a strong drive to lose weight and great fear of weight gain are central to anorexia nervosa, intensifying the drive to develop rules and safety behaviours related to food and eating. Although there are efforts from many sources to counter it, Western and Western-influenced societies place high value on thinness for women, and associate being overweight and obesity not only with health risks, but also with poor self-control and laziness. The social environment, particularly social media, provides a multiplicity of messages about dieting and weight control, not all of them rational or evidence-based. These can easily be integrated into disordered thinking

as rules about 'safe' and 'unsafe' foods, for example avoiding foods high in fat or sugar; fixed times and frequency of eating, such as not eating before a fixed time in the afternoon, or after a fixed time in the evening; strict limits for elements that can be counted, such as calories or grams of carbohydrate or fat, or individual food items. Anxiety about body weight may also be affected by a need to keep weight below a precise target, with weight increase interpreted as evidence of 'breaking the rules'. Thoughts and feelings about eating may assimilate other messages from the social environment, for example concerning healthy eating, or preventing environmental damage, or spiritual observance or purity. For an autistic person, this can easily become a characteristically obsessive special interest, pursued to an all-encompassing and damaging extreme, and needing a treatment approach aimed at reducing the damaging rules and beliefs, and replacing them with healthy ones, rather than abolishing the preoccupation.

Social anxiety about eating and meal times [1]

Meal time conversation, even with familiar people, may be experienced as an overwhelming distraction, and as a difficult challenge, for people who struggle to understand usual social obligations and behaviour. Being expected to join conversation while eating may be experienced as bewildering and stressful, and it may be extremely distressing, especially with unfamiliar people. Difficulty understanding and meeting expectations for behaviour at the table, and the effort required to learn the rules – table manners – which may seem arbitrary and inconsistent, can become a source of anxiety and stress. Some people with autistic traits may have a tendency to clumsiness (Riquelme, Hatem & Montoya, 2016), which may be particularly exposed at meal times, when there are foods and drinks that are easily spilled, and utensils that may break.

This may result in finding eating extremely arduous in many normal social eating situations, for example with friends or visitors, at college or at work, when travelling, and in hospital. These experiences may lead to avoidance of social eating, and eating only when alone, or in the company of familiar people.

---

1   See also Chapter 2 on social anxiety.

Need for predictability and familiarity

Unfamiliar places, or changes in the environment, may cause distress for people with ASD. Eating away from the familiar environment can create an unbearable burden of distraction, confusion and bewildering expectations, sometimes leading to extreme agitation.

Unfamiliar foods may be rejected because of anxiety about how they may taste, or the effect they may have, for example on body weight or the feeling in the stomach. Foods which seem to have caused discomfort on one occasion, for example by tasting unpleasant or causing uncomfortable fullness, may thereafter be refused completely in an effort to avoid a recurrence.

Particular foods may be eaten frequently, almost to the exclusion of other foods, for a period and then suddenly be rejected, which is experienced as getting bored with the food or 'going off' it. It may be replaced with a different food, or not replaced, which then leads to continuing reduction of the acceptable range of foods.

A need for predictable routine can result in eating only at regular times. This may mean that a meal is missed altogether if the expected meal time is missed.

These experiences may lead to a need to eat in the same place every time, with no changes in the environment, and to keep the eating environment calm, quiet and free from distraction. Acceptable food may be limited to a very few items, which always have to be presented in the same amounts and the same way, for example the same brands and packaging, leading to a very limited range of acceptable foods. Some individuals may find it difficult or impossible to eat if these conditions are not met, because of the anxiety triggered by any changes or deviations from the expected.

Sensory processing difficulties

Sensory hypersensitivity, hyposensitivity, and abnormalities of sensory processing are associated with ASD in adults (Tavassoli *et al.*, 2013; Horder *et al.*, 2014) and children (Nadon *et al.*, 2011). There may be difficulties with filtering out irrelevant sensory stimulation, resulting in confusion and distractibility. Flavours, odours and textures of many ordinary foods may be experienced as too strong, unpleasant or even disgusting, so many foods are rejected after one encounter, or even before trying them (Nadon *et al.*, 2011), or there may be a strong preference for particular flavours and textures. Foods may be refused because of fear or expectation that they may be disagreeable or repulsive, or contaminated or spoiled. People may need to touch or smell food, or taste a tiny sample, before feeling safe to try it.

The sound of other people talking, eating, and using crockery and cutlery may be distracting and off-putting.

A variety of different foods on the plate, with different colours, shapes and textures, may be confusing and distracting. Composite dishes, such as casseroles or pizza, with several ingredients of different flavours and textures, may seem bewildering and difficult to identify, or rejected because they contain (or may contain) one disliked food. If different food items touch each other on the plate they may seem to be contaminating each other, or appear confusing.

Difficulties with sensory processing may reduce the awareness of the position of food in the mouth (Aswathy, Manoharan & Manoharan, 2016), and hamper ability to control it, leading to an instinctive fear response to a perceived risk of choking, which is naturally powerfully reinforced by any actual experience of choking. This leads to rejection of foods that feel unsafe, so only foods with a smooth and homogeneous texture or foods that quickly dissolve in the mouth are accepted.

In both anorexia nervosa and ASD there may be reduced sensitivity to internal bodily sensations, including normal hunger and fullness (Pollatos *et al.*, 2008; Fiene & Brownlow, 2015), leading to feeling unsure about what and how much to eat, and more dependent on rigid eating routines and rules, or an eating plan, rather than responding to natural physiological signals.

These experiences may lead to rejection of all but a very limited range of foods, often bland in flavour, smooth and homogeneous in texture, of similar neutral colours, placed separately on the plate, presented in the same way every time. This then gives rise to a set of entrenched internal rules about what is safe to eat.

Some of these sensory processing difficulties appear to improve with increasing age, but this improvement may arise from learning to apply management strategies, so the need for exhausting effort persists.

Disorders of sensory processing may also result in extreme distractibility, so that a person may easily be diverted from eating by surrounding noise, activity and disturbance (Twachtman-Reilly,

Amaral & Zebrowsli, 2008). This can affect the ability to attend to eating, slowing the pace, or halting it altogether. Some individuals may find it difficult to manage more than one behaviour at a time, for example cutting up food for the next mouthful while chewing, and this also can slow the pace of eating.

Physical discomfort provoked by eating

People on the autism spectrum seem to have increased risk of digestive disturbance, including nausea, gastro-oesophageal reflux (GORD), abdominal bloating, diarrhoea and constipation (McElhanon *et al.*, 2014). This may be related, at least in part, to disruption of the healthy gut microbial population (Cao *et al.*, 2013; Li *et al.*, 2016; Strati *et al.*, 2017). Restricted variety and amount of food intake, and multiple courses of antibiotics, probably contribute to the imbalance of intestinal microflora (Parracho *et al.*, 2005). These symptoms naturally cause an increase in anxiety which may add to the discomfort, creating a vicious cycle of distress and food rejection.

Some individuals may be hypersensitive to physical pain and discomfort (Riquelme *et al.*, 2016), so that symptoms, and even normal gut sensations, which are not very troublesome for most people, can cause serious suffering. Any food that causes, or seems to cause, pain and discomfort, naturally may be restricted or avoided

Low muscle tone may make sitting at the table without suitable support uncomfortable and tiring, and motor processes associated with eating, such as cutting up food and chewing it, may require fatiguing effort, so smooth-textured foods that require less motor effort are easier.

Anxiety and guilt about breaking rules
or not getting eating quite right

It is natural that a person experiencing such distress will seek ways to reduce it and make it more manageable. People resort to behaviours and internal rules in their efforts to find control. Some of these strategies are rational, and may be helpful, at least in the short term, for example refusing to eat a food that tastes unpleasant. For many reasons, these rules can become difficult to manage and damaging. Some may be baffling and exasperating for family members and others.

A rigid thinking style leads to rules that are 'all-or-nothing' rather than allowing flexibility, for example 'Cake is fattening so I must never eat cake', rather than 'Cake is a food high in fat and sugar so I try not to eat cake too often'. Similarly, information may be over-interpreted, leading to excessive strictness, for example it is well known that excessive sugar intake is harmful to health; this may be interpreted in an over-simplified and very extreme way, such as 'sugar is toxic'. It is easy to find validation and reinforcement of such extreme ideas on social media. Rules may lead to increasing restriction over time, for example 'I must not eat more calories today than yesterday'. Some may seem like an over-reaction, for example 'That food made me feel too full, I won't ever eat it again'. Anorexic thinking creates high sensitivity to information – and mis-information – about food, dieting and weight, so that any suggestion that a food is likely to cause weight gain may lead to total rejection of the food, even if the information is out of context or incorrect. There may be a drive to seek safety by knowing detailed information about food, for example the number of calories in the pack, and this information may be relied on to provide a feeling of certainty about food, even though it is illusory. With time and repetition, these thoughts and behaviours become consolidated as habits.

Rules may relate to:

- which foods to eat, including particular types or brands, and which to avoid

- times to eat, times to avoid eating, and how often to eat

- places to eat, and the details of the environment

- amounts to eat at each meal, or each day. This may be measured in calories; grams of particular food elements such as fat or carbohydrate; serving sizes or package size, or size of items such as pieces of fruit; number of food items, such as slices of bread or biscuits, or even small items such as raspberries or peas. This can lead to a need to weigh food, to know every ingredient in a food item, or nutrition analysis information, before accepting it

- how many different foods to eat, for example at one meal, or on one plate, or on one day

- pace of eating.

Rules give rise to behaviours aimed at helping to keep to the rules, for example:

- eating a very limited variety of foods, sometimes only bland, smooth-textured and neutral-coloured foods (Marí-Bauset *et al.*, 2014). This may be severe enough to exclude whole food groups. In ASD this is most commonly fruit and vegetables (Ledford & Gast, 2006), while in typical anorexia nervosa it is more likely to be foods high in fat or sugar, sometimes including dairy foods, meat and others that contain fat. This can impair overall nutrition (Johnson *et al.*, 2014)

- restricting the amount of food eaten to the point of weight loss and becoming harmfully underweight

- separating, mashing, mixing or smearing foods on the plate

- slow (or occasionally rapid) pace of eating

- eating only in 'safe' places

- avoiding social eating

- hiding food, pushing it off the plate or off the table, giving it to others.

They also lead to efforts to compensate for, or punish, perceived rule-breaking by:

- increasing food restriction further

- increasing exercise

- purging by using laxatives or self-induced vomiting.

Articulating an individual's personal thinking and feeling about eating is a helpful first step in making changes to improve eating and nutrition, by supporting change in unhealthy thinking. Change can be made possible by setting long-term aims, and agreeing priorities, then making and consolidating small steps towards changing the specific behaviour, thoughts and feelings that drive the damaging and unhealthy ways of using food. This challenging process needs time and sensitivity (Kinnaird *et al.*, 2017).

References

Aswathy, A., Manoharan, A. & Manoharan, A. (2016) 'Addressing oral sensory issues and possible remediation in children with autism spectrum disorders: Illustrated with a case study.' *International Journal of Medical, Health, Biomedical, Bioengineering and Pharmaceutical Engineering, 10*(7), 400–403.

Cao, X., Lin, P., Jiang, P. *et al.* (2013) 'Characteristics of the gastrointestinal microbiome in children with autism spectrum disorder: A systematic review.' *Shanghai Archives of Psychiatry, 25,* 342–353.

Fiene, L. & Brownlow, C. (2015) 'Investigating interoception and body awareness in adults with and without autism spectrum disorder.' *Autism Research, 8*(6), 709–716.

Horder, J., Wilson, E., Mendez, A. *et al.* (2014) 'Autisitic traits and abnormal sensory experiences in adults.' *Journal of Autism & Developmental Disorders, 44,* 1461–1469.

Karlsson, L., Råstam, M. & Wentz, E. (2013) 'The Swedish Eating Assessment for Autism Spectrum Disorders (SWEAA) – validation of a self-report questionnaire targeting eating disturbances within the autism spectrum.' *Research in Developmental Disabilities, 34,* 2224–2233.

Kinnaird, E., Norton, C. & Tchanturia, K. (2017) 'Clinicians' views on working with anorexia nervosa and autism spectrum disorder co-morbidity: A qualitative study.' *BMC Psychiatry, 17,* 292.

Johnson, C., Turner, K., Stewart, P. *et al.* (2014) 'Relationships between feeding problems, behavioural characteristics and nutritional quality in ASD.' *Journal of Autism & Developmental Disorders, 44*(9), 2175–2184.

Ledford, J. & Gast, F. (2006) 'Feeding problems in children with autism spectrum disorders: A review.' *Focus on Autism and Other Developmental Disabilities, 21*(3), 153–166.

Li, Q., Han, Y., Dy, A. *et al.* (2016) 'The gut microbiota and autism spectrum disorders.' *Frontiers in Cellular Neuroscience, 11,* article 20.

Marí-Bauset, S., Zazpe, I., Mari-Sanchis, A. *et al.* (2014) 'Food selectivity in autism spectrum disorders: A systematic review.' *Journal of Child Neurology, 29,* 11.

McElhanon, B., McCracken, C., Karpen, S. & Sharp, W. (2014) 'Gastrointestinal symptoms in Autism Spectrum Disorder: A meta-analysis.' *Pediatrics, 133*(5), 872–883.

Nadon, G., Feldman, D., Dunn, W. *et al.* (2010) 'Mealtime problems in children with autism spectrum disorder and their typically developing siblings: A comparison study.' *Autism, 15*(1), 98–113.

Nadon, G., Feldman, D., Dunn, W. *et al.* (2011) 'Association of sensory processing and eating problems in children with autistic spectrum disorders.' *Autism Research and Treatment,* article ID 541926.

Parracho, H., Bingham, M., Gibson, G. & McCartney, A. (2005) 'Differences between the gut microflora of children with autistic spectrum disorders and that of healthy children.' *Journal of Medical Microbiology, 54,* 987–991

Pollatos, O., Kurz, A., Albrecht, J. *et al.* (2008) 'Reduced perception of bodily signals in anorexia nervosa.' *Eating Behaviors, 9,* 381–388.

Riquelme, I., Hatem, S. & Montoya, P. (2016) 'Abnormal pressure pain, touch sensitivity, proprioception and manual dexterity in children with autism spectrum disorders.' *Neural Plasticity,* article ID 1723401.

Rogers, L., Magill-Evans, J. & Rempel, G. (2012) 'Mothers' challenges in feeding their children with autistic spectrum disorder – managing more than just picky eating.' *Journal of Developmental & Physical Disabilities, 24,* 19–33.

Spek, A., van Rijnsoever, W., van Laarhoven, L. *et al.* (2019) 'Eating problems in men and women with an autism spectrum disorder.' *Journal of Autism & Developmental Disorders, 50*(5), 1748–1755.

Strati, F., Cavalieri, D., Albanese, D. *et al.* (2017) 'New evidences on the altered gut microbiota in autism spectrum disorders.' *Microbiome, 5,* 24.

Tavassoli, T., Miller, L., Schoen, S. *et al.* (2013) 'Sensory over-responsivity in adults with autism spectrum conditions.' *Autism, 18*(4), 1–5.

Twachtman-Reilly, J., Amaral, S. & Zebrowsli, P. (2008) 'Addressing feeding disorders in children on the autism spectrum in school-based settings: Physiological and behavioral issues.' *Language, Speech and Hearing Services in Schools, 39,* 261–272.

Chapter 11

Supporting Recovery of Eating and Nutrition

Kate Williams

Most of the research on the links between eating disorders and autism spectrum disorders has related to anorexia nervosa. People with ASD may also develop other eating disorders, including bulimia nervosa, with binge eating and purging dominating, and binge eating disorder, often leading to obesity. We know that the mix of experiences, thoughts and feelings that underlie all eating disorders are similar, and so similar strategies to support recovery can be used to help.

Having an eating disorder is exhausting and distressing. Years of trying to feed an autistic person with an eating disorder leave carers feeling drained and de-skilled. Setting out recovery in a series of stages helps to make the process manageable and achievable.

SUPPORTING CHANGE TOWARDS RECOVERY

1. Identifying and exploring behaviour, thoughts and feelings that maintain disordered eating.

2. Setting priorities for recovery.

3. Agreeing aims for recovery.

4. Collaborating to make changes in eating and nutrition.

5. Consolidating recovery.

In this way, strategies to manage food and eating to achieve and sustain safe and effective nutritional recovery, while minimizing the anxiety and distress that impede change, can be planned and tried. To make the work of recovery less daunting, and as safe and effective as possible, it is important to identify immediate priorities for action, and challenges that can be set aside for later.

Stages of recovery

1. Medical stabilization.

2. Nutritional recovery and return to healthy, stable weight.

3. Comfortable and acceptable social eating.

Strategies to prevent relapse need to be integrated at every stage.

Medical stabilization

For safety, the first priority must be medical stabilization and dealing with any immediate risk to health.

Risks that need immediate attention include:

REFEEDING SYNDROME

There may be a risk of refeeding syndrome for individuals at low body mass index (BMI). Refeeding syndrome occurs when refeeding is not controlled carefully, and can result in fluid retention, confusion, and weakness of muscles, including the heart and breathing muscles. Blood tests for electrolyte levels will help to assess the risk. Low white cell count is associated with severe malnutrition, and indicates increased risk (O'Connor & Nicholls, 2013). People with low BMI (below 16 kg/m²), especially if they also have had very little recent food intake and are losing weight (NICE, 2006), should be assessed by a doctor or dietician for risk of refeeding syndrome. If there is severe and immediate risk to health, it may be necessary to manage the early stages of refeeding in hospital, where close medical monitoring and treatment can be given. For some people, tube feeding may be the best option at this stage. In extreme cases, tube feeding may need to be applied without the person's consent, under the Mental Health Act.

In community settings, where close monitoring may not be possible, slower refeeding is safer, and usually easier to tolerate.

DEHYDRATION AND LOW FLUID INTAKE

Fluid intake may be deliberately restricted, to keep weight down, to avoid feeling full, or to comply with other internal rules. If overall fluid intake is restricted to less than six drinks over the day (about 1200 ml total, not including water contained in foods), there may be a risk of dehydration and low blood pressure, causing symptoms such as dizziness, fainting and headache, dry mouth, lips and skin. Purging by vomiting or using laxatives increases the risk by increasing fluid loss from the body.

VERY EXCESSIVE FLUID INTAKE

There may be excessive fluid intake (over four litres daily) to manipulate weight, suppress hunger, or facilitate vomiting. This can lead to dilution of the blood and resultant fall in electrolyte levels. Symptoms include nausea and headache, muscle cramp, and even seizures and coma if very extreme.

CONTINUING WEIGHT LOSS

Individuals at very low BMI (below 14 m/kg^2) who are continuing to lose weight, especially if the weight loss is rapid (0.5 kg/week or more), are at risk of organ failure and death, so nutrition support should be instigated immediately.

ELECTROLYTE ABNORMALITIES

Electrolytes (salts) in the blood may be abnormal because of low intake of food, or restricted or excessive fluid intake, though the most likely cause of severe abnormalities is purging by vomiting or laxative use. If it is very severe, this can cause heart or kidney abnormalities, and urgent medical supplementation is required.

ANAEMIA

If food intake is restricted overall, or food sources of iron such as meat, bread and green vegetables are avoided, body stores of iron become depleted, leading to anaemia. This risk is ameliorated in women as menstrual losses stop at low weight, but anaemia may still develop, causing extreme tiredness, faintness and headache.

Other conditions that need early consideration include:

- nutrients related to bone health: calcium and vitamin D

- other vitamin or mineral deficiencies

- managing mouth and gut symptoms such as dental pain, reflux, bloating and constipation

- low protein intake and poor protein status

- bone marrow suppression, indicated by low white cell count, and risk of infection.

Recovery of nutrition and weight

After stabilization of medical risk, the next priority is improvement in overall nutritional status, including weight gain if necessary. For an underweight individual, this needs an increase in the amount of food eaten, to establish steady weight recovery, and often also an increase in the variety of foods eaten, to provide the full range and amount of all essential nutrients. There may have been poor intake of micronutrients (Hadigan *et al.*, 2000), so it is usually helpful to supplement vitamins and minerals to make up deficits quickly, and replenish body stores. This may also need some modest increases in the range of foods accepted, so that enough foods are present in the diet to ensure adequate provision of all essential nutrients, and this usually requires at least some foods from every food group (see the NHS Eatwell Guide, www.nhs.uk/live-well/eat-well/the-eatwell-guide).

SUSTAINING RECOVERY AND PROTECTING
HEALTH FOR THE LONG TERM

Eating disorders may relapse, especially at times of stress, so the prevention and management of relapse must be part of recovery. Alongside nutrition recovery, work on changing the thoughts and beliefs related to food and eating is part of the process. Experiments and practice with healthy and adequate eating, and experience of the effects of better eating, can be integrated into recovery to support confidence in new, healthy beliefs, rules and habits. These can form the basis of well-consolidated eating routines that resist relapse, and be quickly resumed if lapses occur. Building a modest amount of flexibility into new rules makes them more practical and increases resilience.

Comfortable and acceptable social eating

Family and social eating is one of the greatest challenges for the people who care for a family member or friend of an autistic person or someone with an eating disorder (Sharp, Burrell & Jaquess, 2014). The websites of support organizations for both types of disorder reflect this distress. Most families expect shared meal times to be relaxed and enjoyable, and they often provide one of the best routine opportunities for socializing together. An eating or autistic disorder can rob families of this positive experience for years, replacing it with distress, and making social eating away from home so challenging that it comes to be avoided. Avoidance of social eating results in social isolation and limits life activities.

Because of this, progressing towards more relaxed, confident and acceptable social eating is an important aim of therapy. However, change may be very difficult and slow, and needs to be taken in small steps, without seeking to work on too many different changes at one time. Working too early on changes in social eating behaviour may impede nutrition recovery by making the total challenge too great. For this reason, it is usually better to make sure that physical recovery is well established before beginning work on the additional changes needed to make social eating easier.

Agreeing aims for recovery

The process of change usually is achieved by agreeing broad, long-term aims, and negotiating short-term, specific and clear goals as steps on the way to achieving them (Table 11.1). For people with autistic traits, especially if there is a life-long history of food selectivity and other quirks related to eating, the aim of entirely socially normal eating, with all its variety, flexibility, novelty and unpredictability, may not be appropriate, even for the long term, though it is always possible to work towards it.

Table 11.1. Possible short- and long-term aims to consider

Starting point	Short-term aims	Long-term aims
Restricted amount of food.	Adequate amount of food to recover healthy weight and correct nutritional deficiencies.	Enough food to sustain health in the long term and prevent relapse.
Restricted variety of food. Repetitive meals.	Enough variety to include all essential food groups.	Enough variety to meet long-term psychological and social needs.
Rigid meal times.	Eating often enough to achieve nutritional recovery and restore natural appetite regulation.	Enough flexibility and spontaneity to join family and social eating, and cope with unexpected changes.
Counting calories, fat, carbohydrate, food items. Weighing food. Using foods only in known pack sizes.	Using portion exchanges as a more approximate measure. Trusting others to serve food, at home and in other environments.	Using household measures, judging serving size by eye. Successfully managing eating away from home in a variety of settings.
Eating only foods of known nutritional content. Limiting to known brands and products. Repetitive meals.	Including enough options to achieve nutritional recovery, and to be manageable for practical purposes.	Enough flexibility to maintain adequate nutrition in a variety of settings, and cope with changes that may occur.
Eating behaviour that interferes with adequate eating and/or is not socially acceptable.	Eating behaviour that enables adequate food intake in an appropriate amount of time, and is not distressing to others.	Eating behaviour that enables normal family and social eating.
Irrational rules about eating that impede good nutrition and normal eating behaviour.	Healthy rules about eating to support recovery and long-term nutritional health.	Increasing flexibility and spontaneity with meal times, food choices and other aspects of eating.

Collaborating to make changes in eating and nutrition

Changing eating behaviour is very challenging for people with eating disorders, especially for those with ASD, and needs continuing support. Understanding the individual barriers to change can help to develop and use appropriate strategies to sustain efforts to improve eating and nutritional health. Intense fear of change in eating is central to anorexia nervosa. Starvation makes thinking rigid, and impairs learning and memory. Difficulty with understanding some communication idioms, such as metaphor or imagery, is characteristic of ASD. These features make it difficult to understand, remember and believe the reasons for change, so building trust and maintaining motivation are challenging. Recovery is a process of continuing collaboration, planning, experimenting, reviewing and adapting.

Setting, reviewing and building on goals

Goals for nutritional recovery often take the form of a meal plan, or a plan for a particular meal or snack. This ensures goals for change are positive things to do, as this is easier than trying *not* to do something. Goals for change need to be specific enough to review usefully, so it is clear if the goal has been attained. Goals need to be challenging enough to gain progress while being achievable. Each experimental change offers opportunities for learning and building. Making a time limit for achieving the change focuses efforts and prompts review and learning. If it has gone well, it may need more time to embed it, or it may be possible to make it more challenging, or add a new goal for change. If it was achieved with difficulty, it could stay the same for a further time period, to allow more practice. If it proved too challenging, it is helpful to consider the difficulties and ways to overcome them, or adjust the goal to make it more achievable. Part of the process is to embed the idea that change is always an experiment, a learning opportunity, and progress towards the long-term aims. Progress is not linear, there will be changes of direction, pace of change will vary, and breaks may be needed. Even when things seem to slip back, the learning and experience are never lost, and will support further improvement. Criticism and punishment are not helpful to the process – they distract from recovery and drain energy and motivation. Swift and encouraging acknowledgement of progress and achievements, however modest, helps to consolidate and build on them.

Goals and strategies for medical stabilization

It may be necessary to make some changes urgently, to halt weight loss and manage medical risk. This may need a period of intensive support, from professionals, family and friends. Carers may feel very anxious about a loved one who is seriously unwell, and feel their confidence and skills in feeding that person have drained away.

Carers can find themselves feeling very unsure and anxious about what to. Understanding the priorities can help make this situation less overwhelming.

At this stage, the undernourished brain cannot change rigid beliefs, and anxiety is elevated, so changes need to be limited to what is needed for safety, and as clear and straightforward as possible. For example, a meal plan with few or no choices, repeated for several days, may be easier than one with a range of choices (see www.peacepathway.org for a sample plan). It is usually possible to reduce risk safely by making small changes, progressing gradually over the first few days. For example, it may be possible to increase intake by escalating quantities of foods that are acceptable, without changing the type of food. It may be possible to increase fluid intake by adding to the frequency of taking drinks without changing the type or amount of fluid at each drink. Liquid oral nutrition supplements may be useful, if they are more acceptable than food.

The only rule for this stage is: 'This is really difficult, I have to do it for my health, my safety and my recovery.'

REFEEDING SYNDROME

To reduce the risk of refeeding syndrome, it is important that the increase in food intake, especially carbohydrate, is very gradual; to give supplements of thiamin and other B vitamins; and to ensure adequate provision of potassium, phosphate and other essential nutrients, by using foods high in those nutrients, and supplements as required. It is usually safe to start with the amount of food that will prevent further weight loss, without seeking to achieve weight gain immediately. The safest foods include milk, especially whole milk, plain yoghurt, especially whole milk or Greek-style, and cheese. It is possible to achieve safe refeeding with a very limited variety of foods, given in small amounts, at frequent intervals, increasing gradually over several days (see www.peacepathway.org for a sample eating plan). If foods high in phosphate (milk and milk products) or potassium (fruit and vegetables) are not acceptable, medical supplementation may be needed until the risk of refeeding syndrome is past.

Rapid change of weight due to fluid shifts is inevitable, and may be extremely alarming. Explanation of the reasons for this, and in particular reassurance that it is self-limiting, may be helpful. The main reasons for fluid retention at first are shifts in fluid and salts in the body, and rebuilding essential stores of carbohydrate, which holds fluid. Unless there has been severe purging, the gain is likely to be two to three kg at the most, over seven to ten days.

VITAMIN AND MINERAL DEFICIENCIES

A diet very limited in both quantity and variety can give rise to vitamin and mineral deficiencies, such as iron-deficient anaemia. To correct these, a multi-vitamin and mineral supplement is simplest and safest. A variety of preparations is available from pharmacies, in liquid, capsule and other presentations, making it easier to select an acceptable product. In the longer term, preventing deficiencies is a significant reason for improving nutritional mix.

FLUID

Changes in the amount of fluid may be needed. Fluid intake can be increased in small steps, changing the amount taken at each drink, or the frequency of drinking. A written plan with clear aims for fluid intake may be helpful. For individuals who find increasing fluid difficult because of feeling full or bloated, an oral rehydration solution, available from pharmacies, may be easier than plain water.

If fluid intake is dangerously excessive, reductions can similarly be made in small steps. Hot drinks, such as tea or decaffeinated coffee, are sipped more slowly, so may be more comfortable for this process, though it is best to avoid extremes of temperature. To manage perceived thirst, sucking ice chips may help.

Goals and strategies for nutritional recovery

The next stage is recovery of healthy nutritional status. This may take some time, and maintaining motivation can be a challenge. It may be helpful to agree short-term goals, such as improvement in sleep or bowel function, which can be achieved with relatively modest changes. Weight gain is usually the most apparent, and the most feared, result of this process, so it is important to give continuing attention to all the elements of nutritional recovery, and the subjective benefits that follow, so that the focus is widened beyond body weight. As nutrition improves, most people will feel improvements in energy and reduced tiredness, improved muscle strength, feeling warmer, improved sleep and mood, and resolution of symptoms such as constipation, dizziness and faintness. Blood tests will also indicate improvements. Looking out for these benefits can help develop confidence that the direction of change is healthy, the people encouraging it can be trusted, and the long-term gains will be worth the effort.

MANAGING PHYSICAL DISCOMFORT

Increasing food intake after a long period of very restricted eating is physically uncomfortable, and many people feel worse as they increase eating, which makes it difficult to persist, and even to believe it is the right thing to do. These discomforts usually improve as nutrition recovers, and there are some measures that may help. Consult a doctor about severe or persistent symptoms.

Bloating and constipation are common, as gut motility is reduced, and the population of gut micro-organisms is abnormal. Increasing dietary fibre intake may help, but as the gut muscle is weakened by starvation, this must be taken slowly. Foods such as oats, fruit and vegetables contain soluble fibre, and are the best foods to use at first, in gradually increasing amounts, spread over the day. Very high fibre foods such as bran cereals are best avoided.

Supporting recovery of the micro-organisms in the gut may help to reduce discomfort. Some people find pro-biotic products such as live yoghurt are helpful; they must be taken regularly for several weeks before the full benefits are achieved. Regularly eating fermented products such as sauerkraut, kimchi and kombucha may be beneficial, but the flavour and odour can be unacceptable for individuals with hypersensitivity.

To keep gut bacteria healthy for the long term, as wide a variety of foods as possible is helpful, ideally including fruit, vegetables, pulses, nuts, wholegrain cereals, fish and dairy products.

Symptoms usually improve as the gut recovers.

FOOD VARIETY

Expanding what may be a limited range of acceptable foods is not a main focus at this stage, but there is a need to provide all essential nutrients and food elements. To achieve this, it is necessary to include at least one or two foods from each food group. Using the Eatwell Plate as an objective guide may be helpful. Care is needed to avoid information about healthy eating that is aimed too much at weight control.

There are balances to be achieved, which need specific discussion and agreement. Some individuals may find it very difficult to take more energy dense foods (usually higher in fat and sugar), and feel able to eat only low energy density foods such as wholegrain cereals, beans and pulses, fruit and vegetables. Achieving adequate energy intake with only low energy density foods requires a large volume to be consumed, which may also be difficult, so an achievable compromise must be found, for example adding olive oil as a dressing. Some find it very difficult to take fluids that provide calories, such as milky drinks or fruit juice, which means that more solid food must be consumed. Finding the best balance may take some patient discussion. Small experiments may help. Supplement drinks may be a useful addition at this stage.

MEAL PATTERN

Meal times and frequency of eating may need to be changed. It may be necessary to work with a temporary meal pattern that is not completely socially normal, in order to achieve adequate intake. For example, most people find it easier to increase intake by having two or three snacks daily, in addition to regular meals, rather than having larger meals than normal. Meals may need to be more substantial than average, for example by including two courses at all meals. There is no flexibility to miss meals. A short-term aim for three meals and three snacks, at regular intervals, is usually needed. If some meals have previously been missed, they can be built up by beginning with small food items, or even drinks, at the agreed meal time. Some people may feel distressed by having to eat more often than others seem to. A gentle reminder that the eating plan is a temporary measure to support recovery may help. Eating needs to be given priority at this stage. It may be necessary to plan social, education and work commitments to ensure meals and snacks are not missed. Making a habit of carrying snack items such as cereal bars or packets of nuts may help.

PORTION SIZE

It is not usually necessary to increase portion sizes beyond normal, but they must be large enough to achieve continuing recovery. Where increases are needed, they can be taken in agreed steps, working on a few items at a time, perhaps just one at each meal. It may be helpful to use information on food packs, or pre-portioned food, or pictures and lists of normal portion sizes. Ready meals may be more acceptable as they are standard and predictable, but are expensive, not always ideally healthy, and may change or become unavailable, so are best used very explicitly as a short-term or limited strategy. They may be useful as an alternative when other household members are sharing an unacceptable meal, or stress is depleting motivation.

WEIGHT GAIN

It is usually necessary to adjust food intake as progress continues, to maintain an adequate rate of gain. The body needs more energy as it recovers, to support increasing metabolic rate, body size, and sometimes activity. It is important to be aware well in advance that this is likely to be needed, and to plan for it, so that it is clear what will happen if weight gain slows or stops. Although this is difficult, it is usually easier than having to make changes quickly if weight gain is too slow. It is, however, important to resist any wish to micro-manage body weight by making frequent small adjustments to food consumption. There are many factors that influence body weight other than food, so weight does not respond in a highly controllable way to changes in food intake. Such efforts create confusion, and can impede recovery. It may help to agree an acceptable rate of weight gain, as a range, perhaps 0.3 to 0.7 kg per week (usually more for hospital inpatients), and calculate the calorie requirement together, then make a meal plan to meet it.

Useful rules might include:

- 'I need to eat three meals and three snacks every day. The exact times of these may need to change sometimes.'

- 'If my weight gain is less than the agreed amount, straight away I need to add an item every day from my planned list of extra foods.'

- 'Eating my meals and snacks is the most important thing right now. I may need to limit other activities to make sure I eat everything I need.'

- 'I need the foods from every food group to recover good nutrition.'

ANNA'S RECOVERY

Anna had been at low weight all her adult life. She worked in an accountancy firm, and lived alone. She was very anxious about portion sizes, and used pre-packed foods or weighed food. She also struggled with intrusive thoughts about numbers, and counted food items. She had kept to a limited variety of foods for some years. She wanted to improve her eating because of health concerns, including osteoporosis, so her broad overall aim was reducing nutritional risk. She was able to build a new eating routine for herself, which remained rather repetitive, as she felt more comfortable with that, and she continued to use several portion-packed foods. This enabled her to eat enough to achieve some weight recovery, and a healthier mix of foods, in particular adequate intake of calcium and vitamin D. For example, Anna knew that her breakfast of a single sachet of microwave oats made up with water was not an adequate breakfast, though it had been her habit for a long time, and felt safe. She built on it in stages, as shown below, with a particular focus on taking more milk to increase calcium intake.

Current breakfast	Goal	Week 1	Week 2	Week 3
1 sachet instant porridge, made up with water, on weekdays only, eaten before leaving for work.	1 sachet instant porridge, made up with skimmed milk, eaten before 9am, every day for a week.	Achieved on work days, not at the weekend. Try with the same goal for another week, with a time target of 10am at the weekend.	Completely achieved, feeling confident to continue.	New goal to change to semi-skimmed milk to make up the porridge, every day.

She worked on other goals at her other meals and snacks, for example she had always eaten six pretzels when she arrived home from work, and chose to change it to 12, as she felt comfortable with the number 12.

She spent a little time on Sunday afternoons reviewing her progress on the phone with her mother, who was able to offer some support.

Some individuals, like Anna, find a regular review with a supportive friend or family member, or professional is helpful. Others find food diaries a helpful tool. They can build to form a record of progress over time, so reviewing them can be an encouraging reminder of gains that have been achieved.

To support making changes in eating:

- Discuss aims and priorities, to agree what to work on, where to start, and what can be set aside for later. This makes the task less daunting.

- Provide clear explanation of the risks, the aims and likely results of making changes, using concrete information about blood tests and other medical evidence, related to symptoms and experience. Because memory and learning may be impaired by starvation, this may need to be repeated. Straightforward written information, free of redundant detail, and ideally adapted to the individual's circumstances and thinking style, may be a helpful aid to understanding and remembering. Some people may work better with more visual tools such as timelines, a chart or pictures.

- Agree a clear plan and a timescale for changes. Keep changes small and specific, and avoid too many changes at once. Provide a written copy of the plan, showing the agreed changes and the timescale.

- Agree that the plan will not be discussed at meal times. Instead, arrange to set aside time with a supportive person, ideally each day at first, to review progress, consider how to tackle problems that have arisen, and plan for the next steps. Use results of blood tests, other measures such as temperature and blood pressure, and improvements in symptoms to reinforce success.

- If the plan has been recommended by a doctor, therapist or dietician, remind the person of this, and that the advice must be followed until the next review meeting with the professional – this technique is called 'calling on a higher power' and it allows you to have a discussion without taking personal responsibility for the details of the plan or the need to implement it. You can say something like, 'The dietician explained why you need to follow this plan until the next meeting. We can note the difficulties to discuss the next time we meet her, but for now we need to work on sticking to it', or, if it is relevant, 'You remember that the doctor told us that if you can stick to this plan, you should be able to avoid an admission to hospital.'

At this stage, alongside challenging goals for change, it is useful to make an alternative meal plan to use when eating is more difficult, so that improvement can continue. The back-up plan must provide enough food to maintain progress with nutritional recovery, while feeling as safe and manageable as possible. This plan can then be used at stressful times, when other people are eating foods that are outside the acceptable range, or when motivation falters. It should be planned so that it can be used easily, with as little effort and stress as possible, using foods that are consistently acceptable and can easily be kept in store, such as cereals, ready meals, frozen or canned foods (see www. peacepathway.org for an example).

Goals and strategies for comfortable and acceptable social eating

One of the effects of an eating disorder is avoidance of social eating, which can lead to extreme social isolation, which is distressing and contributes to entrenching the disorder further. Many people wish to feel more comfortable eating in social groups in a wider range of places, for example at work or college, when travelling, or to join friends eating out or in their homes. Many people with ASD, especially females, develop strategies to camouflage their difficulties in social situations. It can be helpful to explore these masking skills to find the most effective ways to use them without becoming stressed and exhausted. Strategies to manage social eating will be a mix of the individual's own skills at camouflage, the efforts of friends and family to make the environment more comfortable, and selection of occasions and places, and the mix will be applied differently, depending on circumstances and individual choices.

When there is a strong incentive for managing social eating better, improvements can be made, with time and a clear plan. Incentives may relate to long-term health and nutrition, eating at work or college, or to share family and social eating. Ways to keep these aims clearly in mind can support motivation. It may be that keeping to familiar foods and routines at home, to conserve energy to use when it is most needed, will make achieving these aims easier, or practice at home in a familiar environment may be helpful.

When nutritional recovery is well established, aims for developing more socially normal eating can be considered. These may include increasing variety of accepted foods; improved ability to try new foods; more flexibility with meal times and settings; reducing damaging and socially unacceptable eating behaviours such as counting food items, slow pace of eating or excessive manipulation of food. The priority remains maintaining nutrition and health, but many people want to eat in a socially normal way to achieve life aims for a career or education, or developing relationships with friends and a partner. Clarifying specific skills and behaviours to support these aims makes them less vague and more manageable. It can be reassuring to know that neurotypical people constantly adjust their behaviour according to the situation, but can sometimes find it an uncomfortable effort, and this is normal.

It remains important to keep in mind the need to eat enough to maintain good nutrition, and not to allow efforts to improve social eating to impede this.

INCREASING VARIETY

Once a basic, nutritionally adequate variety of foods is in place, work can begin on expanding further, if the person wants to do that, for example to make it easier to eat with friends. It is useful to reduce reliance on a very small range of foods which may not always be available.

It is helpful to clarify the reasons for expanding variety, so that there are clear benefits for the individual, and aims can be related to specific needs. Consider how food selectivity is interfering with activities and aspirations, such as going out with friends or going to college. Agree on modest, achievable, short-term aims, that are relevant to the individual's needs and wishes, so that the task does not seem overwhelming.

Most of the strategies used for reducing food selectivity have been developed for children. They include behavioural approaches (Sharp *et al.*, 2014), food chaining (Fishbein *et al.*, 2016; Fraker & Walbert, 2011) and the sequential oral sensory approach (Toomey & Ross, 2011). These approaches may be adapted for adults, who are often able to select the most useful strategies for themselves and progress more quickly. Adults may have strong personal incentives to build tolerance of foods, be able to manage their own anxiety successfully, and adjust the pace of change and the timing of breaks, so maintaining a sense of control and enabling them to sustain progress.

Minimizing anxiety supports success with experiments with new foods. A calm environment without distractions can help to control anxiety, though gentle music may be soothing. A supportive seat with enough space to move freely can help to make meals less tiring and stressful. Keeping wipes on the table allows cleaning of hands whenever that is needed. Agreeing what kind of encouragement is most useful, so that supporters understand what to do, is helpful. Plan one experimental change at a time, with an agreed time schedule, so it is predictable and not too overwhelming. The next change can then be planned to build on success. It can support confidence and motivation if it is clear that at home, while experimenting with new foods, it is acceptable to behave in a way that is not generally socially acceptable, for example to touch food with the fingers, touch to the lips, sniff food, or spit out a new food that is too unpleasant to swallow. Whatever strategies are used the pace of change can be adjusted to make progress without excessive distress, and breaks can be taken.

Behavioural techniques include gentle prompts and reminders, and consistently rewarding small achievements with praise and encouragement from others or self-rewards. This can help to maintain motivation and pace of progress. Adults are able to find for themselves the rewards and incentives that will be effective for them. Aims usually are to improve nutrition and protection of long-term health; and to make social eating easier. To progress towards these aims small goals can be planned, implemented and achieved, and rewarded.

Food chaining involves identifying acceptable foods and the flavours and textures they have in common, for example smooth foods like custard or yoghurt, or crisp foods like crackers. It is then possible to find new foods with similar characteristics, and to build variety with a series of small changes. For example, if mashed potato is an accepted food, it might be possible to try plain boiled potato, which has a similar flavour but a different texture; or mashed sweet potato, which has a similar texture but different colour and flavour. The next step might be jacket potato, or mashed carrot. Success with one change can help build confidence to make further changes. It may help to begin with some of the accepted food and a little of the new food together on the plate, to take alternate bites, or to mix foods together, for example a little sweet potato mixed into mashed potato. Masking a new food with an accepted condiment or sauce may help.

In planning experiments with food chaining, it is helpful to move away from an extreme position of perceiving foods as simply 'acceptable' or 'not acceptable', to build a hierarchy. For example, if a type of low-fat portion-packed cheese spread is acceptable, a strong flavoured high-fat type of cheese such as Stilton may seem completely impossible, but it might be possible to try a mild, low-fat type which is more similar to the accepted item, such as pre-sliced Gouda. If sliced white bread is acceptable but wholegrain, crusty granary bread seems impossible, sliced wheatgerm bread might be possible. The variety and nutritional mix can be improved by moving along the hierarchy in small stages. Choice of foods to try may be influenced by individual aims, for example if constipation is a problem, increasing fruit, vegetables and wholegrain cereals might be a priority.

A full description of the process is set out in *Food Chaining: The Proven 6-Step Plan to Stop Picky Eating, Solve Feeding Problems, and Expand Your Child's Diet* by Cheri Fraker, Mark Fishbein, Sibyl Cox and Laura Walbert.

The sequential oral sensory approach (Toomey & Ross, 2011; Benson *et al.*, 2013) uses very small increases in exposure to build tolerance, without any expectation that the food will be eaten until the final stages. The full process identifies 32 steps, beginning with visual tolerance of the food increasingly closer; manipulating the food with utensils; experiencing the smell and feel of the food; tasting the food, at first without swallowing, and finally chewing and swallowing. More information is available at https://sosapproach-conferences.com.

Increasing familiarity with foods can be presented to children as playing with the food. This approach can seem infantilizing to adults. This can be re-framed as practice with handling food as part of buying and preparing food. With supportive help, this can provide graded opportunities to become more familiar with foods, and to think about and use food in a calm and productive way. Some adults find it much easier to use online shopping, as they can take it at their own pace, in a familiar place, and may even use the same order repeatedly. Others can find this leads to obsessive information-seeking and product comparison. Opportunities to practise, with a supporter, making food plans and shopping lists; visiting food shops (perhaps initially without any expectation to buy food); putting food into a supermarket trolley; handling food in the kitchen, for example washing and peeling vegetables, pouring, mixing, cooking, and dealing with waste, can help to overcome individual difficulties. Stress associated with these activities can be minimized if they are well-planned, take place in a calm environment, and without expectation to eat the food, so that tolerance can build.

Tolerance of a new food may be lost if it is not used regularly. Repeated practice with a new food in a comfortable and supportive environment then builds integration of the new food into routine eating.

Adults can learn about these approaches, and choose for themselves which techniques feel most suitable for them, how to implement them, and what support is most helpful for them.

EATING IN UNFAMILIAR SETTINGS

A planned visit to a new café or restaurant at a quiet time, with a familiar, supportive person, can help make the environment more familiar, and offer an opportunity to look at some of the food available, to help plan. A first visit can be made with clear agreement there is no expectation to eat or drink, or perhaps have just a cup of tea or coffee, or whatever may be possible.

Knowledge of the food available in new settings can help to set specific aims which are achievable. Most restaurants and cafés have menus on their websites, so it is possible to choose a place which offers acceptable options, and plan choices, including alternatives, in advance. It is generally possible to find a meal that is a reasonable match to the usual meal. If the meal is likely to be larger, it can be taken in place of the meal and the next snack, but no more than that. Once a planned meal is agreed, it is important also to find possible alternatives, in case the chosen items are not available.

Portion sizes may be unpredictable, and larger than usual. A plan for this can help prevent anxiety about it. If possible, it is good to have a supportive friend briefed to help. They can than check the portion size together, and if it seems too large, remove the excess. It can be offered to others at the table, or moved aside on the plate, or put on a separate small plate, whatever is most comfortable. Planning useful phrases to use in talking to restaurant staff, and reassurance that they are happy to help, may reduce anxiety. For example:

- 'May I have another small plate please?' (No explanation is needed.)

- 'May I have it without sauce/dressing please?'

- 'It was delicious, just a little too much' is an acceptable response to a question about whether the food was all right, often asked if food is left on the plate.

It is also useful to plan how to manage knocking over or spilling something, if this may happen.

It may help to plan taking a break, with a supporter if possible, if anxiety rises too much. It is always acceptable to leave the table, with a quick 'excuse me', to go outside or to the toilet for a few minutes to calm down.

UNEXPECTED EATING
A spontaneous invitation to join a person for coffee or to eat is often automatically refused.

Learning to accept can be very difficult, but is worth trying to do to support social connection. Developing a repertoire of responses that stop short of total rejection can help, for example:

- 'I would love to, but I can't now, but how about next week/ tomorrow...'

- 'Would it be okay if I just have tea/coffee?'

- 'Would it be okay to go somewhere small/quiet/nearby/to this place that I know?'

SOCIALLY UNACCEPTABLE BEHAVIOUR WITH FOOD
Habits that have evolved to avoid eating, to check or test foods before eating them, or otherwise make eating seem subjectively more comfortable or controlled can make social eating difficult. Some of these behaviours may interfere with adequate eating, so need to be addressed, at least enough to maintain healthy weight and good nutrition. It may be necessary to work on pace of eating, cutting food into tiny pieces, spitting out food, touching or sniffing food, smearing it on the plate or hiding it, separating or mixing or mashing foods, or other similar behaviours. The aim may not be total abolition of these behaviours, but reducing or modifying them enough to achieve the desired gains, for example it may be possible for an individual to eat in a more acceptable way when

eating out, but revert to more entrenched behaviours at home. It may be reassuring to know that most people adjust their eating behaviour and manners to the environment and the company, and are more casual at home alone or with close family. It is not necessary to work on making progress at every meal time; a break may help maintain efforts.

It is helpful to explore the drivers of these behaviours, and the gains to be achieved from abolishing them. Some may have developed in childhood, before the eating disorder, and it may be possible to view these as childish behaviours that can be left behind. Some of these habits may have developed to restrict eating, to suppress hunger, or avoid physical discomforts, so no longer serve any useful purpose as recovery progresses. There may be personal incentives to reduce, modify or abolish these behaviours, for example to maintain recovery and join with normal family and social eating. Identifying these is helpful in motivating work on change. When a better understanding has been achieved, small goals can be set to progress towards the aims.

Some of these behaviours may have developed to help manage hunger, so they are easier to reduce when nutrition has been restored and hunger is less overwhelming, and there is less incentive to suppress it. Work to establish regular eating with a healthy mix of foods supports improved appetite regulation and improved confidence with eating.

Reducing these behaviours raises anxiety, so managing anxiety supports change. A calm, familiar environment is easier. A few moments of slow breathing and muscle relaxation before and after eating is helpful. Planning with others what support will be most helpful allows the right support to be given, and reduces stress in other people at the table, as they know what to do. Identifying the thoughts and feelings that drive the behaviour can address it directly, for example:

- 'I have got into the habit of eating slowly to make a small amount of food feel like more. Now I eat enough, so I don't need to do that.'

- 'I have got into the habit of smearing food on the plate to make it look less obvious that I am not eating it. Now I eat enough, so I don't need to do that.'

- 'I have got into the habit of mixing and mashing food to try to prevent it giving me indigestion. Now my stomach is functioning better, and I feel less anxious, stomach pain is not such a problem.'

- 'When I was little, I felt a need to make sure the different foods on my plate didn't touch. Now I am grown up, I can eat more normally.'

It may be possible to identify foods and situations which are most likely to trigger these behaviours, or environmental triggers, and plan to find alternatives. It is helpful to avoid the most triggering foods and situations if possible, at least at first, and then gradually work towards managing more challenging situations.

Consolidating recovery

Especially at first, recovery of eating may be fragile. Planning to prevent and reverse relapse reduces risk and makes relapse more manageable. It should be possible to anticipate high risk situations. Risk rises at times of stress, such as exams, moving house, changes at work or in the family. Some events may be challenging, such as holidays or celebrations. Unfamiliar events or places may make eating more challenging. Many of these situations can be anticipated, so plans can be negotiated to be ready to manage them successfully, identifying the difficulties and planning ways to minimize, avoid or overcome them.

Sustaining recovery and protecting health for the long term

Examples of useful rules include:

- 'I will aim to keep my weight above 48 kg. I know this is still underweight, so if my weight increases, I will try to tolerate that, so that I continue to approach a healthy weight gradually.'

- 'I know everyone needs at least five servings from the fruit and vegetables group every day, but too many will make me feel too full, so I will have five to seven.'

- 'To protect my bones, I need at least four servings every day from the dairy foods group.'

- 'To help make sure I get enough iron, I will have a serving of red meat or eggs five times a week.'

- 'At every meal, I will have a starchy food, a protein food and a serving of fruit or vegetables.'

- 'To get essential fats for my brain and body, I will have a serving of olive oil, or nut oil, or rapeseed oil every day.'

- 'I need a variety of foods to support the healthy bacteria in my gut, so I will build a repertoire of at least seven different cooked meals and seven different light meals that I can eat regularly.'

Preventing and managing lapses

Preventing relapse must be integrated into the process of recovery. Ensuring that small lapses are perceived positively, as opportunities to learn and plan, can help reduce feelings of failure and enable people to deal better with difficulties.

At stressful times it may be helpful to set aside time with a supporter to review eating and check that it remains healthy and adequate. This can help to identify lapses quickly, and set in place a recovery plan. This may need additional support for a while, or a return to using tools such as a meal plan or eating diary.

If weight loss is a risk, regular weight monitoring is necessary, but should not become obsessive, or trigger attempts to micro-manage it. An agreed plan for how it will be done, perhaps by a health professional, can ensure the weight record is used positively to support recovery. It is helpful to have a plan to make appropriate changes to eating to maintain body weight within an agreed range, so that decisions do not have to be made under stress. For example:

- 'I will aim to keep my weight between 54 and 56 kg. If my weight falls below 54 kg, I will add a cereal bar to my lunch and a banana to my breakfast every day until it recovers to 55 kg.'

- 'When my weight reaches 58 kg, I will not need to gain more. I will stop having a pudding with my main meal every day, and have yogurt and fruit most days. I like puddings, so might have just one or two each week.'

Any lapse or setback is an opportunity to learn, to identify risks, and implement strategies to manage them, making recovery and confidence more robust for the future.

Conclusion

Eating is necessary to sustain life. Eating habits that are damaging to health and life cannot simply be abolished, they must be replaced with eating in ways that sustain life and health, are practical to achieve, and acceptable in all the settings needed. For anyone with anorexia nervosa, this is a complicated and arduous process, made more challenging by the particular difficulties associated with ASD. Every individual faces a unique mix of challenges, and to overcome them must explore the barriers to change, and develop strategies to overcome them. The time, planning and effort invested in this can be rewarded by a life of health and achievement.

References

Benson, J., Parke, C., Gannon, C. *et al.* (2013) 'A retrospective analysis of the sequential oral sensory feeding approach in children with feeding difficulties.' *Journal of Occupational Therapy, Schools, & Early Intervention, 6*(4), 289–300.

Fishbein, M., Cox, S., Sweeny, C. *et al.* (2016) 'Food chaining: A systematic approach for the treatment of children with feeding aversion.' *Nutrition in Clinical Practice, 21,* 182–184.

Fraker, C., Fishbein, M., Cox, S. & Walbert, L. (2007) *Food Chaining: The Proven 6-Step Plan to Stop Picky Eating, Solve Feeding Problems, and Expand Your Child's Diet.* Cambridge, MA: Da Capo.

Fraker, C. & Walbert, L. (2011) 'Treatment of selective eating and dysphagia using pre-chaining and food chaining therapy.' *Perspectives of the ASHA on Swallowing and Swallowing Disorders, 20*(3), 75–81.

Hadigan, C., Anderson, E., Miller, K. *et al.* (2000) 'Assessment of macronutrient and micronutrient intake in women with anorexia nervosa.' *International Journal of Eating Disorders, 28*(3), 284–292.

Harris, G. & Shea, E. (2018) *Food Refusal and Avoidant Eating in Children including those with Autistic Spectrum Disorder.* London: Jessica Kingsley Publishers.

NICE (2006, updated 2017) *Nutrition support for adults: oral nutrition support, enteral tube feeding and parenteral nutrition* (CG32). Accessed on 08/07/20 at www.nice.org.uk/guidance/cg32.

O'Connor, G. & Nicholls, D. (2013) 'Refeeding hypophosphatemia in adolescents with anorexia nervosa.' *Nutrition in Clinical Practice, 28*(3), 358–364.

Sharp, W., Burrell, L. & Jaquess, D. (2014) 'The Autism MEAL Plan: A parent-training curriculum to manage eating aversions and low intake among children with autism.' *Autism, 18*(6), 712–722.

Toomey, K.A. & Sundreth Ross, E. (2011) 'SOS approach to feeding.' *Perspectives of the ASHA on Swallowing and Swallowing Disorders, 20*(3), 82–87.

Westwood, H. & Tchanturia, K. (2017) 'Autism spectrum disorder in anorexia nervosa: An updated literature review.' *Current Psychiatry Reports, 19,* 41.

SECTION 6

Sensory Sensitivities

ASSESSING, UNDERSTANDING AND ADAPTING

In this section, we provide information on sensory sensitivities and how you would recognize, understand and adapt to them to better support an autistic person with an eating disorder. The final chapter in this section provides a case study of an autistic person with bulimia nervosa written by an occupational therapist.

Chapter 12

Assessing Sensory Sensitivities Co-Occurring in Autism and Eating Disorders

Emma Kinnaird, Isis McLachlan, Katherine Smith and Kate Tchanturia

Our senses refer to the way in which we perceive stimuli in the world around us. We process these senses unconsciously and automatically, starting with the detection of stimuli and then flowing to how this information is processed and integrated in the brain. For example, we detect the taste of food through taste buds in our mouth. This information then goes into the brain, where it is integrated with other inputs, including how it smells, whether it tastes nice, or how hungry we are. This integrated information creates our overall perception of the food and informs our reaction. If we are hungry and the food smells nice but tastes bitter and unpleasant, we are likely to avoid that food and try something else!

We traditionally think of having five senses: hearing, smell, taste, touch and vision. However, we also have other senses. Our vestibular sense helps us judge our balance and spatial orientation, while our proprioceptive sense tells us about the position and movement of our body. We also have an interoceptive sense, allowing us to sense our internal bodily sensations. This is how you can tell if you feel hungry, or whether you're feeling pain. Our ability to feel these senses is fundamental to how we relate and react to both the world around us and ourselves. For example, researchers think that if you can't identify your internal sensations, you might struggle to identify your emotions (Brewer, Cook & Bird, 2016). If you feel angry, you might feel your body temperature rising, your heart rate might speed up, or you might have a tight chest. If you cannot sense any of those processes, you might find it difficult to identify the fact you feel angry in the first place.

A person may experience difficulties with sensory processing, meaning there is a problem in how sensory information is detected, or in how it is processed in the brain. Someone who is autistic may experience **under-sensitivity (hyposensitivity) or over-sensitivity (hypersensitivity)** to different stimuli. Often, the easiest way to tell if someone has sensory processing difficulties is to look at how they react to stimuli. If someone is under-sensitive, they do not process enough information about a stimulus. They may appear disengaged or indifferent, and may be drawn to stronger stimuli: if someone has under-sensitive taste, they may prefer stronger flavours. If someone is over-sensitive, their brain may process more information than it can handle. This can lead to them deliberately avoiding certain sensations, or feeling overwhelmed and unhappy when the sensation cannot be avoided. Importantly, whether someone is under-sensitive or over-sensitive can vary across the different senses, and can even vary across time and situations.

Sensory differences are very common in autistic people, to the extent that they are now included as a diagnostic criterion for autism in the most recent *Diagnostic and Statistical Manual* (DSM-5; APA, 2013). Interviews with autistic people who have anorexia nervosa and their carers suggest that sensory differences in autism can both contribute to the development and maintenance of the eating disorder, and make engaging in treatment very difficult (Kinnaird *et al.*, 2019). Sensory issues appear to impact eating disorders and their treatment in two key ways: they can impact someone's diet, and they can make the treatment environment feel unpleasant or overwhelming. For example, if someone is over-sensitive to certain food textures, they may avoid all foods with these textures, contributing to restriction (see detailed information in Chapters 10 and 11). They may also refuse to eat these foods if placed on a meal plan during treatment, causing distress. Sensory differences can also make the treatment environment itself overwhelming for autistic people: if someone is over-sensitive to sound, the sounds of a busy ward or dining room can be very unpleasant.

Accommodating someone's sensory differences can be relatively simple: for example, if someone is over-sensitive to sound, they could wear ear defenders in loud spaces. Table 12.1 gives an overview of different types of sensory difficulties, signs to help you recognize these problems, and some simple strategies to consider. One thing to always first explore if someone is presenting with hyposensitivity is whether there is a medical reason for their problems. For example, someone presenting with hyposensitive hearing could benefit from a medical assessment to check for hearing loss. Additionally, if someone presents with sensory problems around food or movement together with an eating disorder, you might want to discuss these with a clinician before making adaptations. For example, sensory difficulties around food are very common in avoidant restrictive food intake disorder (ARFID), and people experiencing this condition could benefit from seeing a dietician to create a meal plan that adapts to and accommodates these issues.

Table 12.1. Sensory sensitivity and helpful strategies to support people who experience similar states

Sense	Signs of hypersensitivity	Possible strategies	Signs of hyposensitivity	Possible strategies
Hearing	Distress around loud noises. Covering ears. Avoidance of loud events (e.g. concerts). Trouble blocking out background noise in conversation.	Wearing ear defenders. Minimizing background noise or possible distractions. Providing a quiet space.	Enjoys listening to loud music. Does not pay attention to quieter sounds, despite no medical hearing difficulties.	Providing headphones to allow the individual to listen to loud music without affecting others. Speaking loudly and clearly.
Smell	Reacts to smells that other people do not notice. Finds apparently mild smells overpowering.	Carrying a familiar or comforting smell (e.g. lavender) to use when overpowered by other smells. Using unscented cleaners or soaps.	Enjoys strong smells (e.g. essential oils). Does not notice smells that appear obvious to other people.	Using strong essential oils or incense. Cooking foods with strong smells (e.g. using spices) may help stimulate appetite.

Sense	Signs of hypersensitivity	Possible strategies	Signs of hyposensitivity	Possible strategies
Taste	Strongly dislikes and avoids certain tastes. Prefers bland food tastes.	Developing a meal plan around familiar and acceptable tastes.	Enjoys food with strong tastes. Adds condiments to food (e.g. salt, chilli sauce) to make it taste stronger.	Exploring cooking with foods with stronger tastes (e.g. curry).
Touch	Avoids touching certain textures (e.g. not wearing jeans due to rough fabric). Does not eat foods with certain textures. Dislikes being touched.	Buying clothes made of acceptable fabrics. Adapting diet around food texture sensitivities. Seeking permission before touching the individual.	Appears to be less sensitive to pain. Drinks tea at a temperature that seems too hot to other people. Enjoys and seeks out physical contact. Not noticing light touch.	Using fidget toys. Providing textured objects to help with self soothing (e.g. a soft blanket). Careful monitoring to check for unnoticed injuries.
Vision	Prefers to turn the lights off as low as possible. Finds flickering lights unpleasant and distracting. Becomes overwhelmed in visually cluttered rooms (e.g. by a cluttered noticeboard).	Using dimmer switches. Avoiding fluorescent lighting. Where lights cannot be changed (e.g. sunlight), wearing sunglasses. Decorating rooms in calm colours, minimizing visual clutter.	Enjoys bright or moving lights (e.g. fireworks). Gets distracted by moving images (e.g. a spinning washing machine, a film playing on the television).	Using light toys to help with calming. Adding colours (e.g. highlighters) to text can help with attention and learning.
Interoception (internal awareness)	Often experiences unpleasant physical sensations (e.g. skin prickling, stomach pains). Gets distracted by physical sensations (e.g. feeling hungry). Experiences anxiety.	Using calming relaxation techniques. Exploring therapeutic techniques that could help with anxiety.	Does not feel hungry and forgets to eat. Finds it difficult to identify emotions. Does not notice that they are feeling tired until they are completely fatigued.	Using body scans to become more mindful of body sensations. Creating routines to avoid relying on internal signals (e.g. creating a meal plan with specific meal times).

Proprioception (body awareness)	Avoids sudden, fast or extreme movements. Appears to be overly careful about banging into things.	Exploring activities that involve different types of non-strenuous movement. Using repetitive movements to help calm anxiety (e.g. rocking chair).	Appears to be clumsy or un-coordinated. Has difficulty with tasks involving complex movement, e.g. sports. Finds sitting still difficult, and enjoys physical movement.	Using fidget toys. Incorporating movement breaks into daily routine.
Vestibular (balance and spatial awareness)	Experiences travel sickness. Feels dizzy easily. Avoids extreme movement.	Using repetitive or predictable movements (e.g. rocking chair). Incorporating gentle physical activities (e.g. swimming). Avoiding busy spaces.	Struggles with balancing and appears un-coordinated. Enjoys fast movements, e.g. can spin without getting dizzy. Enjoys constantly moving.	Encouraging physical activity or exercise (note: this should be introduced carefully and with the guidance of a clinician in eating disorder treatment).

In order to develop these strategies, it is important to understand whether the person experiences sensory differences, and exactly how their sensory differences manifest. Whilst Table 12.1 gives examples of behaviours associated with sensory problems, exact sensory differences and how they manifest will vary from person to person. Even the same person may feel that their sensory differences change across certain situations. For example, the degree to which someone experiences sensory difficulties might be affected by how anxious they feel at the time, or how far they feel in control of the situation. Therefore, it is important to assess an individual's sensory profile early on in treatment.

A sensory profile simply means an overview of whether someone is under-sensitive, over-sensitive, or experiences no differences across their senses. This can be more or less detailed depending on individual needs and available resources. Once a sensory profile is in place, this gives clinicians more information to make adaptations. A low resource option that can be carried out by anyone is to simply ask individuals to rate their sensitivity in different areas on a scale. An example of this type of assessment is included at the end of this chapter. The benefit of this kind of assessment is that it is straightforward, practical and brief to use, and does not require specialist assessment or access to specific resources. However, this kind of assessment should be used as a starting point for a more detailed conversation about sensory needs: it does not include information about specific triggers, or whether sensory differences vary across situations, or how the sensory differences impact the particular individual. For example, one person might rate themselves as hypersensitive on sound, but then specify that this only applies to loud environmental sounds outside of their control, and feel that they enjoy listening to loud music through headphones to block out environmental noise. It also does not give information on whether that person seeks out sensory stimulation, or whether they try to avoid sensory stimulation.

Therefore, autistic people with eating disorders could benefit from a more detailed assessment of their sensory needs. In treatment, this would often be done by an occupational therapist. Potential types of assessments that might be used by the occupational therapist are outlined below.

General sensory sensitivity

The Adolescent/Adult Sensory Profile provides a more in-depth assessment of the traditional five senses and proprioception. It seeks to explore how the patient responds to different senses, categorizing them into four quadrants:

- low registration

- sensation seeking

- sensory sensitivity

- sensation avoiding.

Once the occupational therapist has explained the assessment, the person can complete it themselves. The occupational therapist can provide further assistance with completing the assessment if required and it may also be useful for the person to discuss the assessment with someone who knows them well. The sensory profile self-report questionnaire asks the patient to answer a series of statements by rating them from 'Almost Never' to 'Almost Always'. The statements are broken down into the following sections:

- Taste/Smell processing (e.g. 'I add spice to my food').

- Movement processing (e.g. 'I trip or bump into things').

- Visual processing (e.g. 'I like to wear colourful clothing').

- Touch processing (e.g. 'I dislike having my back rubbed').

- Activity level (e.g. 'I work on two or more tasks at the same time').

- Auditory processing (e.g. 'I am distracted if there is a lot of noise around').

The occupational therapist can then total up a score for each quadrant which provides an overall sensory profile. From here, it is helpful to discuss the findings with the patient (and people close to them) and to explore examples specific to the patient. This will help inform interventions and strategies to support the patient. These may be adaptations to the environment or activity, strategies for managing discomfort/anxiety, planning or utilizing support from others.

As previously mentioned, it is important to remember that a person's sensory profile can change depending on the circumstances. What might be a helpful intervention in one situation could be unhelpful in another. Therefore it can be helpful to ask them to complete a sensory-motor preference checklist. This is a brief assessment which allows the patient to explore what they find stimulating and calming. This can be useful information for planning interventions and also encourages them to self-manage their symptoms, increasing their independence. Similarly to the sensory profile, the assessment breaks down various strategies and asks the person to indicate if they use the strategies and if so, whether these are stimulating or calming. Below are a few examples:

- Touch: touch, twist or twirl own hair.

- Look: doodle while listening.

- Oral motor input: chew on a pencil/pen/toothpick/straw.

- Move: tap toe, heel or foot.

- Listen: listen to nature sounds.

The assessment also provides some questions to consider. It is important to discuss the assessment with them not only to explore the strategies they are already using to self-regulate, but to understand when they use them and why. These can then be used or avoided in a planned way to help manage over- or under-stimulation of the senses.

Interoception

It can also be helpful to assess interoception to understand how well a person can notice their body's signals and connect those signals to a meaning. This is important in managing both physical and emotional needs. There are several assessments which can be completed to help inform this:

- *The Interoceptive Awareness Interview*: This is an informal question and answer format using a mix of open-ended questions and a rating scale. The person's responses will indicate if they are aware or unaware of their bodily responses. It can be useful to ask these questions during real-time activities, rather than asking them to reflect on something that has previously happened or is yet to happen.

- *The Assessment of Self-Regulation*: This is a series of pictures with corresponding questions. It examines the understanding and thought processing around causes of bodily or emotional reactions in themselves and others, and what strategies they use to manage this.

- *The Caregiver Questionnaire for Interoceptive Awareness*: The caregiver answers 24 questions using a rating scale, circling the questions they feel apply to the person or situation. It can be difficult for someone experiencing interoceptive sensory differences to assess how this impacts on them so getting the perspective of someone close to them can help shed some light on this.

Using more in-depth sensory assessments can be more time-consuming, so deciding whether to use them and how many to use depends on the individual and their needs. However, having an understanding of a person's sensory differences is essential in supporting them to manage over- or under-stimulation with specific interventions, tailored to their individual needs. Even minor adjustments to the activity or the environment can have a transformative effect for an autistic person!

Our group has developed and piloted the basic sensory self-assessment below to help patients and their clinical team work collaboratively to support any sensory sensitivities. Using this tool can help create an individualized approach in adapting the environment, diet and social interaction in the best possible way for patients.

SENSORY SUMMARY

Mark where you think you are on the below scales. Hypersensitivity means you are *highly sensitive* to sensations and may try to *avoid them* where possible; hyposensitivity means you have *lower sensitivity* and may try to *seek out* these sensations. There are examples below each scale. If you think you are neither hyper/hyposensitive and have no sensory differences, mark yourself in the middle as a 5.

Taste

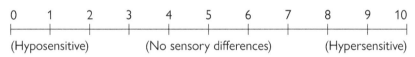

(Hyposensitive)   (No sensory differences)   (Hypersensitive)

If I am hyposensitive, I might add lots of salt to my food to make it taste stronger. If I am hypersensitive, I might prefer to eat bland foods as I find other foods too strong.

Smell

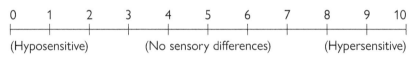

(Hyposensitive)   (No sensory differences)   (Hypersensitive)

If I am hyposensitive, I might not notice strong smells and enjoy smelling essential oils. If I am hypersensitive, I might dislike smelly places like a canteen and find smells overpowering.

Vision

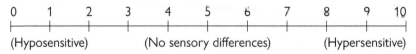

If I am hyposensitive, I might really like watching bright light displays. If I am hypersensitive, I might prefer to have lights dimmed or turned off.

Sound

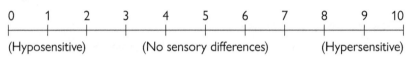

If I am hyposensitive, I might enjoy rubbing my hands on soft fabric or a soft toy. If I am hypersensitive, I might dislike and avoid touching certain fabrics.

Texture

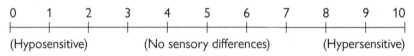

If I am hyposensitive, I might really enjoy the feeling of certain food textures in my mouth. If I am hypersensitive, I might strongly dislike and avoid eating certain food textures.

We have piloted this brief, pragmatic questionnaire in our clinical services. At the moment this is small exploratory study, and these are early results. We are presenting the results here with the hope that it will be a useful resource for the clinical and treatment teams to adapt and use in their programmes.

Our findings are presented in Figure 12.1.

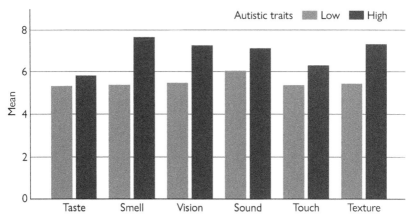

Figure 12.1. *Comparing sensory sensitivity for those with high autistic traits and for those with low autistic traits*

From this exploratory survey, it looks like people with anorexia nervosa and high autistic features scored themselves as more hypersensitive on all scales. This data suggests that the strategies we choose to make the environment more friendly to our patients who are over-sensitive to all types of sensory input could make a difference for patients in this clinical pathway.

We used these research findings to develop psychoeducation materials and sensory wellbeing workshops. The protocol for this is available online on our website at www.peacepathway.org.

We have evaluated these workshops in the inpatient and residential care settings asking participants to complete the assessment pack on our website. Self-reported sensory awareness, strategy knowledge and confidence using the strategies highlighted in Figure 12.2 increased. Participants commented:

'Making sensory bag was fun and useful.'

'This is the best thing I've attended since being in the ward.'

'I hope to attend more of this.'

'Thank you offering this workshop, earbuds will be very useful to have on ward.'

'I enjoyed doing my own hand cream and thinking about my own sensory bag.'

We had very positive feedback from the staff members who found the workshop content meaningful and the process of the group relaxed and engaging, and it was helpful for them to see patients outside of the dining room and community group setting where the dynamic is very different.

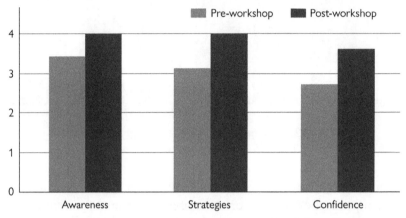

Figure 12.2. *Self-rated pre- and post-assessment of workshop participants*

Encouraged by the pilot work, we are planning to do more of these workshops and improve and create more as we go along. We will share them on our social media platforms (@PEACE_Pathway) and our website (www.peacepathway.org).

References and further reading

American Psychiatric Association (2013) *Diagnostic and Statistical Manual of Mental Disorders* (5th edition). Arlington, VA: American Psychiatric Publishing.

Brewer, R., Cook, R. & Bird, G. (2016) 'Alexithymia: A general deficit of interoception.' *Royal Society Open Science, 3*(10), 150664.

Kinnaird, E., Norton, C., Stewart, C. & Tchanturia, K. (2019) 'Same behaviours, different reasons: What do patients with co-occurring anorexia and autism want from treatment?' *International Review of Psychiatry, 31*(4), 308–317.

Kinnaird, E., Stewart, C. & Tchanturia, K. (2018) 'Taste sensitivity in anorexia nervosa: A systematic review.' *International Journal of Eating Disorders, 51*(8), 771–784.

Kinnaird, E., Stewart, C. & Tchanturia, K. (2020) 'The relationship of autistic traits to taste and olfactory processing in anorexia nervosa.' *Molecular Autism, 11*, article number 25.

Chapter 13

Occupational Therapy Benefits for an Autistic Patient with Bulimia Nervosa

Jake Copp-Thomas

Editor's note: We have already discussed in the book research and lived experience involving co-morbidity of anorexia nervosa and autism spectrum disorder; however, in the PEACE Pathway we tried to learn about other eating disorders with which the autism co-morbidity also exists but for which less research and clinical evidence is collected.

Jake, our outpatient occupational therapist, has done some very interesting work presented below. It is impressive how the small changes Jake and Tashi (made-up name to anonymize the person) introduced in daily life can produce meaningful changes for someone who spent long hours and invested lots of energy sticking to rigid rules around shopping and hobbies. Jake contributed to PEACE Pathway development showing us how occupational therapy benefits could be added to treatment package for adults with variety of eating disorder presentations and autism spectrum co-morbidity.

TASHI'S STORY

Context of referral

Tashi is a young lady in her early twenties with a diagnosis of Asperger's syndrome and bulimia nervosa, who could also experience panic attacks and has a history of self-harm. She was referred to our outpatient clinic for treatment with diagnosis of bulimia nervosa. When first referred,

Tashi was experiencing binge–purging cycles approximately six days a week whilst exercising daily in isolation. She received psychological therapy for 22 sessions in the outpatient eating disorder clinic, during which she was gradually able to stop binge–purging completely, and worked on a variety of difficulties using cognitive-behavioural therapy. Towards the end of psychological therapy input, she was referred to the outpatient Occupational Therapy team for ongoing support regarding her routine and life as a student. At the time of referral, Tashi was a student living in halls of residence.

GOAL SETTING

Within Occupational Therapy we used a goal setting and review format to structure the intervention. We used the experience of these goal-focused changes as the basis for discussions to then develop ways to enable Tashi to change and develop her routines. The goals set were always experiential in nature and activity orientated; for some of the goals the engagement in the activity was the goal and for others it was the experience of trying it. Sessions lasted one hour and were fortnightly to allow time for change between sessions; seven sessions were offered and attended during the follow-up period from psychological therapy. Tashi had many interests, including embroidery, badminton, botany, translation, ballet and anatomy. The initial goals agreed upon for Tashi were to start swimming or badminton, be able to visit her grandparent when they went into hospital due to ill health and attend a social club at university. However, due to a bereavement Tashi deferred her year at university, which changed the course of intervention after our second session. Goals were then adapted to swimming, visiting her grandparent when unwell and finding temporary employment during the deferred year, with the focus remaining on routines. From breaking these goals into smaller steps, two primary areas of focus emerged and these were explored during the sessions and then challenged between the sessions. The focus areas identified were rigidity and lack of flexibility of routines, and hypersensitivities to the sensory environment.

Rigidity and flexibility

We identified that Tashi was incredibly rigid in her routines and behaviour. Psychoeducation was provided on rigidity being a known trait for individuals with both Asperger's syndrome and eating disorders. This compromised Tashi's ability to easily change her routines and engage in identified goals. The primary end goal for this area of focus was for Tashi to be able to stop her usual daily routine and visit her grandparent when they went into hospital, as previously Tashi had been unable to be flexible with her routines and had not visited the hospital, leaving Tashi with difficult emotions. To begin exploring the act of being flexible we used other ways to experience this within Tashi's routine that felt less anxiety-provoking. For instance, we changed the time of Tashi's alarm clock from 6am to 7am to experience a change in routine, as Tashi had the same alarm time for many years despite not needing to leave the house until 10am. The predictions of change and the likelihood of these predictions were explored, as Tashi often predicted that her day would fall apart or be ruined.

The flexibility challenges were used to develop confidence gradually and were always meaningful to challenge the predictions. These behavioural changes would then be considered in tandem with Tashi's sensory and eating disorder difficulties. It appeared helpful in session to use Tashi's examples rather than fictional scenarios when discussing acts of change. The next flexibility challenge was to use a different supermarket. Tashi had used the same supermarket on the same day and time despite living in a different city for over four years, and therefore would travel for over two hours to keep this the same on a weekly basis. In addition to changing supermarket and alarm clock time, we explored an incident when Tashi was waiting for her friend who was a few minutes late and Tashi left due to rigidity of her timings, her emotional response and predicted impact on her day. We began to explore the advantages and disadvantages of being both flexible and rigid, whilst acknowledging that these may differ depending on the activity and neither is right or wrong. For these specific flexibility challenges advantages to being more flexible included spending time with her friend and not feeling guilty about leaving her; different supermarkets are quieter, better stocked and Tashi saved time commuting as they were convenient and local. We also explored Tashi's predictions that her day would be ruined and although the change could leave Tashi with difficult emotions for some time afterwards, the prediction was never fully confirmed. The flexibility challenges were always set by Tashi and agreed together, as there were a few that Tashi felt were not meaningful and felt like change for the sake of it, with little impact on daily life. For instance, changing brand of shampoo both felt like a meaningless task but also had the additional challenge of a sensory experience attached to it, which unnecessarily impacted Tashi throughout the day.

Over the course of our joint work, Tashi was able to tolerate waiting 20 minutes for her friend, start attending multiple supermarkets based on practicalities rather than familiar rigid routines, and could begin to use the time differently when things didn't go to plan, such as Christmas shopping when she didn't see her friend despite planning to.

When Tashi began swimming again, rigidity came up as Tashi had reserved hours in her day according to previous use of that time. For instance, at 7am on particular weekdays Tashi historically took a family member to the GP. We then explored what it meant to use this slot differently now, the probability of needing it again for this purpose, how this impacted predictions, and the consequences and limitations of never using the time differently. With the application of these ideas, alongside Tashi's motivation, she was able to start swimming again in a time of the week historically left empty due to previous responsibilities at that time.

Unfortunately, during treatment Tashi's grandparent did become unwell and was admitted to hospital just before our final Occupational Therapy session. During this time Tashi was able visit them, thus achieving her longer-term therapy goal around flexibility. We used the last session exploring how this felt, the benefits of tolerating the change of plans, experience of uncertainty/spontaneity and how Tashi could continue challenging rigidity going forward. Tashi described adopting a frame of thinking that everything is approached as 'novel', with no pressure for it to be become part of her routine if she didn't like it or felt it was meaningless. Going forward Tashi independently planned to begin changing the seat she sits on on the bus, as when this particular seat is not free she is unable to use the bus and gets off it, resulting in being late for work, lectures and seeing friends.

Sensory hypersensitivities

In addition to the focus on rigidity, we focused on hypersensitivities to the sensory environment. We used the brief sensory screen described in Chapter 12 alongside the sensory-motor preference checklist both as an exploratory intervention and as a means to enable completion of Tashi's fortnightly goals. Tashi identified hypersensitivity to auditory, tactile, visual and olfactory senses, with textures and gustatory senses scoring at a more average degree of sensitivity and arousal. Tashi was prompted to give real-life examples of these to contextualize the experience and she named: crunchy food/keyboards/sewing machines/cutlery/some public and work environments being too noisy; certain clothing/bedding being too difficult to touch or wear; smells such as shampoo; and feeling hyperaroused by visual stimuli in particular environments. Some of this was apparent during therapy sessions; for instance, when the noise of the wind, people talking in the background or the hospital helicopter could be heard this could temporarily disrupt Tashi's attention and appear to startle her. Tashi would appear to visually scan the room when entering and could appear quite alert initially; however, she would gradually appear more relaxed throughout the session. We acknowledged that in some environments it may be unrealistic to make adaptations to completely meet Tashi's sensory needs, but in others there could be both adaptations and sensory strategies applied to minimize over-stimulation. For instance, Tashi chose to swim at 7am due to the volume of noise in a public swimming pool, in addition to body image concerns. Tashi trialled using a gel or sensor touch-based keyboard for her computer, which allowed her to work without noise-cancelling headphones. In regards to employment, Tashi had a history of quitting jobs due to feeling over-stimulated and anxious within work settings but was passionate about embroidery and anatomy laboratory work. During sessions we discussed reasonable adaptations such as hand-stitching/picking rather machine use or ripping fabrics, requesting not to work with certain fabrics, quieter spaces in the room, having de-stimulation breaks to reduce arousal and other sensory strategies such as sipping a hot drink. These strategies were developed from Tashi's sensory-motor preference checklist. At the time Tashi would sit in a dark room at the end of each day or listen to sports statistics to de-stimulate herself, which may not always be fully replicable outside of her home and could be time-consuming. Tashi began using the insight of sensory stimuli to not only identify and adapt challenging sensory environments but to also use as a means for self-soothing after flexibility challenges, social anxiety or difficult feelings such as irritation, discomfort or guilt. Over the course of intervention, Tashi confirmed temporary part-time employment and had been offered another temporary job which she declined. We discussed the anticipated sensory environments, reasonable adaptations, sensory soothing and the role of Occupational Health for each of these.

Both Tashi's rigidity and sensory experiences impacted her ability to eat with others; for instance, due to the noise of crockery, she would wear headphones and would eat in a separate room. We explored a graded approach to adapt this and Tashi was able to begin with having hot drinks when visiting her grandparent in hospital. Tashi was then able to change her day's plans to visit her grandparent and have a drink with them, and this progress was noticed by her family and remarked upon. Going forward after discharge, Tashi had independently planned to continue transferring this to other settings such as having a hot drink with a friend in a café, with the aim of managing the sensory experience differently.

Reflections from working with Tashi

As an occupational therapist working with Tashi I learned a lot from the experience and identified the following considerations for when providing treatment for an individual with both an eating disorder and an autistic spectrum disorder:

- Use live and recent experiences rather than fictional narratives – this allowed Tashi to reflect in more depth and consider emotional responses and impact on other areas of her own life.

- Give time and prompt for emotional experiences and thoughts, as occasionally when asked about an experience Tashi would provide a description of the event rather than how it felt. Be explicit that you are interested in how it felt as well as what happened.

- Ensure consistency in therapist behaviour and being organized for the session. Given being flexible and spontaneous could evoke anxiety, being consistent felt important to reduce additional and unnecessary anxiety within the sessions. Lateness of staff had previously resulted in Tashi leaving the waiting room and experiencing anxiety before attending sessions. An exception to this was doing flexibility challenges within the session, for which pre-planning and prior agreement would be important.

- Ensure goals feel meaningful. Due to the variety of issues that you could choose to work on, willingness to work on changing a behaviour that felt like purely an experiment or meaningless would understandably be limited.

- Use concise and clear language. I attempted to reduce the use of metaphors, and the idea of using proverbs was not useful on this occasion.

Fast food

Skilling Up the Clinical Team and Implementation

In this section, we focus on what can be done to skill up clinical teams from an individual level up to a wider systemic implementation level. We discuss the different options for autism screening and assessments and how you might implement PEACE in your clinical team, and take a broader look at quality improvement.

Chapter 14

What Can Clinicians Do Differently in Sessions?

Kate Tchanturia, Katherine Smith and Yasemin Dandil

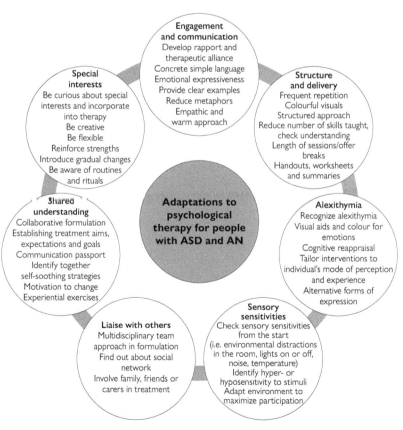

Figure 14.1. *Adaptations to therapies for autistic people with anorexia nervosa*

Adapting psychological therapies for autistic people with eating disorders

Autistic people with eating disorders (EDs) benefit from psychological therapy; however, it must be adapted to meet the individual's cognitive and communication needs. Modifying therapy to facilitate engagement and build a therapeutic relationship is vital. There is a no 'one size fits all' approach; nonetheless, Figure 14.1 highlights some possible adaptations that can be applied to psychological therapies for each person. Some of these adaptations were inspired by the core characteristics of autism spectrum condition (ASC) and some are relevant to all people in psychological therapy.

Making the environment user-friendly for someone with ASC and ED

Once you have your scheduled appointment, we suggest you think about the environment of the session.

People on the autism spectrum can be overwhelmed with sensory input, often leading to high anxiety and preoccupation. It is important to be mindful of lighting, background noise and strong odours. Sometimes just a simple change can make a big difference to a session; it is important to be mindful and to ask.

Below are some possible sensitivities to watch out for:

- Lighting

  - Trying to find a room with no fluorescent lighting is hard. Would it be possible to use natural light?

  - Screen monitors can have a harsh light that some find distracting.

- Noise

  - Corridor noise can be tricky to deal with. This might be something you take into consideration when planning session times to when footfall would be at a minimum.

  - Are your bracelets clinking? Is the computer humming? Sometimes noises we don't even notice can be excruciating to people on the autistic spectrum. In the busy ward we found it useful to have keycaps to reduce the noise.

- Is there a choice of rooms? Try to think about avoiding noises from outside too such as traffic.

- Odour

    - Especially to patients with co-morbid eating disorders, the smell of food can be particularly anxiety-provoking. It might be worth thinking about session times and them not overlapping with meal preparation times when odours may be particularly strong.

    - Some autistic people can find perfumes and colognes suffocating. It might be an idea to ask the patient or to skip that extra spray on the days of your appointments.

- Physical comfort

    - Consider the temperature: someone with an ED may be hot but may feel uncomfortable taking off their jumper.

    - Type of chair can be important; perhaps if possible offer the patient a cushion.

    - Some patients are very sensitive to food temperature so try to accommodate this to make it easy to feed them.

Another question worth asking is how they might like to sit: some patients may find it less anxiety-provoking to sit side-by-side to avoid the added pressure to maintain eye contact. This will reduce the amount of extra information processing and attention of the social situation.

All of these environmental and sensory needs vary from person to person. One of the best ways to find out what works for the person you are seeing is to ask them directly.

We have seen patients being more comfortable during the sessions once we have explored and calibrated the environment according to their individual needs. We have seen differences in rapport too by making it very explicit and clear to the patient that we are trying to support their individual needs in the session.

What we learned from trying to make these changes and asking these questions is that less really is more. Making these small adaptations from the start can make a big difference, especially to people with both eating disorders and autism spectrum condition, or ASC features.

Simple surroundings

The importance of regularity

If you are meeting with someone who is on the autistic spectrum for a certain number of sessions, try to keep it regular with time and location! This is important for every patient but particularly for those with ASC. In general, we try to encourage flexibility and decrease rigidity; however, with autism spectrum co-morbidities we can try to support people with low tolerance of uncertainty to make them less anxious. This is very important for some people on the autism spectrum who can be very specific about their routine.

A useful tip is to discuss during your first session what the protocol will be for a missed session to reduce anxiety and unpredictability around a potentially anxiety-provoking situation. Advanced warning is the best way to avoid this anxiety, but we know that cannot always be done. From our experience, this is very important in establishing the therapeutic alliance – you can then start exploring if some of the rigid behaviours can change.

Another important aspect to have in mind when planning sessions is that people on the autism spectrum may have difficulty planning ahead and organizing. It may be beneficial to write down appointment reminders or help them make an alert on their phone.

Engagement

Introduce yourself clearly. Make sure patients know who you are and what your role in the clinical team is. It is important to outline how the clinical encounter works, and what the expectations of both parties are.

For rapport building, we have found that involving the patient's special interest (if they have one) can be very helpful at building rapport and spending extra time on that can be very beneficial. Some patients have favourite films or book characters and bringing these to the session can help to express how patients think and feel. For example, one of our clinicians had a patient with a specific interest of Anime cartoons. In a group formulation session, we thought of creative ways this special interest could be used to engage the patient, such as looking at storylines and emotions of different characters.

One thing that is important to be aware of when working with the eating disorder/ASC co-morbidity is the use of language to describe autism. It can often help the clinician–patient alliance if the clinician asks the individual patient at the beginning of their work together what phrasing the person prefers (e.g. 'on the autism spectrum' as opposed to 'autism spectrum disorder' or 'autism spectrum condition'). Note that this may change as people explore their new identity more if someone is newly diagnosed in treatment. From our experience, we learned that 'autism spectrum condition' is the preferred terminology for patients and families. As well as this, we have found our patients prefer identity-first language, for example 'an autistic person'.

We have provided helpful reading and website links on our website (www.peacepathway.org). These materials may be helpful to give to patients and families out of sessions to support them.

Importance of pace

Some autistic people may take longer to process information. Being able to slow it down and allow someone the time they need to answer is essential. This might mean you have to block out a longer time period than you might do with non-autistic patients. Again, the resource pack we have provided can be helpful. You may want to break it down and give one piece of information after each session.

Changes to meal plans, for example, may need a while to process, as this might make anxiety worse. Similarly, in occupational therapy or psychological therapies, when setting goals or homework, it is better to give enough time for patients to process what it is you are asking. On the other hand, patients may have no difficulties with this at all so it is important to check in and ask.

As well as processing difficulties, autistic people may have difficulty concentrating, dividing attention or shifting attention from one activity to another. As Pooky explains in Chapter 3, having both an eating disorder and autism feels like 'autism on steroids'. This is important to bear in mind when using something like Cognitive remediation therapy where you might typically do two activities in one session. You also may need to be more detailed and specific than you might ordinarily be.

According to our research evidence and work from other groups, people who have both conditions seem to need a longer time to adjust to the clinical services and take longer to have similar outcomes to non-ASC patients (for the overview and related work see Tchanturia *et al.*, 2019).

Make it visual

Often having a visual representation can make it much easier for an autism person to process information. However, it is always important to ask if this is the case. Try asking outright and then maybe ask about how the person thinks. Some autistic people think in pictures and it may be helpful to know this. This might mean you write your session plan out at the start of the session and share it. For dietetic work, having a print-out of the menu might be less distracting than on the screen and it allows the patients to take the information away to process in their own time. This is often helpful with therapeutic handouts too. After ward rounds and other important meetings, our consultants have found it helpful to write a summary of what has happened. Often, in these fast-paced meetings with lots of people talking, anxiety can take over and the information can be lost. In the PEACE Pathway we have produced photos of the food options in our clinical service, created communication passports, and encouraged patients to create 'mind maps' when relevant and to produce their own collages for the table mats. We suggested in our reading list *The Autistic Brain* by Temple Grandin and Richard Panek (2014), as well as Grandin's online lectures.

She speaks and explains very clearly how some people with ASC think in pictures, not in words. This reflection helps us as clinicians to make communication easier and give our patients an opportunity to express their needs non-verbally.

A picture is worth 1000 words

Language use

Keep it simple, keep it literal. Avoid the use of metaphors, sarcasm and humour whenever possible unless you know that people are okay with these forms of communication – again, just ask!

Hungry eyes

Let your mind wander

In terms of how you speak: do it slowly and clearly, and repeat the main points if necessary. Autistic people may not always respond well to Socratic questioning styles. Asking more straightforward questions with a yes/no answer might help. Open-ended questions can be difficult to answer for an autistic person. Some therapists find that multiple-choice answers provided to the autistic person can useful.

If possible, try to talk about concrete examples rather than abstract concepts. Abstract thinking could extend into reflecting on past experiences for autistic people, so it is important to understand if this might be a challenge for your patient.

It may be helpful to use language such as 'sometimes' and 'usually' – that way fixed views are not developed.

The power of positive communication

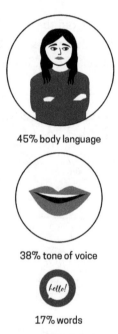

Figure 14.2. *Key elements of social communication*

We tried to highlight to our patients and healthcare professional staff the power of positive emotions. To illustrate how powerful the way we say things can be, we use psychoeducation materials in the format of cognitive remediation and emotion skills training (CREST) in individual and group format and we do pop-up workshops about the power of positive communications. For example, it is often forgotten that words have less of an impact on what you are trying to say; the tone of your voice and your body language are often the most powerful (Figure 14.2). Having attended actors' training (Kate Tchanturia) in the National Theatre, I have observed and adapted some of the exercises to make sure that we used experiential techniques jointly with experimental and science-based findings.

Developing positive bias

Our research of tolerance of socially frustrating situations in groups of people with and without eating disorders (Harrison *et al.*, 2011) showed us how the majority of eating disorder patient groups reacted in different way compared with non-eating disorder comparison groups. We believe that it is possible to train ourselves in adaptive and better social responses once we are aware of what we do and how to do better. We know that politicians, actors and those in business settings do that, and we can do more work in clinical settings to support people in their recovery journey and aid better social functioning if they choose to make some adaptations (Figure 14.3).

Figure 14.3. *Positive bias*

We take every opportunity in our treatment programme to address and practise the power of positive thinking. It can be hard to do, but it is worth persevering!

Session endings and therapy ending

Preparing for endings is very important for all patients and in the context of the ASC/eating disorder co-morbidity it becomes even more important. It is helpful to set clear expectations from the beginning around the number of sessions there will be. Advanced warning for the ending of sessions is also helpful. It might be beneficial at the end of sessions to outline clearly where patients may go to seek further support. This can be done in an ending letter to ensure they have a copy of the information to keep and refer back to when needed. If providing written information, it might be worth including any information available on recovery or relapse prevention plans.

Writing a letter before the therapy ends can be very useful to summarize and prepare the person for saying goodbye and session endings.

In terms of aftercare, more work is needed. It is difficult to find clinical or community services which are ASC/eating disorder co-morbidity friendly. We always must try to remember: we treat eating disorders and make ASC-friendly adjustments, and on the road of recovery people also need similar ASC-friendly services to function at their optimal level in society. The PEACE Pathway is a little step in this long journey to develop and innovate clinical and community services for people with eating disorders…but every journey starts with a simple step.

References

Grandin, T. & Panek, R. (2014) *The Autistic Brain*. London: Rider.

Harrison, A., Genders, R., Davies, H. & Tchanturia, K. (2011) 'Experimental measurement of the regulation of anger and aggression in women with anorexia nervosa.' *Clinical Psychology & Psychotherapy, 18*(6), 445–452.

Tchanturia, K., Adamson, J., Leppanen, J. & Westwood, H. (2019) 'Characteristics of autism spectrum disorder in anorexia nervosa: A naturalistic study in an inpatient treatment programme.' *Autism, 23*(1), 123–130.

Chapter 15

Therapy with People on the Autistic Spectrum with Eating Disorders

REFLECTIONS OF AN EXPERIENCED THERAPIST

—— *Elaine Smith* ——

My long experience of working with eating disorders in the outpatient department at the Maudsley Hospital has brought different challenges over the years. Co-morbidity between autistic spectrum conditions and eating disorders was not as clear in the earlier days as it is now. The growing thought that there is a link between anorexia nervosa and autism spectrum conditions does help to make sense of some of the challenging behaviours I have worked with. That is not to say that everyone with anorexia is autistic, but the similarities of behaviours are interesting to compare. The behaviours that have been most challenging are the rigidity of thinking, patients feeling unsafe when their routine is changed and wanting to isolate themselves when feeling overwhelmed by others or by life. Their need to feel safe can also lead to some obsessive-compulsive behaviours.

What it feels like for the patient

One of my patients who actually had a diagnosis of ASD tried to explain how he felt when trying to make sense of the world. He told me that he felt he had been abandoned on an alien planet when he was young and was still waiting for someone to come and take him home. The only way he could cope with life was by copying behaviours and ways of expressing himself from others, particularly his siblings. He said he soon came to realize that *he* was the alien and if he was to survive in his community he had to learn how to behave and express himself in the same way as others. He could manage this most of the time but every now and again he would revert to what he thought of as his 'natural self', which seemed to upset everyone around him. His family commented that he had two different personalities, and he would have to struggle to slip back into the personality that fitted in with his family and friends.

A number of patients have talked about behaviours being learned and not instinctive. This meant they had to learn what is acceptable in different situations, and when you are developing through childhood this is an extra pressure; sadly, they often get it wrong, leading to outbursts of frustration and temper and emphasizing their difference. One patient described to me a situation where his best friend had lost something that he was very fond of and shed tears over it. The patient simply could not understand his friend's attachment to something that could be bought again. He often brought incidents to the session which he did not understand when certain powerful emotions were shown and he wanted some understanding and confirmation that this was not strange behaviour from friends. Interestingly, he was able to show sympathy because he watched how others behaved and not necessarily because he understood it. He found it difficult to form long-term close relationships, but instead he had a lot of casual friends who would be okay with him tagging along if they were going out. He often felt that he was not automatically included but had to ask if he could join them. When he was on his own at home he would spend most of the time alone in his room working on his computer as he found it easier to communicate using social media channels.

Women with both conditions

In female patients with whom I have worked it has been more difficult to assess whether they have autistic traits as many have had social anxiety which they connected to food and drink being a part of social activities. It was never very clear if the major cause of the anxiety was wanting to be seen as 'normal around food' or concern that they would be expected to eat something while appearing to be friendly and unconcerned. One of the areas that caused a lot of anxiety was plans changing at the last minute, particularly if they had planned to meet friends for a meal and the restaurant was changed at the last minute, in which case they would generally cancel. Others have also described to me that going to a supermarket to buy something in particular only to find they did not have the exact item in stock would then lead to major anxiety and not being able to think about a substitute. In extreme cases the patient has left the store without buying anything.

Several patients had grown up in families where they felt very different from the other family members, and although their parents knew something was different they had been unable to get a diagnosis and therefore did not get the support they needed to help their child develop in a way that would help them fit in. One young lady told me that she was very reserved as a child and chose not to mix much with other children as she only felt safe with her family. If visitors came to the house, she would hide behind the sofa and sometimes sit there for long periods until they went away again, and her family learned there was no point trying to coax her out. As she became an adult she preferred living on her own and staying in a safe routine, i.e. eating the same foods every day and not having people in her home. It wasn't until she had a child of her own that she realized she needed help to plan a routine for him and contacted social services for their help. Looking after a child did not come naturally, but she felt safer in a structured routine. She did not get the help she needed because she was autistic, but because she had an eating disorder.

Much of the work we did together in outpatients with autistic behaviours has been about structure. We worked carefully to meet needs by structuring the day; yet at the same time trying to make it a little less rigid. We did a lot of work on paper, making small changes to a daily schedule that did not feel so major that the patients would become anxious about it. Also, patients would often email me to share thoughts and ideas if they could not talk about them in the session, although they would be okay if I talked about them in following sessions. Some of the paperwork we did had to be quite explicit, such as timing meals and quiet times and fitting in other activities. If it wasn't on the worksheet, they would not be able to fit it in, particularly if it meant making changes to the day. When the daily routine became more automatic they were able to follow it without thinking too much about it and then they were able to make small changes themselves. We would also write down what their anxieties were around change and what would lead up to the feelings of being unable to cope.

Autistic characteristics in families

Other work in outpatients has been with those who have autism spectrum conditions within the family. One person described her mother as 'emotionally unavailable' and this made her feel unloved. She never received praise or encouragement, but was given her 'orders' on what she had to do that day. Her mother was a keen gardener and knew the botanical name of every plant; she also could play the introduction to every piece of classical music she had heard. We discussed whether ASD had been mentioned and she said the more she thought about this, the more understanding she felt towards her mother. It was also helpful for her to know that her mother was behaving in the only way she knew how and not because she simply did not like her daughter. She learned to forgive her mum, realizing it must have been really difficult for her to bring her children up and to fit into social surroundings. Unfortunately, this patient married a man who was also unable to support her emotionally and she would have to look outside the marriage and have her own needs met through a group of very close friends who gave her the support she needed.

So, patients who have grown up with ASD in the family, although not diagnosed themselves, often mentioned not having their emotional needs met and family members being distant and changeable or not being interested in what they were doing. They themselves are unsure of what behaviours are acceptable and although they do better working on an instinctive or intuitive level, they still feel the need to check out correct behaviours.

I have also worked with patients who, although not diagnosed, clearly have some autistic behaviours; some of these patients told me that they had to learn to socialize, particularly when they had children. They forced themselves to take their children to toddlers' groups and meetings with other mums, because they were aware that if they did not then their children would suffer or become alienated. Often there was someone in the family telling them what they should be doing to help their children. One patient told me she was not the slightest bit interested in other people's children and could not wait to get back to her own house, her own routine and thoughts. However, she continued to socialize for her daughter's sake and to help others to see her as 'normal', hoping that they did not realize she was copying social behaviours from others. She said it could feel like a role play every day.

The common pattern with ASD is that behaviours are not instinctive and have to be learned, and often people with ASD find themselves involved in things that they don't really want to do. They prefer to spend time on their own, although that does not necessarily mean they don't want any social contact at all. I have found that they shy away from loud, bright and noisy places where they find it difficult to focus. They may prefer to communicate with their friends through technology as they can think about what they are saying rather than feel it.

Patients who have a diagnosis of anorexia nervosa and not ASD may exhibit similar features but they often want to change even if they find themselves unable to do so. They often want to lose the rigidity of the eating disorder but again find it difficult. There can be a fear of fatness and/or a dislike of their body image which does not seem apparent in an ASD diagnosis. In ASD this appears to be more a fear of changing previously learned behaviours, as they can't rely on instinct. Similarities are rigid behaviours, wanting to stick to a routine, and wanting help yet at the same time rejecting it. The more you work with ASD, the easier it becomes to actually see the differences.

Autistic people do not exhibit just one specific trait; the spectrum appears to be a mix of different traits and different needs. Most people struggle to understand exactly what autism means and see it as a neurological condition or just being 'wired differently' to other people. The frontal lobe of the brain processes changes of plans, which means it's more difficult for autistic people to make changes at the last minute and they are unlikely to perform well in tasks that require mental flexibility.

Understanding others

Autistic people have difficulty knowing what other people are feeling, and this makes it difficult for them to develop relationships. They may want to be around other people but don't understand how to do this and fit in. Although ASD can mean that you struggle with social interaction, this alone does not mean you have ASD. Other traits that have been present is that quite often people with ASD don't see the value in 'sugar-coating' things or not being honest, which can sometimes lead to hurt feelings. Women on the spectrum don't present in the same way men do and there is not much research on this. Women are better at masking their inability to feel comfortable in strange situations, such as social situations, and can often laugh at a joke even if they don't understand what it means (as discussed in Chapter 1). Trying to mask socially doesn't come naturally and it is likely that when they get home they will go into a dark room and not want to speak to anyone until they feel safe again.

Sensory sensitivities in autism (discussed in Chapters 12 and 13) mean that people experience things such as bright lights, strong smells and touch differently. These can cause anxiety, be painful and cause a shutdown.

Our joint work on the PEACE Pathway hopefully will help families and clinicians to recognize the importance of timely diagnosis and learn from our examples and reflections on how to support people with both conditions.

Which therapies worked and which didn't

As a cognitive analytic therapy (CAT) therapist,[1] I always use the CAT structure, but may change the content if someone is having difficulties understanding the formulation. In the first session where we discuss the assessment letter and process, I usually know if this person is different and may need a bit more help understanding. For example, I give out the psychotherapy file (PF) for the patient to fill in at home, but if I feel the patient has difficulty understanding it then I wait until the second session and go through it with them, explaining it in a different way so that they are able to understand. For example, there are questions about certain 'traps' they may feel caught in, such as a 'trying to please trap' – in other words, do they try to please others to avoid upsetting them? The answer to this is often no, they don't try to please because they don't know how to please others or what they would like. The same with 'Fear of hurting others': they don't hold their feelings in for fear of hurting others, but if they inadvertently upset someone, they are more afraid of

---

1   Cognitive analytic therapy (CAT) draws upon and integrates understanding from both cognitive therapies and psychoanalytic therapies resulting in an effective, time-limited talking therapy.

the reaction they get because they struggle to understand rather than the concern that they have upset someone. So there are many questions in the PF that are not designed for someone who struggles to know what they are actually feeling.

CAT is generally about relationships and exploring feelings within those relationships, but we convert this to thought and understanding rather than feeling, although feelings do also play a part, notably in helping someone to understand what they are feeling, particularly if it is anger and frustration.

Encompassed in that is an amount of planning and drawing up of charts they can follow on a daily basis, and giving them plenty of time to think about things. This can sometimes feel a bit repetitive as we have to go over things a lot until they have formed the routine otherwise they easily slip back to their old pattern. This is particularly important if patients are of low weight.

Sometimes I have felt that just being listened to is important, especially if no one has really listened to what they are experiencing before. They can explain what goes on inside when they feel like cutting off from the world. People have explained to me that sometimes staying in the dark and not having to communicate or think about anyone else helps them to come out of their shutdown and feel calm again. It's like learning a new language which only a few people speak so you have to search for someone who understands.

Working through rapport

I try to develop a rapport with someone with ASD as soon as I can as I realize it is not as easy as it is with someone who is not on the spectrum. I used to try to work with patients with co-morbidity in therapy rooms where it was quieter and there were fewer unexpected noises like doors slamming. I keep my voice quiet and calm and don't react to sudden outbursts other than with quiet questioning. We try to keep everything in the room calm and let them tell me things in their own way. I let them feel that being different is okay, not wrong but just different, yet we need to learn to understand each other. I tell them they can do a lot to help others understand the way they think, as people are only afraid of what they don't understand and that leads to difficult behaviours on both sides.

Reflections

I enjoyed working with people with both ASD and eating disorders, particularly developing a rapport with them and learning more about how difficult life could be for some of them if they grew up with siblings who were not on the spectrum and who were sometimes afraid of them, or if they grew up without siblings and therefore had no one to learn from and parents who expected a lot from them. Even those who grew up with a parent on the spectrum did not seem to develop much understanding or parental rapport. Each person on the spectrum has their own individual personality alongside their feelings of just being different and misunderstood. In a similar way to anorexia nervosa, you are not just working with an illness but how lots of different personalities experience it.

The difficulties I felt were that patients with co-morbidity really needed more time and perhaps the eating disorders treatment setting was not necessarily the right place for them, as eating disorders on their own can be quite tough without adding an extra 'string' to work with. It was more frustrating as it took longer and, as I said, could be more repetitive. Quite often, these patients needed to be referred on to other services that could help after treatment. Sometimes they needed social groups or social services support if they had children.

They stayed in my mind longer as I knew that when they meet something in life that puts them into a 'meltdown' situation where they cut themselves off for a while then they are very likely to fall back into old routines. As a therapist I felt frustrated early on when it was really difficult to get a diagnosis of ASD and often on writing to various clinical services to get help I received no response. Patients themselves were frustrated, knowing something was wrong but again they had received no help. There was less of a sense of satisfaction on ending with a patient with whom I felt I had not been able to make significant changes that would stay with them. Most of what I learned about autism spectrum conditions was from my patients themselves in those earlier days. I was so glad when the PEACE project began to plan clinical pathway for patients with co-morbidity and more light was thrown on the subject so that we could develop a better understanding. I think that is the key word for the future: 'understanding' of differences rather than rejecting differences when supporting people.

Chapter 16

The Importance of Assessment

AUTISM EVALUATION IN HEALTHCARE SETTINGS

James Adamson, Jess Kerr-Gaffney,
—— *Katherine Smith and Kate Tchanturia* ——

About assessments

Much could be gained from integrating routine autism evaluation in healthcare settings with almost no time or financial costs for patients or services. Benefits would include greater insight into patients' psychopathology, especially considering that research has shown that up to 37 per cent of patients with anorexia nervosa (AN) have high levels of autistic traits and respond to treatment differently than those without autistic traits (Tchanturia, Larsson & Adamson, 2016; Tchanturia *et al.*, 2019; Adamson *et al.*, 2018). Consequently, clinical services can adapt existing treatment to provide improved outcomes as a result of tailoring treatment in line with patients' autism evaluation results. Furthermore, it allows clinical services to evaluate the level of possible co-morbidity in their settings and compare it nationally and internationally with other treatment centres and across other mental health settings. There are many ways that clinical services can introduce autism evaluation; in this chapter we will go over how to implement routine screening in clinical settings and the benefits and compromises that may develop with the introduction of an evaluation programme. Furthermore, we consider some of the implications for both the patient and multidisciplinary healthcare teams when introducing autism spectrum condition evaluation and how to reflect on the findings. Although this chapter will focus on what we have done across our eating disorder services, the process can be replicated across any clinical service and in any population, especially if a routine audit is already taking place.

One of the easiest ways to introduce evaluation into clinical services is to add a screening questionnaire to any pre-existing audit or service evaluation process. This might be at assessment, during admission or start of treatment, depending on the type of setting. Since autism is a neurodevelopmental condition, we would expect the scores from these questionnaires to remain reasonably stable over time, so it only needs to be asked once at the start of treatment. Findings from our eating disorder national service in South London and Maudsley NHS Foundation Trust support the theory that scores remain stable over time, as we did not find any significant difference in scores between admission and discharge in our inpatient settings (Tchanturia *et al.*, 2019). Which screening measure you choose is often a balance between participant burden due to the time it takes them to complete it and the predictive validity of the questionnaire, i.e. how good it is at predicting a diagnosis. Often with questionnaires, the more questions there are, the better it is at predicting what it was designed to predict; however, it would be wholly unreasonable to expect someone new to treatment to fill out long questionnaires.

Autism Quotient (Baron-Cohen *et al.*, 2001; Allison, Auyeung & Baron-Cohen, 2012)

One of the most popular questionnaires used as a screening tool in research and in clinical contexts to aid the decision as to whether to refer an individual for a full assessment is the Autism Quotient (AQ-50). The AQ is a 50-item self-report questionnaire devised by Professor Simon Baron-Cohen and his team. Eleven years later the same team conducted a large-scale study with 4000 participants to deduce which questions predicted a diagnosis of ASC better than the others. They were able to reduce the AQ-50 right down to 10 questions whilst still holding very similar predictive validity and they called it the AQ-10 (Allison *et al.*, 2012). We were very interested to explore in our clinical settings the feasibility of using this measure (for details of this pilot work see Tchanturia *et al.*, 2013). Research conducted one year later found that the AQ-10 was just as good as the AQ-50 in predicting an ASC diagnosis (Booth *et al.*, 2013). The AQ-10 comes in variants for adults, teenagers and children and these can all be accessed for free online (https://www.autismresearchcentre.com/arc_tests). In our eating disorder services, we use the AQ-10 at the beginning of treatment for all patients in inpatient, outpatient and day care programmes. It provides a means of assessing for autism in clinical services in a very fast and efficient way with very little time burden for the patient or clinician. We found that this approach helped us to calibrate our care pathway for people with ASC and eating disorder co-morbidities with full insight that it is not an ideal measure (because it is based on self-report and is very brief), but it is better than ignoring the co-morbidity or ASC features even if patients are not autistic.

Social Responsiveness Scale (SRS-2; Constantino & Gruber, 2012)

The SRS-2 is a 65-item questionnaire, available in both informant-rated and self-report formats. It is currently recommended by the National Institute for Health and Care Excellence (NICE) for assessing ASC in clinical settings. It comprises five subscales: social awareness (ability to recognize social cues); social cognition (interpreting social behaviour); social communication (reciprocal communication in social situations); social motivation (motivation to participate in social interactions); and restrictive interests and repetitive behaviour (circumscribed interests and stereotypy). The benefit of this questionnaire is that along with a total score, T-scores can also be calculated in order to give an indication of the severity of an individual's symptoms. T-scores falling within the mild, moderate or severe range suggest clinically significant symptoms with varying degrees of impact on everyday social interactions.

Although the SRS-2 has been used extensively in individuals with ASC, our research group is the first to use the measure in individuals with AN (Kerr-Gaffney, Harrison & Tchanturia, 2019). We found that around half of people with AN scored in the 'moderate' or 'severe' range, compared to about 30 per cent of those who had fully recovered from AN. In our control group, only 5 per cent scored in the 'moderate' range, and none in the 'severe' range (Figure 16.1). This shows that the SRS-2 is sensitive to the difficulties experienced by people with AN. We do not yet use this self-assessment systematically in our clinical setting yet, but these preliminary findings from Kerr-Gaffney and colleagues are helpful.

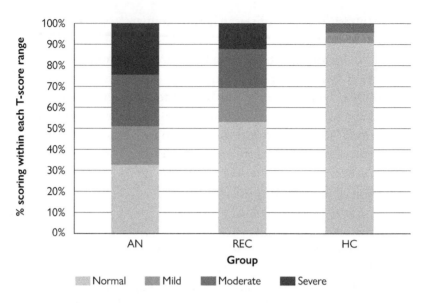

Figure 16.1. *Proportions of adults with anorexia nervosa (AN), recovered AN (REC) and healthy controls (HC) scoring within each severity category of the Social Responsiveness Scale (SRS-2). N=142*

In addition, we found that scores on the SRS-2 were associated with scores on the ADOS-2, meaning that the SRS-2 could be a useful tool in identifying those who may benefit from a full diagnostic assessment. Relatedly, those with higher SRS-2 scores were found to have more problems in daily living, suggesting the SRS-2 could provide meaningful information about the specific areas of difficulty an individual presents with.

Autism Diagnostic Observation Schedule (ADOS; Lord, 1989)

A more belt-and-braces approach would be to use clinical interviews such as the Autism Diagnostic Observation Schedule, Second Edition (ADOS-2) which not only gives us an overall quantifiable score, like the AQ-10, but also assesses multiple domains which can be helpful to evaluate individuals' areas of difficulty and strength. Furthermore, it is the gold standard diagnostic tool that is often used in combination with developmental history and comprehensive clinical assessments to diagnose ASC. Although there are many benefits to using the ADOS-2 there are also a few compromises to consider. First, the assessment itself typically lasts 40–60 minutes and can take that time again to score it, especially when we need to review the video, double score and check reliability. Second, we need professionals that are trained in using this tool. Training typically is a four-day workshop with some additional homework and being part of a specialist group. It can be costly to train multiple clinicians. Furthermore, it is expected that those using the ADOS-2 attend regular consensus meetings (specialist groups) in order to make sure they are administering and scoring the assessment accurately. If clinical services are willing to invest the time, training and financial commitments then it can offer a more detailed assessment of autistic traits and the strengths and weaknesses of the individuals in related domains. One other important point to note when using the ADOS-2 is to be aware that the algorithm has been criticized in the research literature for missing females who have developed an ability to camouflage their symptoms, especially in social domains, and therefore do not meet criteria in these areas. There have been recent developments to the algorithm, and research from our group has shown that the latest version is superior to the old version in picking up autistic females (Sedgewick *et al.*, 2019).

Feeding back results

One important aspect to consider as a team is what and how we feed back the results to the individual who completed the measure or assessment. Assessments can feel like a tick box exercise, if used as such, but can be used as an exploratory exercise in collaboration with the patient if you ensure that the results can lead on to further discussions that might elicit real change for the individual. In the case of the AQ-10, considering it is a self-report measure that will likely be combined with other psychometric measures as part of an initial assessment or admission, it can be treated very similarly. In that case, the results can help to inform clinician decisions such as potential treatment adaptations, and it would be best practice to feed back the results to the individual who completed it. Should someone score above cut-off on the measure you decided to use, it can be extremely useful to have a conversation with the individual about whether they would like to be referred for a formal assessment, what that would entail and the pros and cons of getting a diagnosis. It would also be important to consider that scoring above cut-off on measures does not mean that the individual meets the criteria for a diagnosis, nor should it be introduced as such; instead, it gives indications as to individual differences that might be characteristic of autistic traits. Most importantly, it should be used as the start of a conversation, with the results giving points for discussion and exploration. That being said, our experience of patients going on to receive a diagnosis after undergoing a full formal assessment, often later in life, is positive. It is often especially positive if it allows systems – teams, families and patients themselves – to adjust treatment to better meet the individual's needs and if it brings greater understanding to the individual's experiences across their lifespan.

We still learn from each individual case how best to provide individual feedback. We know from our clinical experience and work on the PEACE Pathway that feedback and psychoeducation around testing results done well can be therapeutic, useful and engaging. For an insight into an individual's experience of being diagnosed with autism at age 35, please see Pooky Knightsmith's YouTube video: 'Adult Autism: what's it like to get a late diagnosis? My story' (https://www.youtube.com/watch?v=Sim9Vk4urSo).

Treatment development

Once the decision is made on which measure to implement in any specific clinical service you need to think about how best to use the information that you are now obtaining. Evaluating autism in clinical services not only allows you to increase awareness of the condition amongst your team and patient group, but it also allows you to start to analyze how effective your current treatment is for these individuals. Evaluation of current treatment options in healthcare settings can help us to evaluate the efficacy for patients with high levels of ASC traits, those who score above cut-off on screening measures, and those with an official diagnosis. Furthermore, it can help to identify what aspects of treatment currently work and what is not working so that we can modify treatment options and clinical pathways accordingly for patients with autistic traits or a diagnosis. For example, we can identify whether an intervention would work best in a group setting vs. individual work, whether an increase in treatment length would be beneficial, the type of

THE IMPORTANCE OF ASSESSMENT

therapies offered and what modifications can be made to the delivery of treatment including the environment in which they are delivered. Furthermore, autism evaluation in clinical settings can open up conversations about other related adaptations to treatment, for example potential sensory difficulties for the individual that can be catered for within the treatment settings, the power of positive communications and how to be more effective being around social situations.

Although the possibilities for improving outcomes using routine autism evaluation are exciting, it is extremely important to not forget individual differences. Separating those that score below and above cut-off can be useful for research purposes, but grouping data and generalizing is not always helpful in a clinical setting. As with all measures, clinicians should exercise caution in making large causal inferences based upon the results of a measure and should always use them in combination with a wider picture of the individual, with the individual taking a central role in any conversations around interpreting results and making any adaptations. With all diagnoses, and especially with autism spectrum conditions, there is a massive spread of strengths and difficulties – two individuals can be very different. It is, therefore, more important to consider how a potential diagnosis or high levels of traits affect an individual so that you can tailor the intervention with their own strengths and difficulties in mind. However, having an indication can start useful conversations, improve understanding, formulation of problems, therapy aims and expectations for everyone involved and therefore improve treatment for everyone. Assessment helps teams to calibrate, formulate and remind us that we treat eating disorders within neurodiversity, whether people are on the autism spectrum or not.

References

Adamson, J., Leppanen, J., Murin, M. & Tchanturia, K. (2018) 'Effectiveness of emotional skills training for patients with anorexia nervosa with autistic symptoms in group and individual format.' *European Eating Disorders Review*, 26(4), 367–375.

Allison, C., Auyeung, B. & Baron-Cohen, S. (2012) 'Toward brief "red flags" for autism screening: The short autism spectrum quotient and the short quantitative checklist in 1,000 cases and 3,000 controls.' *Journal of the American Academy of Child & Adolescent Psychiatry*, 51(2), 202–212.

Baron-Cohen S, Wheelwright, S., Skinner, R., Martin, J. & Clubley, E. (2001) 'The Autism-Spectrum Quotient (AQ): Evidence from Asperger Syndrome/High-Functioning Autism, males and females, scientists and mathematicians.' *Journal of Autism and Developmental Disorders, 31*(1), 5 17.

Booth, T., Murray, A.L., McKenzie, K., Kuenssberg, R., O'Donnell, M. & Burnett, H. (2013) 'Brief report: An evaluation of the AQ-10 as a brief screening instrument for ASD in adults.' *Journal of Autism and Developmental Disorders, 43*(12), 2997–3000.

Constantino, J.N. & Gruber, C.P. (2012) *Social Responsiveness Scale—Second Edition (SRS-2).* Torrance, CA: Western Psychological Services.

Hus, V. & Lord, C. (2014) 'The autism diagnostic observation schedule, module 4: Revised algorithm and standardized severity scores.' *Journal of Autism and Developmental Disorders, 44*(8), 1996–2012.

Kerr-Gaffney, J., Hall, D., Harrison, A., & Tchanturia, K. (2020) 'The Social Responsiveness Scale is an efficient screening tool for autism spectrum disorder traits in adults with anorexia nervosa.' *European Eating Disorder Review, 28*(4) 433-444.

Lord, C., Rutter, M., Dilavore, P., Risi, S., Gotham, K. & Bishop, S. (2012) *Autism Diagnostic Observation Schedule, Second Edition (ADOS-2) Modules 1-4*; Western Psychological Services: Los Angeles.

Sedgewick, F., Kerr-Gaffney, J., Leppanen, J. & Tchanturia, K. (2019) 'Anorexia nervosa, autism, and the ADOS: How appropriate is the new algorithm in identifying cases?' *Frontiers in Psychiatry, 10*, 507.

Tchanturia, K., Adamson, J., Leppanen, J. & Westwood, H. (2019) 'Characteristics of autism spectrum disorder in anorexia nervosa: A naturalistic study in an inpatient treatment programme.' *Autism, 23*(1), 123–130.

Tchanturia, K., Larsson, E. & Adamson, J. (2016) 'How anorexia nervosa patients with high and low autistic traits respond to group Cognitive Remediation Therapy.' *BMC Psychiatry, 16*(1), 334.

Tchanturia, K., Smith, E., Weineck, F., Fidanboylu, E., Kern, N., Treasure, J. & Baron-Cohen, S. (2013) 'Exploring autistic traits in anorexia: A clinical study.' *Molecular Autism, 4*(1), 44.

Chapter 17

Can You See Me?

HOW TO BUILD A BUSINESS CASE IN YOUR TEAM — CLINICAL LEAD PERSPECTIVE

Danielle Glennon

The NHS is a complex organization, with clinicians, patients and carers striving for better patient-centred care, but with restricted resources. There is not usually a shortage of wonderful ideas in how to improve patient care and quality to ensure that patients get needs met. The budget, however, is set annually, and this means that the long-term strategy and changes to patient pathways can be arduous and difficult to achieve. As part of managing NHS resources, services have had to become diagnosis-led. This can be extremely helpful and also a curse, restricting the treatments which can be offered. As we know, co-morbidity in eating disorders is a norm rather than an exception, and yet a lot of eating disorder services continue to be restricted in what 'bit' of a patient they can treat, i.e. only the eating disorder part. However, working in this way with patients with ASC and eating disorders doesn't work, therefore how treatment is offered when ASC and the eating disorder are inextricably linked needs further consideration. When you marry quality improvement initiatives with investment, change does happen; however, these changes can be in isolation, and need a whole team and wider organizational engagement to ensure longevity. This chapter aims to give you key information as part of your business case for change, and top tips in how to improve the care of people with ASC and eating disorders.

We know that treatment outcomes for eating disorder still need improving, with just under 50 per cent of patients fully recovering, over

30 per cent of patients improving somewhat, and 20 per cent continuing to have a chronic eating disorder (e.g. Steinhausen, 2002; Steinhausen & Weber, 2009). Services need to adapt and change as new evidence and improvement in treatments emerge, and the traditional 17-year delay of generation of research evidence being translated into real-life services and treatment adaption needs to be shortened.

At South London and Maudsley NHS Foundation Trust eating disorder clinical service, we are lucky to be have received support from The Health Foundation and Maudsley Charity to explore and implement adaptations to treatments in real time. This support has allowed our service to move towards true patient-centred care, ending the myth that one model fits all, and developing a service which is built around the patient rather than asking the patient to fit into the service (not to mention that the service is usually designed for neurotypical people). We have a good track record of piloting and scaling nationally innovations and novel approaches. One such innovation is the evidence-based First episode Rapid Early intervention for Eating Disorders (FREED) which is now being rolled out nationally, thanks to its evidence influencing policy and guidelines in how eating disorder services should be set up in real time. We now hope to do this for patients with ASC and eating disorders through our PEACE Pathway (Pathway for Eating disorders and Autism developed from Clinical Experience).

Patient-centred treatment may seem obvious, and many clinicians will argue they adapt and formulate treatment for each individual patient; however, this is done still with a traditional set of treatment principles for neurotypical patients in mind. It is only recently the link between ASC and eating disorders has been explored, and therefore we are in a process of learning what may work better for those with both ASC and eating disorders. As we learnt in Chapter 2 about social anxiety disorder, people with ASC can develop negative core beliefs about their abilities, and therefore it is essential as clinicians we don't inadvertently solidify further these negative core beliefs when the treatment-as-usual approach doesn't work. Therefore, how can we adapt treatment to fit patients' needs? What is good enough and what is needed to implement changes which meet the needs of patients with ASD and eating disorders?

Service within a service

The PEACE Pathway can be embedded into any evidence-based eating disorder service. In an eating disorder outpatient setting, our audit data shows 25 per cent of patients being treated report heightened ASD symptoms compared with a community, age and socio-demographic matched non-eating disorder control group of women where only 2 per cent report above-threshold scores on AQ-10.

As an evidence generating service, we have learnt that there are key ingredients to successfully develop, implement and sustain any new initiative within a service, so that the service can be a patient-centred one, meeting the needs of individual patients and their carers. We hope our top tips will help you to think about how you may need to adapt your service to incorporate the ASD and eating disorders pathway, and so patients and their individual needs can be seen.

We suggest you use a simple Plan, Do, Study, Act (PDSA) cycle as a way of putting in any quality improvement initiatives such as this. It may be useful for you to hold in mind Rogers's Bell Curve (2010) approach to conceptualize the scaling and growth of new ways of working within your team. It describes the diffusion of innovation as progressing through five categories, namely, 'innovators' (2.5%), 'early adopters' (13.5%), 'early majority' (34%), 'late majority' (34%) and 'laggards' (16%). As Elaine Smith explained in Chapter 15, understanding there will be differences rather than rejecting people for being different is essential. This applies to the team in which you work as well as the work with patients and carers.

Champion

A champion is essential. A champion is someone who can take the lead on the development of the new pathway for people with ASD and eating disorders. The champion can be from any discipline of the multidisciplinary team, but we have found they need certain characteristics to be successful in the role. Any change can be difficult, especially in busy services, and therefore they will need to be able to bring everyone from administrators to clinicians and managers on board. Any potential change must also involve patient and carer expertise in shaping the new principles and adaptations in treatment. A champion therefore is someone who has energy, and who is good at communicating with and has the respect of the wider team. They will have a particular interest in this patient group, and be confident engaging with wider stakeholders outside of their eating disorder service.

The champion's role will need the support of the clinical lead and/ or service manager. They will take the lead in examining the current processes within the service, and evaluating what potential tweaks there need to be in order to adjust what and how the service is offered to people with ASD and eating disorders. We have included many resources in this book which will help you to start the project; however, from patient, carer and team feedback you may have different ideas and want to improve and adapt your own resources.

Also it may be worth getting support from the service leads to be trained and accredited in ADOS-2 for adults. This won't lead to you being able to clinically diagnose someone with autism, but will mean you can diagnose if autism is likely, and therefore support a forward referral for a full clinical diagnosis. Some patients welcome a full diagnosis and others are happy with this mini assessment and report, which a champion trained in ADOS-2 can do. If you are able to go down this route, then it will be important to link with other ADOS assessors to check validity of the assessment each time. You may choose to train up several members of the team together, so that they can become peer support checkers.

'Buy in'

Get 'buy in' from anyone who will listen. You may be surprised where resources can then be found for things like decoration, training, funding changes etc.

As champion, there are opportunities to be creative in how you implement the ASD and eating disorder pathway. This may include taking a lead on changing the environment, getting some resources printed up, training some of the team, and engaging senior members of the Trust. As an example, in one NHS Trust we supported in scaling up our First episode Rapid Early intervention for Eating Disorders (FREED), they engaged with the Trust's communication team and disability team, and secured a dedicated parking space for FREED patients. Engage your communications team, hold celebration events, sign up to Twitter or get your communications team to tweet about anything ASD and eating disorder related.

Engage with any local ASD teams that exist. By doing this, we learnt a lot about how they adapt treatments for social anxiety, depression and impulsive behaviours for people with ASD, and this is all relevant for your work with ASD and eating disorders.

Mini team

Depending on the size of your team, we recommend that you create a mini team to drive this forward, and engage in repeated PDSA cycles. The South London & Maudsley NHS Foundation Trust eating disorder service covers a population of 2.4 million people, and stretches across two sites, therefore we chose to have two mini teams. Each mini team consists of between four and six people. Building a reflective team which has time to think, formulate and adapt treatments for patients even when there are limited resources is essential for the success of improving treatments and outcomes for patients with ASD and eating disorders. As patients move across the pathway of these two sites, learning and formulation is shared as part of any transitions.

In the mini team, discuss all possible cases of ASD even if patients present with pseudo-ASD symptoms and eating disorders, and work together in developing the pathway. The mini team can help ensure that learning is captured, and that any adaptations are manageable. As a mini team, you can provide peer supervision, share ideas and develop new ways of working. The mini team could consist of anyone who is part of the multidisciplinary team, and it is useful to have representation from all disciplines.

Huddle and extended huddle

A huddle is a 15-minute get-together to discuss any ASD and eating disorder pathway issues, identify any possible cases, and update on any changes to the pathway which are currently happening, such as changes to the environment.

In our PEACE Pathway we have introduced extended monthly huddles where the cases are discussed in full, to formulate the patient, share learning, hear other people's ideas, and plan treatment going forward (more details can be found in Chapters 19 and 20). This is particularly useful for the multidisciplinary team in adapting their approach depending on the work they are doing with a patient. For the nurses this could be adaptations to the approach supporting patients in the dining room; occupational therapists might be helping patients who want to widen their social network; psychological therapists might be working with patients on breaking negative core beliefs, for example. The extended huddle is open to all members of the team, not just the mini team.

Team meeting

In our team meeting we have a slot on the agenda to update everyone on any quality improvement, pathway developments, and nuggets of information which would be useful for the team. You can also remind people of when the extended huddle will be taking place. Having this on the agenda in team meetings helps keep the pathway development alive and ensures that any changes can happen in real time with the team's buy in. It is also a chance for the team to feed back on any aspect of the work, so that any further adaptations can be implemented.

On a final note, it takes a village to support change and we want to hear from you about anything you are doing for patients with ASD and eating disorders. Please do follow us on Twitter @peace_pathway and get in touch.

References

Rogers, E.M. (2010) *Diffusion of Innovations* (4th edition). New York: The Free Press.

Steinhausen, H.C. (2002) 'The outcome of anorexia nervosa in the 20th century.' *American Journal of Psychiatry, 159*(8), 1284–1293.

Steinhausen, H.C. & Weber, S. (2009) 'The outcome of bulimia nervosa: Findings from one-quarter century of research.' *The American Journal of Psychiatry, 166*(12), 1331–1341.

Chapter 18

Adopting, Adapting and Improving

TAKING A QUALITY IMPROVEMENT APPROACH TO CROSS THE CHASM FROM EVIDENCE TO IMPLEMENTATION

Anna Burhouse

I hope that you are feeling inspired to integrate the ideas in this book into your own practice and across the organization you work for. This chapter explains why putting evidence into practice can often be a challenging and complex process and how the use of a structured quality improvement (QI) approach to implementation can help. Use of QI by adopters allows the ideas in this book to be tested and refined in order to best meet the needs of your local context and organizational culture.

Our hope is that, having implemented this work, you will then be willing to contribute your learning by connecting with the team from South London and Maudsley via social media with the Pathway for Eating disorders and Autism developed from Clinical Experience (PEACE) community. This will help to increase the body of knowledge about how to provide services for people with both autism and an eating disorder because we know that innovative concepts and interventions tend to be improved when tested and refined by others.

Getting evidence into practice is difficult

The improvement ideas in this book are a culmination of years of research combined with the insight gained from the authors' lived experience as patients, carers, champions and clinicians. The ideas have been co-designed, tested and evaluated during an 18-month period from January 2019 to April 2020, in an inpatient and community mental health service in the UK. This research is now ready to be adopted and tested by others.

This sounds straightforward, doesn't it? But it's estimated that the complex process of getting evidence from research into clinical practice takes an average of 17 years (Balas & Boren, 2000; Grant, Green & Mason, 2003; Wratschko, 2009). There is strong agreement from within the research and health communities that the adoption of new evidence, innovations and technologies into health care takes far too long and that the cost to patients of these delays in terms of life and health are too high.

One of the main reasons that this process takes so long is that most of the investment of time, energy and resources goes into the creative idea development, testing and dissemination phase, rather than into supporting the process of adoption and spread. Many brilliant ideas and inventions are published and then fail to scale or suffer from a noticeable gap between the early, creative design phase of development and the adoption of these concepts/products by the mainstream population. Geoffery Moore (1991) calls this gap, between design/research and mainstream adoption the 'Big Scary Chasm' and argues that crossing this 'chasm' takes different skills and approaches than are needed in the earlier design or research phase.

Despite the growing body of evidence about the specialist skills needed for adoption, we typically see an assumption in healthcare that the move from research/design into practice is a simple, logical linear process or 'pipeline' of diffusion and dissemination. It's also a common assumption that this process should and could be led by the same person or team that originated the work, despite it requiring a fundamentally different mindset and set of technical skills and capabilities.

What commonly happens in NHS healthcare is that we hope that people will read original work or see a breakthrough technology being demonstrated or hear about a new way of working at a conference and then will have a go at putting it into practice. However, dissemination through these routes is often patchy and slow to evolve.

Alternatively, in the NHS we rely on the introduction of a new policy, NICE guidance or national call to action or an invitation to take part in a 'vanguard' or 'pilot' programme, or are subject to a financial 'quality' incentive/penalty to make change happen. However, we increasingly realize that when the NHS 'mandates' adoption from the 'top' via arm's-length bodies, commissioners or government, this does not automatically lead to the desired changes in clinical practice, patient experience or health outcomes that were predicted to occur (Greenhalgh *et al.*, 2004). We know from national audits in the UK that uptake through these routes is often variable. This is not surprising given that behaviours and habits in organizations are hard to change and that the contexts and environment of real-world clinical settings do not always replicate the trial conditions of the study.

Rarely does national guidance come with a detailed implementation guide and adequate resourcing to allow the adopting site to embrace the intervention in a sustainable methodical way. We know from a study undertaken by the Health Foundation (Horton, Illingworth & Warburton, 2018) that adopting teams say they need:

- access to materials and resources about the intervention

- a way of understanding how the idea could be operationalized

- a space to ask the originating team clarifying questions and share their local implementation dilemmas

- training in the intervention (and often in the process of adoption)

- funding or release to create the time it takes teams to undertake this process.

Horton *et al.* (2018) argue that:

> It requires teams on the ground to adapt and implement a new intervention in ways that will enable it to work in their own setting. Staff may need to develop new skills or learn to use new techniques. There may be a need for culture change, relationship building, new ways of working or undoing entrenched habits – none of which can be achieved purely through compulsion. (p.3)

They also stress the importance of understanding that the likely success of adoption depends on the 'context: the underlying systems, culture and circumstances of the environment in which it is implemented' (Horton *et al.*, 2018, p.4) and that this often requires re-work or changes to the original idea or 'a long journey to build new relationships, shift the prevailing team culture or develop new skills' (Horton *et al.*, 2018, p.5). If this is correct then it places a key emphasis on the role of what Everett Rogers (2010) calls the 'early adopters' in helping to test and refine the original ideas and to discover what it takes to adopt complex change ideas in other contexts and environments.

Early adopters may well help to surface contextual, social or behavioural elements of the original work that the inventors were not conscious of, such as the importance of coordinated team work, sickness absence levels, the support of an encouraging manager, the passion of a patient advocate etc. for the success of the intervention; these may be factors the original team took for granted or treated as the cultural 'norm' (Bauman, Stein & Ireys, 1991; Bate *et al.*, 2014; Howarth *et al.*, 2016). This highlights the adaptive nature of the process of adoption where 'There is a growing understanding that there is a dynamic relationship between the innovation, implementation, context and people involved. Context is not a static backdrop but an active part of the story' (Albury *et al.*, 2018, p.8).

The early adopters are therefore not passive recipients of the original team's knowledge; instead, they contribute new ideas and improvements to the original idea, helping to test and revise it in order to make it clearer and more effective. Early adopters are therefore better viewed as 'co-designers' than 'consumers' because the gain is reciprocal (Albury *et al.*, 2018). Nationally mandated NHS adoption routes would therefore be wise to routinely capture this vital learning, to help inform the wider adoption process by the groups that follow the 'early adopters', that Rogers (2010) calls the 'early' and 'late' majority of the population.

Achieving adoption and spread of good ideas in a way that leads to consistent, sustainable and measurable change is therefore not an easy task. Its complexity requires us to use as robust a methodological approach to roll out as had been applied to the original invention or research. This is where taking an active decision to use a continuous improvement approach in the early stages of the adoption process can be extremely helpful as it supports the originating and adopting teams to jointly:

- explore and test their underlying theory of change
- find out what is 'core' to the idea/intervention/invention and what can be subject to local adaptation

- discover what it really takes to put an idea into practice in another environment/culture

- measure a range of outcomes to see if there is consistency with the original work

- gain a sense of collective 'ownership' and intrinsic motivation to engage with the intervention, rather than the adopting team feeling that change is being 'imposed' from above

- refine and improve the original idea together through the systematic collation of the revisions, which in turn can support the rate of adoption by the mainstream population.

This is why, should you choose to try to adopt some of the improvement ideas and concepts in this book, we would encourage you to take a quality improvement approach to capture your learning in order to help to inform, co-create and shape the evidence base. So the next part of this chapter will describe what quality improvement is and also why we recommend using it to help with early adoption.

What is quality improvement and why use it?

The term 'quality improvement' (QI) in healthcare generally 'refers to the systematic use of methods and tools to try to continuously improve quality of care and outcomes for patients' (Alder wick *et al.*, 2017). It is a structured and collective way of working together as a team to make small iterative tests of change to systems and processes, to help complex and ever-changing organizations to continuously improve.

QI originated in the 1920s in industry as a way of ensuring production quality control. It was then further developed in the post-war car manufacturing industry as a way of continuously improving the assembly line and flow of goods. It did this through the systematic use of a range of simple tools and methods to map and improve the flow between processes, reduce waste and increase efficiency, and through the development of collective leadership skills and cultural approaches that encouraged all staff to take part in the daily management of quality.

This approach then spread to other industries and was pioneered by thinkers such as W. Edwards Deming (1986, 2000), Armand Feigenbaum (1961), Kaoru Ishikawa (1985, 1990) and Joseph Juran

(1951), It has become an industry standard for complex settings where it can be helpful to take a continuous improvement approach to delivery. QI helps to make improvements in systematic and measurable ways, using improvement methods and tools to reduce unnecessary variation in quality standards and to build quality into the infrastructure in order to minimize human errors and mistakes.

Since the early days, quality improvement has matured and evolved and there are now many different QI tools, methods and commercial brands to choose from. It has spread to other industries and is widely used in the aviation, food production, retail and service industries and the military. It works well in areas where a consistently high quality of service is required in systems that have to adapt in order to thrive.

Whilst there are many different QI methods, a lot of them derive from the same historical roots and share the following key elements:

- They think about the organization as a **complex adaptive system** that continuously needs improving. **They plan** carefully for quality right from the start to create reliable and safe systems that embed a systematic way of **testing** new improvement ideas in real-world settings.

- They strive to know what 'customers' (or in healthcare: patients, carers and families, communities and populations) **value** and understand their needs (in healthcare: through engagement and co-production and use of demographic data) and design ways to capture and make use of regular satisfaction and experience feedback.

- They try to improve the **flow** of processes and reduce **waste** across the system, making it work as effectively as possible.

- They put **improvement** at the heart of the organization's **culture** so that it's 'business as usual'. They ensure that learning from errors is embedded to become a learning organization with a 'just culture', continuously striving to improve, seeking change ideas and solutions from those that know the system best (in healthcare that's patients, carers, families and staff), testing these change ideas rapidly at small scale in real-world settings before scaling. Learning from experience and measurement what works and why. Working together in shared purpose to find out 'What are we trying to accomplish? How will we know that change is an improvement? What changes can we make that will result in improvement?' (Langley *et al.*, 2009, p.29).

- They invest in **staff** and get people involved so that everyone feels a sense of collective leadership where fear of failure is low, psychological safety and compassion for each other are high, everyone can speak up, wellbeing is taken seriously and staff are trained well.

- They use **data** and observation to measure and review. Being willing to hear unexpected results and be curious about understanding that change can alter the 'system' in unpredictable ways.

- They understand the impact of **human behaviour** on the pursuit of perfection, such as disorganization, inertia, ego or habits.

These features are pragmatic and highly adaptable to diverse organizational settings; however, healthcare has been relatively slow to adopt quality improvement compared with other service industries, despite it being a highly complex adaptive system. At first, there was some scepticism that you could translate an 'industrial' approach to healthcare, but slowly improvement leaders began to emerge in healthcare who could demonstrate its applicability and describe how its use had reduced hugely important areas like mortality, infection and healthcare-related injuries.

A breakthrough moment happened in the United States of America in March 2001, when the Institute of Medicine (IoM) published a report called 'Crossing the Quality Chasm. A New Health System for the 21st Century' (Baker, 2001) which called for healthcare organizations to change the way they approached quality and championed the use of QI in healthcare settings.

The IoM helped to describe how QI could be designed for healthcare and called for a focus on six key quality dimensions for healthcare. These dimensions are:

Safe: avoiding harm to patients from care that is intended to help them. Aiming to avoid healthcare related death, injury, infection, mistreatment, over-treatment or harm.

Timely: reducing the time people have to wait for treatment (for instance, to reduce needless pain or surgery) and thinking about prevention and wellbeing, not just illness.

Effective: providing services based on the best available evidence and best suited to people's needs.

Equitable: providing healthcare that does not vary in quality or quantity because of a person's protected characteristics.

Efficient: avoiding unnecessary waste, through duplication, careful use of resources, improved treatments and care pathways etc.

Person-centred: putting patients, carers and families at the heart of all we do.

These six dimensions of quality have stood the test of time and you can see some of these dimensions are applicable to the PEACE Pathway (for instance, offering effective treatment, ensuring people with an autistic spectrum condition have equal access to eating disorder care, improving the care pathway and working in partnership with patients and carers to make meaningful improvements to care).

Whilst no single definition of quality improvement in healthcare has emerged since 2001, it is generally recognized that it is the application of a systematic approach that uses specific tools and techniques to make improvements to the healthcare system, applied within a supportive culture of improvement. Batalden & Davidoff (2007) acknowledge that unlike other industries, health is not just an issue for healthcare organizations and clinicians, but is an issue close to all our hearts and so define QI more inclusively as:

> The combined and unceasing efforts of everyone to make the changes that will lead to better patient outcomes (health), better system performance (care) and better professional development (learning). (Batalden & Davidoff, 2007)

Quality improvement methodologies are very useful when trying to implement a new idea/innovation/invention/process into healthcare, because they allow you to systematically test whether the change idea you have will actually result in an improvement. This is vital in complex adaptive systems, where there can be unintended consequences caused by the introduction of a new idea/innovation/invention/process into a small part of the system that inadvertently has a consequence in another part of the system. For example, introducing a new information leaflet for patients and carers in one locality clinic may be a great improvement, but it could also have an unintended negative impact on a sister clinic in a different locality within the same organization if it inadvertently increases organizational confusion about what people should do.

Getting started

So you've decided you want to take some of the great improvement ideas in this book and have a go at implementing them in your organization. If you have never used a quality improvement approach before and you work in an NHS setting, it is worth looking on your Trust website to see if your Trust has a specific QI method that they use and if there is a central team of QI experts that can help you, either through training or through practical support or coaching.

In the current English NHS, the use of a consistent improvement methodology across provider Trusts is highly variable, but Trusts are being encouraged to use a QI approach following the publication of national frameworks and concordats such as 'Developing People, Improving Care' (NHSI, 2016a) and 'Shared Commitment to Quality' (NHSI, 2016b). Both documents highlighted the need for healthcare organizations to build quality improvement knowledge and skills, create compassionate cultures, and develop improved leadership skills and quality infrastructures.

This national and local variation in England means that depending on where you work or where you access your healthcare, the underpinning QI approach may be different. If you are part of NHS Scotland or Wales, the predominant quality improvement approach is the Institute of Healthcare improvement's 'Model of Improvement' (www.ihi.org).

NHS Trusts are also at very different stages of organizational QI maturity, from those which have not yet adopted QI, through to those that use it systematically across the organization and encourage all members of staff to take part (Jones, Horton & Warburton, 2019). If you are working in an organization that has support in place, you are likely to have access to:

- QI training

- a group of people that have already been trained that can coach or mentor you

- a range of QI tools, templates and resources that your Trust uses.

If you aren't working in an NHS setting, or if the Trust hasn't started its improvement journey yet, there are a range of great digital resources to link in with at national level and free quality improvement training; for example, the NHSE/I Fundamentals or QSIR training programmes, or the Quality Improvement in Healthcare MOOC provided by the University of Bath on the Future Learn platform and the peer to peer support offered by the Health Foundation's Q Community. A good book to read as an introduction is *The Improvement Guide: A Practical Approach to Enhancing Organizational Performance* (Langley *et al.*, 2009).

Most QI training starts with an introduction to the theory and help to understand how to use some basic QI tools. Tools that can be helpful for you to learn in order to implement some of the ideas in this book include:

- a driver diagram (a simple visual way of showing your improvement aim and the key drivers that will help you achieve it)

- a logic model (a simple way of writing down your theory of change)

- Plan, Do, Study, Act cycle (a simple way of rapidly testing your idea in a systematic way in a real-world setting)

- how to measure your progress using a downloadable statistical process control chart (designed to show you if your change has led to statistically significant change)

- communication tools, such as a stakeholder map

- evaluation tools

- Experience-Based Co-Design methods to help involve patients, carers, families and staff in improvement.

Whilst these tools are very helpful, there is also a strong relational side to QI, as 20 per cent of improvement is technical and 80 percent is concerned with the human side of change (Godfrey *et al.*, 2017). The relational components of improvement include the psychological skills required to lead change and inspire collective leadership. These include communication and interpersonal skills, an ability to work well together, creative thinking, the establishment of a reflexive learning culture and support and compassion for each other when things go wrong, to name but a few.

There are many different ways to deliver improvement but helpful starting points include:

Forming a group

Gather together enthusiastic people that want to help you to implement this work. Start with the 'willing', but try to be inclusive and engage a range of people that will offer diverse opinions and thoughts and have complementary skills to you.

Embedding co-production with people with lived experience from the very beginning of the work is likely to strengthen your approach and ensure the improvement aims are aligned with what is really needed in your area.

It can be helpful to contract with one another about how you are going to work together in a QI way, what values are important to you, how you will deal with any conflict that arises and how you will evaluate your progress as a team.

In most improvement groups, it's good to have people:

- with lived experience and subject matter knowledge

- with enthusiasm, passion, creative drive and resilience

- that like working with data and can use a simple Excel spreadsheet

- with good communication skills

- who are good at bringing people together and encouraging people to participate

- who are 'do-ers' and like to 'have a go'

- who are reflective and enjoy synthesizing learning

- who know your local systems and key stakeholders really well

- who can exert strategic influence or know people that can

- who are comfortable with service evaluation

- who have QI skills or are prepared to learn them along the way.

It's helpful to think about what other skills or values you are missing, what external support or senior managerial sponsorship you might need and how you might go about securing this. If possible, consider drawing on the technical support from your Trust's QI team.

Agree your shared purpose, improvement aim and what to measure

Next, agree what your shared purpose is. What are you trying to achieve? What is your improvement aim? Are you going to try to replicate the whole body of work in this book or pick a small idea to test first? Spend some time discussing why you have chosen that approach. Then check you have all the information you need to put this idea into practice. Do you need to ask any clarifying questions through the @PEACE_ pathway Twitter account or ask for any advice before getting going?

Then, have a think about how the originating team introduced the work into their context and discuss what is similar or different to your context and environment. For instance, some of the original work was tested in community and inpatient mental health settings in London, in an urban environment with good transport links. Is your setting the same or different? Will this make any difference to how you have to deliver these ideas in your part of the world? Think about positive contextual elements you have (for instance, a strong and effective team) and those that may be challenging or different (for example, lack of time). What do you think the likely barriers might be to this work and what might help or enable it to be adopted?

It can be helpful to use techniques like Experience Based Co-Design (EBCD, available from www.pointofcarefoundation.org.uk/resource/experience-based-co-design-ebcd-toolkit/) to actively explore how to improve people's experience of your service. It can help you better understand your improvement aims.

Spend as much time as you need in this important planning phase to agree a really clear improvement aim and how you will know that you have achieved it. Make sure it is SMART: Specific (S), Measurable (M), Achievable (A), Realistic (R) and Timely (T) (NHSI, 2019) and that it has a clear process, outcome and balancing measures that you can articulate clearly and capture.

It can be helpful to think through how you might capture qualitative data through team meetings, focus groups, journaling, stories, surveys and through crowdsourcing on social media. For quantitative measurement of progress towards your improvement aims it helps to use a statistical process control (SPC) chart to track whether your PDSA cycles are making a statistically significant difference. A downloadable Excel spreadsheet with a training booklet explaining how to use SPC is available free from NHS Improvement (https://improvement.nhs.uk/documents/2748/NHS_MAKING_DATA_COUNT_FINAL.pdf).

It can be helpful in the planning phase to either use a 'Logic Model' to articulate your 'theory of change' (i.e. if we do X, we believe we will make X change because…) or a 'driver diagram' tool to show what you think the main drivers for change will be. These visual aids help you describe your thinking succinctly on a single page to key stakeholders. Templates can easily be found on the internet, and YouTube videos give clear instructions for use.

Giving it a go

Once you are clear about your aim, it's time to think about your first step. What is the first thing you want to do? When will you start, how and who with? It's helpful to see this next phase as a series of small-scale iterative tests that lead you incrementally towards your improvement aim. Each small test is known as a Plan, Do, Study, Act (PDSA) cycle and there are plenty of good digital guides and YouTube videos to help you understand how to use them in practice. Even better is to find an improvement coach or mentor to help you get used to this way of working in the beginning.

It's often best to start testing on a really small scale. For example, if you were trying to make reasonable adjustments to the physical environment in an inpatient eating disorder unit in order to make it better for autistic people, then your improvement group might decide to make one small therapeutic change on the least busy day of the week at lunch time between 12pm and 1pm and get feedback. This minimizes the risks associated with the change and allows you to test something new in a reasonably controlled way.

Studying the impact of this change allows you to capture what you've learnt and then use this data to inform the next test. The new test might be to make the same change on a busier day of the week to see if you learn anything new or to extend the time of testing to include lunch and dinner time, for example, to see if there is a difference between times of the day. Quite quickly these small tests and the changes they stimulate can lead to significant improvements and gains in local knowledge. Multiple small PDSA cycles form 'improvement ramps' towards your improvement aims. When measured on a statistical process control chart these PDSA cycles can show impact over time on the process, outcome and balancing measures you selected to measure your improvement aim.

There are many change ideas in this book but some of the main ones to consider are:

- adapting approaches to treatment and care pathways

- making reasonable adjustments to the physical environment

- making reasonable adjustments to work practices and behaviours

- increasing co-production and engagement

- external assessment and review of standards.

Measurement and evaluation

Measurement and evaluation should be integral to all of your improvement work. This can include quantitative and qualitative measurement of key outcome, process and balancing measures that will let you know if you have achieved your improvement aim.

Measuring the PDSA small-scale tests of change enables you to see what has worked and what hasn't. Often we learn more from so-called 'failures' than we do from easy successes. In quality improvement, we often think about failure as our 'First Attempt in Learning', as it informs our theory of change and often gives us better and more refined improvement ideas to test in the next improvement cycle.

This is particularly important when trying to adopt an intervention from another area, as it's likely that even if you try to replicate exactly the same number of implementation steps and the same methods as the original team, you may find that because your context, environment and culture will be different you 'fail' to replicate the exact outcomes. What you are likely to learn is how you need to adapt the work to make it fit for purpose in your environment. Bringing the data you generate back to the group for discussion and reflection will help to make sense of what's happening and is likely to generate fresh improvement ideas for the next PDSA cycle.

For example, one of the interventions the original PEACE team did was to work with the National Autistic Society to review their inpatient environment in order to make recommendations about how to make reasonable adjustments to the premises. Let's imagine that you wanted to replicate this, but you couldn't easily get access to this type of support because of cost or access due to your geographical location. It might mean that you have to think about another way of achieving the improvement aim of getting an external expert review of your services. Doing it differently isn't a failure; it's a key learning point for our collective understanding of how to implement this work in diverse settings. We'd encourage you to share your adaptations with us, so that we can understand what you needed to do to make these ideas thrive in your context, so we can learn and grow from your experience. Many adopters improve the intervention.

Sustainability

Once you have tested and refined the ideas from this book and found how to make them work in your own setting it's likely that you will have built a degree of local ownership of the intervention. Norton, Mochon & Ariely (2012) suggest that this process may well help with sustainability, as being involved in creating or making something generates positive feelings of efficacy, which in turn generate higher levels of attachment in the participants.

Whilst this is really helpful, deeply embedding new ideas into practice often also requires changes to structures and processes, such as care pathways, procedures or joint working arrangements, to ensure that the change is not overly reliant on a few key people and instead, becomes the cultural norm.

It can be helpful throughout this process to have a senior sponsor within the organization and to have been reporting your progress into some sort of governance structure. Some major changes will require organizational 'sign off'. This may well involve the construction of a business plan or the development of a new policy or quality standard. Having a senior person and people with operational experience in your improvement team can really help you think through what it will take from an organizational perspective to get things to 'stick' and become the 'way we work around here'. This could include factors such as staff induction, training, supervision, co-production processes, patient experience measures, data, time, money, changes to work plans, reflective practice and communication plans etc.

Continue to measure the work and share progress with others in simple visual formats and through the use of stories. These techniques can help reinforce the change and help it to become a part of the collective social narrative about the work that you do together. Share your work widely across the organization and join the online community of practice to contribute your ideas and to learn from others. Think about how you celebrate your success and help people to feel proud of what they have achieved, so that they feel inspired to continue to improve.

Conclusions

Putting evidence into practice is a challenging and complex process. Using a methodical quality improvement approach can help you organize your efforts, measure your success, help you learn from failure and achieve local organizational ownership for change. This can help you to adopt evidence gained from elsewhere and enable adaptation to fit your local context and organizational culture. The learning captured from this process can influence the process of wider adoption and spread and can be shared via social media with the PEACE community of practice in order to continuously improve services for autistic people with an eating disorder.

References

Albury, D., Beresford, T., Dew, S., Horton, T., Illingworth, J. & Langford, K. (2018) 'Against the odds: Successfully scaling innovation in the NHS.' London: Innovation Unit.

Alderwick, H., Charles, A., Jones, B. & Warburton, W. (2017) 'Making the case for quality improvement: Lessons for NHS boards and leaders.' The King's Fund. Accessed on 16/07/20 at www.kingsfund.org.uk/publications/making-case-quality-improvement.

Baker, A. (2001) 'Crossing the Quality Chasm: A New Health System for the 21st Century.' (Vol. 323, No. 7322, p. 1192). British Medical Journal Publishing Group.

Balas, E. & Boren, S. (2000) 'Managing Clinical Knowledge for Health Care Improvement.' In J.H. van Bemmel & A.T. McCray (eds), Yearbook of Medical Informatics. Stuttgart: Schattauer Verlagsgesellschaft mbH.

Batalden, P.B. & Davidoff, F. (2007) 'What is "quality improvement" and how can it transform healthcare?' BMJ Quality & Safety, 16, 2–3.

Bate, P., Robert, G., Fulop, N., Øvretveit, J. & Dixon-Woods, M. (2014) 'Perspectives on context: A selection of essays considering the role of context in successful quality improvement.' London: The Health Foundation. Accessed on 16/07/20 at www.health.org.uk/publication/perspectives-context.

Bauman, L.J., Stein, R.E. & Ireys, H.T. (1991) 'Reinventing fidelity: The transfer of social technology among settings.' American Journal of Community Psychology, 19, 619–639.

Committee on Quality Health Care in America, Institute of Medicine (2001) 'Crossing the quality chasm: A new health system for the 21st century.' Washington, D.C.: National Academy Press.

Deming, W.E. (1986) 'Out of the crisis.' Cambridge, MA: Massachusetts Institute of Technology Center for Advanced Engineering Study.

Deming, W.E. (2000) The New Economics for Industry, Government, and Education. Cambridge, MA: The MIT Press.

Feigenbaum, A.V. (1961) Total Quality Control. New York: McGraw-Hill.

Godfrey, J., Little, K.J., Cornwall, R., Carr, P. & Samora, J. (2017) 'Increasing brace treatment for distal radius buckle fractures: Using quality improvement methodology to implement evidence-based medicine: Level 4 evidence.' Journal of Hand Surgery, 42(9), S25.

Grant, J., Green, L. & Mason, B. (2003) 'Basic research and health: A reassessment of the scientific basis for the support of biomedical science.' Research Evalution, 12, 217–224.

Greenhalgh, T., Robert, G., Macfarlane, F., Bate, P. & Kyriakidou, O. (2004) 'Diffusion of innovations in service organizations: Systematic review and recommendations.' Milbank Quarterly, 82, 581–629.

Horton, T., Illingworth, J. & Warburton, W. (2018) 'The spread challenge: How to support the successful uptake of innovations and improvements in health care.' London: The Health Foundation.

Howarth, E., Devers, K., Moore, G., O'Cathain, A. & Dixon-Woods. M. (2016) 'Contextual issues and qualitative research.' In R. Raine, R. Fitzpatrick, H. Barratt, G. Bevan et al. 'Challenges, solutions and future directions in the evaluation of service innovations in health care and public health.' Health Services and Delivery Research, 4(16), 105–120.

Ishikawa, K. (1985) What Is Total Quality Control? The Japanese Way. Englewood Cliffs, NJ: Prentice-Hall.

Ishikawa, K. (1990) Introduction to Quality Control. London: Chapman & Hall.

Jones, B., Horton, T. & Warburton, W. (2019) The improvement journey. Why organisation-wide improvement in health care matters, and how to get started. London: The Health Foundation.

Juran, J. (1951) Quality Control Handbook. New York: McGraw-Hill.

Langley, G.J., Moen, R.D., Nolan, K.M., Nolan, T.W., Norman, C.L. & Provost, L.P. (2009) The Improvement Guide: A Practical Approach to Enhancing Organizational Performance (2nd edition). San Francisco, CA: Jossey-Bass.

Moore, G.A. (1991) Crossing the Chasm: Marketing and Selling Technology Products to Mainstream Customers. New York: HarperBusiness.

NHS Improvement (2016a) 'Developing People, Improving Care.' London: NHS Improvement.

NHS Improvement (2016b) 'Shared Commitment to Quality.' London: NHS Improvement.

NHS Improvement (2019) 'Quality, Service Improvement and Redesign Tools: Developing your aims statement.' Accessed on 22/11/19 at https://improvement.nhs.uk/documents/2189/developing-your-aims-statement.pdf.

Norton, M.I., Mochon, D. & Ariely, D. (2012) 'The IKEA effect: When labor leads to love.' *Journal of Consumer Psychology*, *22*(3), 453–460.

Rogers, E.M. (2010) *Diffusion of Innovations* (4th edition). New York: The Free Press.

Wratschko, K. (2009) 'Empirical Setting: The pharmaceutical industry.' Strategic Orientation and Alliance Portfolio Configuration. New York: Springer.

Chapter 19

Following the PEACE Pathway in Your Organization

TEAMWORK MAKES DREAM WORK

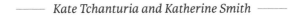

Kate Tchanturia and Katherine Smith

In this book we took you on a journey and shared our experience with you. It really takes a village to support autistic people to allow them to benefit from available treatments. The final chapter of this book presents our views on how to scale up the clinical pathway and we have developed support for health professionals to follow this.

You already heard from our coach Dr Anna Burhouse (in Chapter 18) and from the service lead Dannie Glennon (Chapter 17) on how to build a business case in your clinical service. Twenty people have written the chapters in this book and shared examples from our clinical practice but our team goes on beyond these 20. Below Katherine Smith and I highlight what we *did* to develop the PEACE clinical pathway. We told you about the PEACE acronym at the start of the book – this was chosen by our patients and the more we think about the name of the work we do to make adaptations for ASC and eating disorder clinical pathway, the more we like it. So, if you would like to follow us on the PEACE Pathway:

First of all you need a strong and enthusiastic team. Our thanks to all of you who are listed in the acknowledgements of this book and the funders who supported us.

Building your PEACE team

Building the team and giving clinicians ownership and confidence was one of the biggest challenges for us. In a busy NHS environment where we have lots of innovative projects on top of a busy clinical schedule, our healthcare professional colleagues had enthusiasm but very limited time. We learned some important lessons in how to keep interest, good will and patient care at the heart of the project during implementation:

Regular huddles/'snapshots'

- Having a regular forum to keep the conversation going was one of the key elements in the success of the PEACE Pathway. We implemented 15-minute huddles every week across all of our sites (our inpatient unit is geographically far away from our day care and outpatient site). These 15 minutes were dedicated to discussing the pathway: its adaptations and its patients. These huddles increased communication between the multidisciplinary team.

- We piloted various time slots until we found the best one for attendance and then locked it in. Timetabling it as a part of the teams' weekly calendar was an important strategy. Before choosing a time, it is important to be open-minded and flexible around busy clinical schedules.

- Make your huddle unique. There may already be multiple 'huddles' for various matters. Our inpatient wards had several different huddles a day and it was not standing out enough. We renamed it the PEACE 'Snapshot'. In the outpatient setting we continued to call it the PEACE huddle.

- We evaluated huddles very simply (asking attendees how helpful it was and what to improve). The best huddles were brief, so we made sure we stuck to the 15-minute allocation.

- Minute the meetings and share these widely to all the team (even if they can't attend or are not sharing enthusiasm at the beginning of the pathway development). Due to shift pattern or incidents, not everyone will be able to attend the huddles, but with the minutes in one place people can access them and catch up.

- Use this space in whatever way the attendees want. On one of our sites, the team likes to know what has been going on and to think together about what is needed. On another, the huddle is used more as a group supervision, with people bringing cases to the huddle that they want to think collectively about.

Sense of belonging and group membership

- Appoint champions/mini project leads. Not only does this spread the 'workload' but it imbeds the pathway into the structure already there, meaning it can carry on without external support or a project lead.

- A small, identifiable logo located on a lanyard goes a long way for both patients and the clinicians themselves. We have created badges! Simply handing these to people who were not regular members of our huddles shifted perception of the pathway and demonstrated its inclusivity. People were more inclined to come along and make time for the huddles, feeling that they were wanted and valued there, which they definitely were! We also had PEACE pens, bags and mugs which had similar effects.

- Hear everyone. If someone makes a suggestion or has an idea, follow it up! Different skill sets are needed in different aspects of care, and it may be something you know little about.

Skilling up PEACE team/Power of training

Autism spectrum diagnosis involves specialist training, and specialist assessment and treatment adaptation knowledge. You will know if you have worked on an eating disorder clinical service that there are many training sessions organized which are eating disorder specific. In reality, when we work in busy clinical settings it is hard to keep up with 'what works for whom'. Our clinicians in NHS contexts are often guided by National Institute of Health and Care Excellence (NICE) guidelines, but we all know how beneficial it can be to be skilled up by relevant experts with clinical experience and wisdom. With a high rate of co-morbidity, we benefited hugely from the knowledge and insight of such professionals in the ASC field who helped to skill up our team with knowledge and insight about how we can recognize and support our patients with ASC and eating disorders and allow them to flourish.

We implemented monthly training sessions as part of our PEACE Pathway to skill up all of our health professional multidisciplinary team. These sessions are run by expert clinicians in the autism field of mental health. Although their patients do not necessarily have eating disorders, they have valuable insight into what adaptations can be helpful with autistic people undergoing treatment. Our team was able to learn from these sessions and apply adaptations, combining them with their specialist eating disorder knowledge.

Based on regular feedback from our clinicians, three 'groups' of training have been found to be particularly useful:

Assessment of ASC

This training group was made up of two training blocks. The first we had was for the Autism Diagnostic Observation Schedule, Second Edition (ADOS-2) training. This was followed by Autism Diagnostic Interview (ADI) training. Although most clinicians do not carry out these comprehensive assessments on patients, they reported the training was extremely useful. This was due to being able to recognize what attributes an autistic person may have, understanding how you might best approach patients with potential diagnosis and interpreting reports from the assessors. Another important gain was that clinicians were made more aware of the camouflaging of autism, often seen in women; these assessments gave insight on how to elicit these traits in conversation, and the kind of questions it may be essential to ask to understand the individual. Several clinicians reported after the training that they became more sensitive to ASC features and more confident on how to calibrate sessions with people who might have ASC or display similar traits. Although this training block was focused on formal assessments, these training sessions provided a good reflective space for our eating disorder team to think together about this co-morbidity and how we can support people in their recovery journey.

Treatment adaptations

This training group was made up of ASC clinicians giving insight and sharing their experience into various adaptations which they find helpful. These sessions covered adaptations for cognitive behavioural therapy, Dialectic Behavioural Therapy, cognitive remediation therapy, cognitive remediation and emotion skills training, Formulation and Occupational Therapy approaches for autistic people. In each session, the training clinician would talk about various adaptations which they have found useful. They would then present a few case studies. Our clinicians were then asked to bring vignettes of their cases to be thought about together in that context. Our treatment adaptation training block led to important innovation in the team. Once a month, each of our 'sites' has an extended case presentation and discussion based on a patient's formulation and feedback from the multidisciplinary team. Together we discuss strategies they are using with the patient and this communication helps to give the patient a very consistent, clear message. We have noticed in general that the PEACE Pathway has improved clinical care and communication for *all* patients, not just those who were included in the PEACE Pathway.

PEACE training

This last group of training was to keep clinicians aware of PEACE-specific adaptations. This included what we had introduced as a Pathway so far, what new materials were being rolled out, any new findings from the Pathway, new developments from different areas, e.g. carer's pathway, psychological therapies, dieticians, occupational therapy. These training sessions gave all clinicians of all disciplines a chance to understand how autism was being addressed throughout our service and to allow feedback and collaboration from other clinicians.

Implementing the pathway with your PEACE team's support

From our experience developing the PEACE Pathway, team development is an absolute priority and once we had that collaborative space, we started to make more changes.

Research evidence and experimental work in our department, combined with extensive qualitative interviews and focus groups, gave us important ideas on how to make the treatment environment more friendly for PEACE patients and other patients in our service. We also consulted National Autistic Society experts about changes in the dining room and shared spaces in the inpatient unit. These changes were implemented due to adapting for sensory sensitivities, which can be heightened in busy, anxiety-provoking situations such as a dining room.

What we did to the environment

- Key caps: A quick, easy win was to bulk buy some key covers. These silence the jingling of keys you so often hear in hospital corridors. This noise can be extremely uncomfortable for people with high sensitivity to noises. Small changes make a big difference for people with noise sensitivity. We borrowed this idea from National Autism Unit in our hospital. Which leads to an additional learning point for environmental change – collaborate with your local ASC experts to get more ideas for innovative changes in your clinical settings.

- Muted colouring: We changed the colour scheme of our ward from bright, harsh colours like red to more muted neutral colours like pastels. This was bound to cause controversy in the patient group as not everyone would want neutral colours. We got everyone on board by choosing several colours which would match this neutral scheme and then having all current patients vote for their preference. Once we had reached a consensus, everyone had been heard. Our next job was to then find a date for the redecorating which suited the ward timetable best. We found that doing work over the weekend (if possible) was preferred for our ward environment. Many patients were on home leave which meant that meals were not as disrupted. We had attended

talks from architects and familiarized ourselves with new ideas about mental health and architecture. Thinking big and speaking to experts outside of mental health professionals created a collaborative and constructive approach, allowing small but significant changes to be made, improving the quality of hospital stay and therapeutic engagement.

- 'Going easy on the wall': We had a lot of posters and signs on our walls. These were reduced until only essentials were on display, calming the walls down and making them much less overwhelming. The changes we made to all our clinical settings were based on the principal 'less is more'. Again, we found not only patients on the PEACE Pathway benefited, everyone found it calming.

- Declutter: It is amazing how much stuff you gather over time that no one uses (or even knows what it is!). We decluttered the dining room, the lounges of our ward and the waiting room in outpatients. Before, all surfaces were covered in objects, causing the environment to look cluttered and overwhelming to some people. This was all cleared.

- Addressing sensory sensitivities: We identified 'quiet(er)' session rooms on our clinical sites. These are where clinicians would ideally like to take people who have sensitivity to noises. We also identified rooms which were furthest away from 'smells' such as the kitchen and the laundry room. We put laminated cards on the desks in all treatment rooms to remind clinicians to ask about people's sensory needs as well as to encourage patients to come forward with them.

Changes we made to common procedures
Menu
We implemented a new 'PEACE' menu which is discussed in more detail in Chapter 10 and on our website www.peacepathway.org. This menu was created by Kate Williams and colleagues, an eating disorder dietician who consulted with many ASC sources to develop a new, autism-friendly menu. This enabled us to have a menu adapted to

patients with sensory difficulties, as well as being nutritionally sufficient for patients in the weight gain period. Our intention was for the patient either to be flagged up as a potential referral during the initial sensory profiling during admission or for the patient and dietician to discuss it together and have it included on their care plan. Of course, this menu does not suit all autistic people; some would prefer stronger flavours. This group, we would expect, would choose from the standard menu, which is available to all patients. We made the PEACE menu available to all patients also, but with those who had not had it 'care planned' with a dietician only being able to choose from it three times a week.

Simple food

When we were ready to launch our autism-friendly menu, there was lots of anxiety from the patients. This was due to the uncertainty of the new menu and there being more choice for the patients. Unfortunately, we attempted to launch it in a turn-over time between two dieticians, which did not allow patients to ask the questions they needed answers to. The launch was delayed, and we would recommend anyone implementing this to have the dietician firmly on-board with the pathway and to warn patients ahead of time to avoid anxieties. We then had a focus group with the patients to discuss the concerns with the new menu and answered all of their questions. With regular feedback from the patients, and creative input from our nursing team, we added photos onto one version of the PEACE menu for patients to use on request. This is to allow familiarity and increase predictability around meal times for patients who may be highly anxious around food.

Assessment

In our initial assessments of patients, autism spectrum condition was rarely considered unless a patient was coming to us with a diagnosis. Now, autistic traits are considered throughout the assessment procedure with clinicians, having attended ADOS-2 training, asking specific questions which may reveal autistic traits such as 'What makes you happy?' and 'How do you *feel* when you are happy?' Patients are now often flagged up during assessment, before admission. This allows clinicians plenty of time to think about how they can offer individualized support and to talk about the PEACE Pathway with the patient and family if appropriate. Details of the assessment process are discussed in Chapter 16.

Admission welcome pack adaptation

An admission pack was developed to create a more autism-friendly version. This included all essential information in a 'We can... You can...' way. For example, talking about meal times: 'We can offer support materials such as XYZ; we can try our best to get the meals to you on time', 'You can make sure your meal request sheet is in early; you can bring items which you may need into the dining room with you'.

Adaptations were informed by ASC research and focus groups with our patients. As with many other changes, we found that all patients, whether they had ASC features or not, were positive about this change.

Staff welcome pack

New staff will not have been able to attend the training sessions. We also use bank staff and we felt clear induction was needed for the PEACE Pathway. We have included psychoeducation of the co-morbidity into our staff welcome pack and our bank staff welcome pack. We also invite staff to the huddles and include snapshots in the welcome pack to learn more.

So, now your staff are trained, your environment is 'autism-friendly', your materials have been developed, what's next?

Supporting the patient: Stages of patient identification and individualized care

Table 19.1. Pathway for PEACE patient

Presentation & referral	Assessments of baseline needs	Treatment commences & needs shared with team	Needs reassessed
There are several ways potential autism co-morbidity can be identified: 1. Evidence of traits early on in treatment or in assessment, leading to clinician recognition 2. Carer or patient suspicion 3. Scores of 6+ on AQ10 4. Previous autism diagnosis Once someone has been identified by one of the previous options, they will most likely undergo an ADOS-2 assessment by one of our experienced researchers or clinicians. A report is made and shared with the working clinicians and the patient.	Baseline needs are assessed using several tools: 1. Assessment with psychologist 2. Sensory sensitivity questionnaire completed 3. Assessment with dietician (if applicable) 4. Assessment with OT (if applicable)	This is made up of two phases: 1. Adaptations and considerations are applied to treatment, based on assessment notes 2. These assessment notes, adaptations and considerations are shared with the team in the form of a case study (normally as close to the start of treatment as possible). This ensures everyone is aware of the needs and how to appropriately address the individual's needs. Discussion generated here is often looking at creative adaptations the team can use.	Needs and adaptation appropriateness will continuously be assessed with the patient. Updated information of any change will be shared and discussed in the weekly huddles. If significant changes are made, then the case study is re-evaluated and presented again to the whole team.

Presentation and referral

We will not go into too much detail on this step as implementation of regular screening and assessments is explained in Chapter 18. One important addition to this is how accurate clinician instinct has been in identification, especially in comparison with screener assessments.

Assessment considerations

Now you have identified the patient as having ASC features, they must then be assessed in this context. This can be done with any of the clinicians working with the patient. In this assessment, clinicians should identify several things:

1. First things first: **Does the patient have any sensory needs that need to be met?** E.g. would they prefer the harsh lighting be turned off? This should be the first thing asked when walking into a treatment room. This simple act can instantly demonstrate to the patient that you are interested in supporting their individual needs related to their sensory sensitivity, something which may never have been supported before. Acts like these are essential at building rapport as it allows the patient to feel heard. Although it may not feel possible to have the lights off at 4pm on a January afternoon in the dark, we may be able to be more flexible with our session times, for example, allowing for these adaptations to be possible (refer to Chapter 14 for more details).

2. **What treatment has the patient had before?** What have they **benefited** from and what have they **not liked?** These questions may be able to be answered by reading assessment notes and looking at discharge reports, but it is again so important to explore with the patient and reflect on the things which might change immediately. Someone else's summary of their experience may be completely different to what they experienced. It could be particularly beneficial to adopt (to the best of your ability) a particular style a favoured clinician used. In this book, Chapter 3 gives excellent examples of how personal experience of therapy can change with small adaptations (e.g. Pooky mentions a clock in the room distracting her engagement with the therapist).

3. **How does the patient like to communicate?** Some patients enjoy visuals and handouts, some don't. Exploring at the initial meeting and working with what person says about preferred communication style can be very supportive. In Chapter 15, a therapist with experience of working with people having both eating disorders and ASC gives useful examples.

4. **What can you do as the other person in the room?** It is not unusual for autistic people to find social interactions challenging, especially if there are having a few in a row (e.g. various medical appointments). Asking the person what you can do for them, be

it putting your chairs side by side so that attempting to maintain eye contact does not cause them added anxiety and cognitive demand, or changing the lighting or the volume of your voice. Milly, described in Chapter 5, was not communicating how we could help her. The first time she was able to stay in a session with us was when we had with her followed the adaptations listed above.

Application of each modality
Psychological therapies
What is offered to the patient will depend on what they are looking to get out of treatment. Below are some suggestions based on what the answer to that question may be.

TO BE MORE FLEXIBLE/TO BE ABLE TO USE BIGGER PICTURE THINKING
Our research has shown cognitive remediation therapy (CRT) to be beneficial to people with both an eating disorder and autism spectrum condition. Often, at critical stages of weight loss, brains are malnourished and engaging in therapy can be difficult. CRT aims to engage patients in simple cognitive exercises to help explore thinking strategies and reflect on them and also practise alternative strategies and think about the thinking process more than content. From our clinical audit evaluation and patients' feedback, we know that CRT in an individual format produces significant improvements in cognitive tests in eating disorder patients with or without ASC. In Japan our colleagues conducted a study formally assessing CRT in autistic people with promising results (Okuda et al., 2017).

TO BETTER UNDERSTAND EMOTIONS
Cognitive remediation and emotion skills training (CREST) has been found to help patients with the co-morbidity. In this psychoeducation module with experiential exercises, we try to give patients updates from the research evidence, to talk about key areas of communication and give some skills for positive communications.

From our experience working on the PEACE Pathway, we found that all remedial approaches, CRT and CREST in individual or group formats are positively evaluated by patients. However, significant changes are more evident from individual formats of CRT and CREST. In the resources on our website (www.peacepathway.org) we list the research work evidencing these findings. More work is needed to learn how we can maximize therapeutic benefits for patients with both conditions and this work is in progress.

We also introduced a sensory wellbeing workshop which was received well (outlined in Chapter 12).

Occupational therapies

Sensory sensitivities can be a very useful area of focus for work with occupational therapists. (Please see Chapter 12 for recognizing and supporting specific sensory sensitivities, other ideas for occupational therapy work can be found in Chapter 13).

We very much hope to continue to develop the above information about how to follow the PEACE Pathway. We still are in the process of discoveries with our patients and we are learning a lot about how to support people in their recovery journeys from eating disorders when they are on the autistic spectrum.

Being aware of neurodiversity is the key and improving communication between therapist, patient and family gives us hope that treatment outcomes can be improved.

We would like to share example of specific changes in our inpatients clinical treatment programme. We continue our work and hopefully we will have more to share in few years' time, but for now, as one of my big heroes in psychotherapy Virginia Satir said, 'We have now come to the end of the adventure… If it stimulated you to find new possibilities and provided you with new ideas and information, you can now continue on your own special journey' (1978).

References and further reading

Adamson, J., Leppanen, J., Murin, M. & Tchanturia, K. (2018) 'Effectiveness of emotional skills training for patients with anorexia nervosa with autistic symptoms, group or individual format.' *European Eating Disorder Review, 26*(4), 367–375.

Dandil, Y., Baillie, C. & Tchanturia, K. (2019) 'Cognitive Remediation Therapy as a feasible treatment for a young person with anorexia nervosa and autism spectrum disorder co-morbidity: A case study.' *Clinical Case Studies,* doi.org/10.1177/1534650119890425.

Dandil, Y., Smith, K., Adamson, J. & Tchanturia, K. (2020) 'Individual Cognitive Remediation Therapy benefits for patients with anorexia nervosa and high autistic features.' *European Eating Disorder Review, 28*(1), 87–91.

Kinnaird, E., Norton, C., Pimblett, C., Stewart, C. & Tchanturia, K. (2019) 'Eating as an autistic adult: An exploratory qualitative study.' *PlosOne, 29, 14*(8), e0221937.

Okuda, T., Asano, K., Numata, N., Hirano, Y. *et al.* (2017) 'Feasibility of cognitive remediation therapy for adults with autism spectrum disorders: A single-group pilot study.' *Neuropsychiatric Disease and Treatment, 13,* 2185.

Satir, V. (1978) *Your Many Faces.* Berkley, CA: Celestial Arts.

Tchanturia, K., Larsson, E. & Adamson, J. (2016) 'How anorexia nervosa patients with high and low autistic traits respond to group Cognitive Remediation Therapy.' *BMC Psychiatry,* doi: 10.1186/s12888-016-1044-x.

Tchanturia, K., Larsson, E., Adamson, J. & Westwood, H. (2019) 'Autistic traits in anorexia nervosa: A naturalistic study in an inpatient treatment programme.' *Autism, 23*(1), 123–130.

Chapter 20

Example of Becoming a More ASD-Friendly Inpatient Ward on the PEACE Pathway

—— Pulled together by Claire Baillie ——

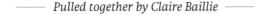

This is a snapshot of what we have done as part of the PEACE Pathway in the inpatient treatment programme. We wanted to translate learning/training and research evidence into practical adaptations which would be of benefit to patients with eating disorder and autism spectrum co-morbidity as well as the wider patient group without ASC.

Anxiety is a significant feature for those diagnosed with ASD and has been linked with atypical sensory function, difficulty identifying and labelling emotions and intolerance of uncertainty (these aspects were discussed in earlier chapters, e.g. Chapter 2 on social anxiety and Chapters 12 and 13 on sensory sensitivies). We have observed that change and flexibility can be particularly anxiety-provoking for people diagnosed with ASC, especially since they may struggle with the emotional regulation skills to manage the anxiety. This means it can be particularly difficult for patients to manage in a busy inpatient environment where the focus is on challenging symptoms and engaging in a process of change. As part of the teaching under the PEACE Pathway we learned how patients with ASD experience sensory hypo- and hypersensitivities which are likely to generate additional anxiety therefore adaptations are required to ameliorate this (Chapters 12 and 13). We learned about the particular challenges and strengths for people living with autistic spectrum condition; this highlighted the importance of ensuring communication is clear and concrete, with visual images to help make information understandable, simple and memorable. We also learned from ASD professionals and organizations that everyone with a diagnosis of ASD is unique, therefore assumptions cannot be made about individual needs and thought has to be given to individualizing care.

Although the work was carried out under the PEACE Pathway, it was important to explore how the adaptations would benefit *all* patients, therefore we considered overlaps in the difficulties of patients with and without the diagnosis of ASD. We know rigidity in thinking styles and a tendency to be detail-focused is associated with anorexia (for more details, see Chapter 1 in this book); we also know that patients with anorexia nervosa experience difficulties around emotions and lack emotional regulation skills (this is also discussed in Chapter 1 and Chapter 21). There are potential further overlaps in the social challenges experienced by both groups of patients; individuals with ASD can expend significant personal resources attempting to mask their inability to interact spontaneously and may use rehearsed internal scripts to navigate interactions. We know individuals with anorexia also experience interpersonal difficulties and report a lot of social anxieties. There are some obvious overlaps in the challenges of all patients regardless of whether they have a formal diagnosis of ASD. For these reasons we had confidence that any adaptations made to improve outcomes for patients with ASD would also benefit the wider patient group.

As stated, feedback from a National Autistic Society visit highlighted the need to avoid a 'one size fits all' approach and to consider creating communication tools/passports with individual patients to avoid them having to re-explain their needs to new people arriving in the ward. It was also felt that our handout for new/agency staff on how to interact in the dining room lacked gravitas since it was named 'handy tips' and could be misinterpreted to suggest social interaction at meals was always helpful. In summary, in this part of the project we considered how to adapt the environment; how to provide clear written information about dining room strategies at the start of admissions; and how to develop guidelines and strategies for managing social conversations on the ward. Within this we hoped to further individualize care by offering tools which aimed to find out what individuals had already discovered which works for them and offer additional ideas to try. As our eating disorder national service is large and very diverse, I will focus on the work we did in the inpatient department.

Environmental adaptations

At the beginning of the work on the PEACE Pathway project, we enlisted the expertise of the National Autistic Society (NAS) to evaluate our environment. We received feedback following the visit with an environmental recommendation which was to redecorate the dining room to make it a more calm, relaxing and pleasant place to eat. The yellow paint was deemed too over-stimulating and there was too much clutter in the room in terms of unnecessary furniture and visual busyness on the walls. Specific feedback was that people with diagnoses of ASD experience less stress in environments where everything has a place and purpose. With the support of senior management we were able to redecorate the dining room (Figure 20.1).

The team identified the key items of furniture required for meal delivery and the dining experience, then arranged for all unnecessary items to be removed. Decisions about paint choices and window blinds were made in consultation with the patients who were on the ward at the time. Paint charts were shown to all patients, who were asked to indicate their preference of colour for the dining room; interestingly, most chose pale neutral colours, which is the recommendation for ASD-friendly environments. The one patient on the ward at the time who had a pre-existing diagnosis of ASD also chose a neutral colour, which was the one selected. Soft furnishings were then chosen to match this neutral colour scheme.

Redecoration work was planned to take place at the weekend when some patients would be on home leave to minimize disruption. We also initiated discussions in the weekly community group to acknowledge the anxiety provoked by eating in a different room (communal lounge) while work took place.

Initial feedback on the changes from the patients was negative: they thought the dining room looked sparse and bare; they missed the images to look at on the walls and stated it made eating harder as there were fewer distractions. We have not received this feedback from subsequent patients, which suggests the initial reaction may have been more about the discomfort of change rather than comments on the actual changes made.

Figure 20.1. *The dining room (left) before and (right) after redecoration*

Welcome pack: Self-help

In the development of written materials we aimed to provide clear written information and signposting to inform patients about strategies they could try to manage difficult situations around meal times and ensure they felt welcome to use resources provided on the ward. Time was spent considering how to translate theory and learning into changes in practice and in particular how we communicated with new patients to ensure they understood the options available to them and how to go about negotiating the types of care they received. As a starting point a draft document was created containing ideas for self-help strategies which could be used in the dining room to manage the various challenges patients faced. This was designed to be included in the patient welcome pack provided on admission and included:

- stickers to indicate whether they wanted to talk during meal times or not

- invitation to take items from the fidget box

- invitation to use conversation starters provided on tables

- suggestion of creating a motivational placemat

- encouragement to use a 'how you can help me' card to have in the dining room to indicate what helps and does not during meal times, especially with less familiar staff

- invitation to use a visualization technique to leave worries in a 'squishie' (originally this was going to be white stones but the Trust risk assessment meant this was not possible so we sourced soft squishy figures as an alternative)

- invitation to discuss with nursing team other strategies which help as these may need to be care planned.

This draft was shared with the patient group in an initial focus group and changes were made based on the feedback, which was: visually a wheel and spoke design (rather than the original boxes) would look better for the first page summarizing the suggested strategies and be more inviting; they suggested information on the first page should be summarized further and more detailed information given on separate handouts; some patients were also keen for the handouts to state that all suggested strategies were optional. Patients understandably did not like the idea of wearing a sticker or badge to indicate if they wanted to talk, which felt too public; they suggested cards which they could more discreetly use to express their preference at a particular meal. Some patients felt the focus was too much on accommodating the needs of patients with ASD – this may have been impacted by the focus group taking place the week after the dining room had been redecorated, unnecessary clutter had been removed and wall decorations simplified in line with recommendations for ASD-friendly environments. We were able to respond to this by highlighting that we hoped the adaptations would benefit all patients and we were also working on pathways for other diagnoses (diabetes and personality disorders). Patients at the time expressed that they missed having distractions on the wall to look at during meals, but subsequent patient groups have not expressed this concern about the dining room environment. This suggests the initial resistance was more related to difficulties with change in the room in which the most important part of treatment takes place and perhaps a feeling of being neglected when other patients' needs are being addressed.

Three months later a further focus group was held to review both the suggested strategies and the handouts/written descriptions for the patient welcome pack. This time the feedback was that it was nice to have the handouts included in the welcome packs; however, newer patients had not known where to access resources, were uncertain who to ask and had not realized they could use the worksheets included in the pack. They suggested more specific signposting and invitations (e.g. 'Feel free to use these worksheets, you will find more copies outside the dining room'; 'You can ask the therapy enablers to support you to complete a "how you can help me card"'. Feedback was that the items in the fidget box were being used and patients requested that we restock this, which we did. As well as having the idea of creating a motivational placemat, patients felt it would be helpful to have a specific handout giving ideas about what might be included on one including a statement that they might want to update and/or change theirs during an admission. Feedback on the 'squishies' was that they appeared sticky and dusty and therefore were not inviting or attractive; worry dolls were suggested as an alternative. Again patients felt there was too much information on the initial page and it would be better to simplify and keep details for the individual handouts. Patients also highlighted that they may feel self-conscious if the resources were kept in the dining room, and it might feel difficult to leave their seat during a meal to collect them; they might be challenged by staff for this or be observed by other patients. Patients sensibly suggested we could store all the materials on a shelf in the corridor which leads to the dining room (Figure 20.2).

Figure 20.2. *The feedback was utilized to update the welcome booklet of dining room self-help handouts and to create a shelf of self-help materials outside the dining room*

Supporting healthy communication: Keeping conversations on the ward helpful

As a team we observed repeated feedback from patients that unhelpful conversations were taking place amongst peers on the ward. We know individuals with ASD may struggle to navigate ordinary social interactions and in general the patient group on the ward tend to report social anxieties and difficulty being appropriately assertive. We also identified that the wider patient group, due to factors like malnutrition, preoccupation with food/weight and shape concerns and/or competitive elements of anorexia, can also struggle to engage in helpful conversations. For example, in spite of being given specific feedback from staff on more than one occasion, a minority of patients (without ASD diagnosis) persisted in starting unhelpful conversations and seemed unaware they were doing this. We considered all of these issues through the lens of the PEACE Pathway and it seemed robust guidance would be needed to adequately address the difficulty and empower the patient group sufficiently. This included considering how direct and clear guidance had to be since the normal subtle social clues may not be picked up on by someone with ASD and/or someone who is malnourished, preoccupied and anxious. It was important that the thinking was done in collaboration with the patient group so we could specify the particular conversations they found helpful/unhelpful, while addressing their specific concerns and needs. We also wanted to create a sense of a shared problem and foster engagement from the patient group rather than having guidelines imposed on them by the staff team. Finally, we had to consider how to support and empower patients to end conversations in socially acceptable ways when they found them unhelpful.

The written information was produced via a process of first issuing a questionnaire for patients to complete anonymously which asked the following questions:

- What kinds of conversations do you find helpful with your peers?

- What topics do you think are okay to discuss amongst patients?

- What kinds of conversations do you find unhelpful amongst your peers?

- What topics do you think are not okay to discuss amongst patients?

- If you accidentally started a conversation about an unhelpful topic, how would you prefer your peers tell you this?

- What support or strategies do you think you would need in order to feel comfortable letting a fellow patient know that what they were saying was unhelpful?

- What rules or guidelines do you think we should have on the ward to keep conversations helpful?

Patients were given the questionnaires in the weekly community group with an explanation about why we were seeking their opinions. Reminders were given over a few weeks and a deadline set. We received five responses from a patient group of 14 over a period of a month, which are summarized in Table 20.1. Following this we held two focus groups, one to produce guidelines and one to explore how assertiveness techniques could be used to end unhelpful conversations.

Table 20.1. Keeping ward conversations helpful
(Based on 5 responses received between October and November 2019, from a patient group of 14)

What kinds of conversations do you find helpful with your peers?
General and normal – about lives, interests, what we have done in the past Recent news headlines Treat conversations like we do not have an eating disorder Unforced/natural The arts; books, films; nature (beauty in the grounds); the world beyond the ward; philosophy New things you have learned about Hobbies and interests Art, literature, film, interesting articles, news items Things which connect with reality and the outer world Finding out about each other – family, friends, memories, interests, likes and dislikes outside the illness

What topics do you think are okay to discuss amongst patients?

Hobbies, events, sports, news and family
Discuss what you are struggling with, with peers or staff
General talk about food, e.g. asking what someone is eating or if it is nice
Normal everyday conversations, e.g. family, holidays, interests
Food is okay to talk about if it is in a healthy way – part of a wider discussion
What people are doing in OT
Current affairs
Arts/creativity
What motivates people outside, what makes people tick
Sharing suggestions of walks for leave or recommending films/TV
Most things as long as it does not stray into obsessive eating disordered thoughts
How we are feeling generally, how has your day been? What have you been up to?

What kinds of conversations do you find unhelpful amongst your peers?

Body shape/image and weight
Food and portions
Talking about coping mechanisms
Talking about individual specific meal plans
Discussing weight/size
Asking personal questions about people's ED/behaviours
Telling others it is their fault they are unwell
Comparing food and behaviours
Telling others to eat
Bringing shame or attention to struggles
Commenting on others' weight
Abuse/self-harm/suicide
It is the staff job to talk through meal plans, emotional regulation etc.
Wonderful to encourage others by talking to the individual person not the ED
Honesty and genuineness is important but not too much detail – save this for staff
Conversations around ward rounds, what leave/passes we have
Meal plans, comparing meals and amounts
Comments about the food you are eating
Comparing past hospital experiences/admissions/treatment

What topics do you think are not okay to discuss amongst patients?

BMIs/weight
Meal plans (yours or others)
Exercise and how to get away with it
Discussing other patients
Physiological changes, e.g. talking about metabolism in rest periods
Medication side effects, e.g. weight gain – discuss in private
Obsessive conversations around food – something beyond normal chit chat
Body shape/image and weight
Food and portions
Talking about coping mechanisms
Medication

If you accidentally started a conversation about an unhelpful topic, how would you prefer your peers tell you this?
They should just gently change the topic of conversation or offer monosyllabic replies so it gets hard to continue
Perhaps gentler and kinder if staff talk to them 1:1 if it was found to be a continuous issue
Just tell me straight out and ask me to discuss it in a more appropriate place/with a more appropriate person
If I can't walk away I say to the person that I don't think the conversation is healthy and the other person may have to talk to staff – if it doesn't cease, ask staff to intervene
To verbally voice this, talk to me outside of the dining room/congregation area or use hand gestures

What support or strategies do you think you would need in order to feel comfortable letting a fellow patient know that what they were saying was unhelpful?
If we all know just to tell each other straight out then it should not be an issue as we all know that sometimes people might want you to stop your conversation (it won't be a shock or meant in a rude way)
Sometimes staff, including consultants, bring up unhelpful topics (even including starvation). Staff (including bank) need a basic understanding of healthy discussions in or out of eating disorder unit
To feel able to have the back-up of staff in a subtle way is positive. Not bringing attention, talking to patient aside later on
Patients being aware of boundaries around what it okay and not okay to talk about
Having a list of unhelpful talking points to refer to would instill more confidence in one's ability to stop, change or challenge unhelpful conversations
If conversations happen in the dining room, subtly alert staff and to receive an intervention/support from them
Maybe letting a staff member know after the meal/event

What rules or guidelines do you think we should have on the ward to keep conversations helpful?
We should come up with them together as a community, every patient should receive a copy, include in welcome packs for new patients
They should be displayed somewhere on the ward, perhaps on a notice board or the dining room
Have others in mind before making comments and to support peers at the appropriate times
Ask yourself if the comment would offend anyone before voicing or not voicing it
Keep conversations away from others, e.g. in bedrooms not corridors so others don't get upset or feel uncomfortable
No conversations about any personal information/behaviours relating to eating disorder

These responses were used as the basis for the first focus group centred on establishing definitions/descriptions of helpful and unhelpful conversations with the aim of producing some general guidelines for the ward. We had eight attendees from a patient group of 14. See Table 20.2 for a summary of the ideas generated from the discussions.

Table 20.2. Defining conversations

Helpful	Unhelpful
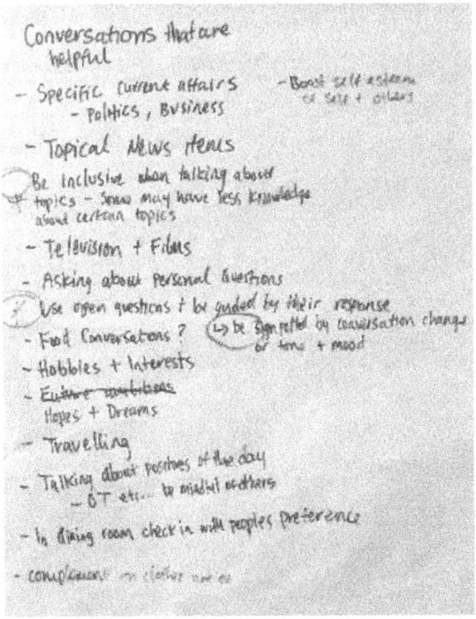 *(handwritten notes)*	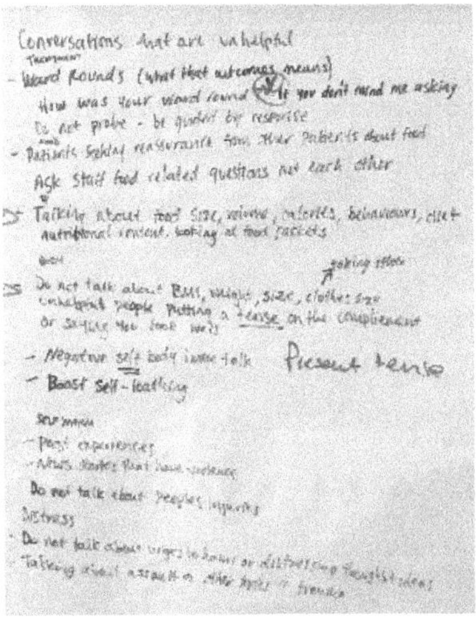 *(handwritten notes)*
Specific current affairs – politics, business	Treatment
Topical news items	Ward rounds – what the outcome means; how was your ward round?
Being inclusive when talking about topics – some may have less knowledge about certain topics	Patients asking for reassurance from other patients about food
Television and films	Talking about food (size; volume; calories; behaviours; diets; nutritional content; looking at food packets)
Using open questions and being guided by responses – be signposted by conversation changes or tone and mood	Talking about BMI; weight; size; clothes sizes
Hobbies and interests	Negative self/body image talk
Hopes and dreams	Conversations which boost self-loathing
Travelling	Self-harm – past experiences; news stories which have violence; asking about injuries
Talking about positives of the day, e.g. occupational therapy	Talking about urges to harm self or distressing thoughts and ideas
In dining room – check people's preferences for conversations	Talking about assaults or other types of trauma
Compliments on clothing are okay, e.g. I like your top, is it new?	

In order to avoid complicated over-detailed lists, which would be too difficult to remember, staff set a limit of five guidelines and explored in the focus group what the priorities would be. Patients and staff felt it would be useful to balance a list of what not to do with ideas about what would be appropriate/positive conversations so we generated a list of both 'Don'ts' and 'Dos'. From discussions we established five themes to be covered in the guidelines about conversations to avoid: food; bodies;

treatment; emotionally distressing subjects; and self-harm. The process was completed by collaborating on establishing a written guideline for each of these themes. The patients felt these guidelines should be provided in the welcome pack for new patients and displayed on the walls of the unit to remind everyone (see www.peacepathway.org).

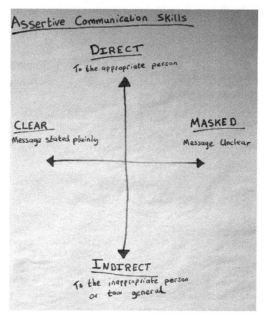

Figure 20.3. *Explanation of communication styles from our focus group*

The second focus group, held a week later, explored how to stop unhelpful conversations and had four attendees out of the patient group of 14. This may indicate the overall patient group's struggles with interpersonal conflict and assertiveness since they knew the topic of the focus group and may have avoided it. The focus group first provided psychoeducation on assertive communication by exploring the differences between aggressive, passive and assertive styles (Figure 20.3). We then highlighted the importance of being clear and direct in order for communication to be more effective. Finally we offered 'I messages' as a structure for scripting an assertive statement. 'I messages' include stating what has happened, how you felt about it, some information about why it had that impact and a request for something different in future (see www.peacepathway.org) (Figure 20.4).

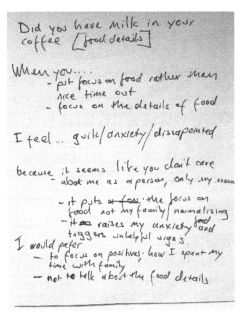

Figure 20.4. *Example of 'I messages' from our focus group*

Following this we generated a list of specific examples of common unhelpful comments the patients had experienced. Patients were supported to identify how they could use the assertiveness skills of being clear and direct via 'I messages' to let others know the conversation was not helpful. This resulted in three varied examples of difficult statements others may say and examples of how to respond to these (see www.peacepathway.org).

Future plans

The plan is to keep these documents live by reviewing and refining them every three months via the use of regular focus groups which will allow input over time from a changing patient group. There are ideas, inspired by the National Autistic Society conference materials, to develop the work further, for example by providing a visual introduction to the ward environment using photos to show the route from the hospital entrance to the ward, as well as the interior of the ward. This will be with the aim of reducing anxiety-provoking surprises or uncertainties, to make arriving on the ward a more predictable and less overwhelming experience.

List of Contributors (in order of appearance in the book)

Prof Kate Tchanturia, PhD, DClin, FAED, FBPS, FHEA

Professor Kate Tchanturia is the lead clinical psychologist for the National Eating Disorder Service at the South London and Maudsley NHS Foundation Trust and Professor in the psychology of eating disorders at King's College London. She is a recipient of Royal Society, the Wellcome Trust, NHS innovation, BRC, Swiss Anorexia Foundation, MRC, Autistica, Maudsley Charity, Psychiatry Research charity and the Health Foundation awards. She has lectured internationally and trained clinicians and researchers in the UK, USA, Europe, South America, New Zealand and Australia in the neuropsychology of eating disorders and how to translate it into remedial approaches. She has published several clinical manuals available in different languages, and more than 200 scientific papers. For more information visit websites: https://kclpure. kcl.ac.uk/portal/kate.tchanturia.html; www.katetchanturia.com.

This book is based on the work Kate is leading called PEACE (Pathway for Eating disorders and Autism developed from Clinical Experience) project funded from the Health Foundation, an independent charity committed to bring better healthcare for people in the UK (Ref:AIMS ID): 1115447 and the Maudsley Charity funding.

Jess Kerr-Gaffney, MA, MSc

Jess is a PhD student at the Institute of Psychiatry, Psychology and Neuroscience, King's College London. Her PhD focuses on social cognition in individuals with anorexia nervosa, and she is particularly interested in the impact of autistic traits on social perceptual abilities. She joined Prof Kate Tchanturia's research group in 2017 from ESRC PhD scholarship.

Dr Pooky Knightsmith, PhD is an expert by experience

Pooky has developed and delivered a range of mental health trainings to over 10,000 students, parents and staff in more than 100 organizations across the UK. Pooky is a member of advisory groups, including Department for Education, Department for Health, Public Health England and National Institute for Health Research. She has created books for children with eating disorders which are used in school and are very well received. Pooky is a collaborator on the PEACE project, contributing her expertise by experience and helpful video links.

Yasemin Dandil, BSc, MSc, MBPsS

Yasemin is the project manager of the PEACE Pathway at King's College London and is responsible for the development and implementation of the pathway at South London and Maudsley NHS Foundation Trust. Prior to working with people with eating disorders, she worked in various specialist forensic mental health services and holds an MSc in Clinical Forensic Psychology from King's College London. She was also a guest lecturer at the Institute of Psychiatry, Psychology and Neuroscience, King's College London. Yasemin has a passion for supporting patients through their recovery journey. Her work has involved the delivery of evidence-based psychological assessments and interventions to meet individual needs. She is also actively involved in innovative clinical research projects and publications in peer-reviewed journals.

Emma Kinnard, MA, MSc

Emma is a PhD student at King's College London. Her PhD is looking at eating disorder treatment adaptations for minority groups, including autistic people. She has a specific interest in sensory problems experienced by autistic people and their implications for eating disorder maintenance and treatment. Emma published her research in needs assessments of main stakeholders in peer-reviewed scientific journals and developed sensory assessments based on her experimental studies on the topic. She joined Prof. Kate Tchanturia's research team in 2017 from MRC PhD scholarship.

Jason Maldonado-Page, BA, DipSW, MA, MSc

Jason is a systemic psychotherapist, lecturer and social worker. Currently Jason is the senior family and systemic psychotherapist at the national inpatient eating disorders service at the Bethlem Royal Hospital (part of the South London and Maudsley NHS Foundation Trust) and is a lecturer in systemic practice at the Tavistock and Portman. Jason has extensive clinical experience having worked at the Great Ormond Street, the Royal Marsden and most recently the Tavistock and Portman in specialist services in autism, gender identity, oncology and bereavement. In all aspects of Jason's clinical practice and teaching he is drawn to the use of self and how we each make meaning from our lived experiences.

Danilen Nursigadoo, BA, MA, PGDip, MSc

Danilen is an associate family therapist and social worker. He currently works in the Eating Disorders Outpatient and Day Care Teams at Maudsley Hospital and has previously worked at the EDU Inpatient service at the Bethlem Royal Hospital. He is orientated by systemic and attachment-based principles.

Jessica Gomularz, BSc

Jess has specialized in inpatient eating disorders for the past two years; she worked across a number of National Health Service Foundation Trusts in various specialisms before finding a passion for psychoeducation in nutrition and promoting body positivity and positive relationships with food. She worked jointly with the PEACE Pathway team in the Bethlem Royal Hospital national eating disorder service and is currently working at St Ann's Hospital as an inpatient eating disorders specialist dietician.

Dr Claire Baillie, BSc, PsychD

Claire is a chartered counselling psychologist who has worked in the eating disorders field for 20 years. Over the span of her career she has worked with the full range of severity of eating disorders and co-morbidity, and in all parts of the eating disorder service including outpatients, residential care and the inpatient ward at South London and Maudsley NHS Foundation Trust eating disorder national service. Pursuing her qualification at Roehampton University, she completed a doctoral thesis exploring the concept of embodiment in relation to anorexia nervosa. Claire also has experience of providing psychological interventions in primary care for a wide range of conditions. She has worked with individuals with ASD traits or diagnoses both within the specialist eating disorders service and the primary care setting.

Katherine Smith MA, MSc, MBPsS

Katherine is research project manager of the PEACE Pathway at King's College London. She has worked in eating disorders for four years and has recently completed her MSc in Mental Health Studies at King's College London under Prof. Kate Tchanturia's supervision looking at wellbeing on eating disorder wards. Katherine has worked on inpatient eating disorder wards in London delivering group and individual interventions. Katherine's current role, as well as overseeing the management of the PEACE Pathway, is in assessment of ASC in patients service-wide and in developing materials for patients, clinicians and carers.

Dr Hubertus Himmerich, Prof. Dr. Med.

Hubertus is a Clinical Senior Lecturer for Eating Disorders at King's College London and a Consultant Psychiatrist at the Inpatient Eating Disorders Service at the Bethlem Royal Hospital, South London and Maudsley NHS Foundation Trust. He is a QED (Quality Network for Eating Disorders) reviewer and a trained CBT supervisor. He has published more than 140 peer-reviewed journal articles as well as 20 book chapters in English and German.

Madeleine Oakley, BA, MSc, Dip. Psych
carer of the young person with ASD

Madeleine Oakley is a UKCP registered psychotherapist, having trained in psychoanalytic psychotherapy initially, followed by family systemic therapy. Her clinical experience has been in the NHS, working with children and families, in adolescent eating disorders at the Maudsley Hospital, the voluntary sector, working as a clinical supervisor of counsellors in the field of bereavement, and in infertility counselling at University College Hospital. She is the parent of a young man with autism and a learning disability and has been active in parent-led groups aimed at supporting families where a member has autism. Madeleine is the Parent and Carer Champion of the Diversity and Inclusion Network at the IoPPN, King's College London.

Madeleine represents the carer community in the PEACE project.

Dr Amy Harrison, PhD, DClin Psych

Amy is a Clinical Psychologist and Associate Professor in Psychology with specialist experience of working with people with eating disorders and their families. Her research has focused on understanding the social and emotional difficulties experienced by people with eating disorders. As part of the PEACE autism pathway at the Bethlem Royal Hospital, she has worked to support patients with autism and eating disorders and their families and carers.

Kate Williams, BSc, MA, RD

Kate is a dietician with work experience in a variety of specialities, including oncology, diabetes and cardiology. She has worked in primary care and all areas of mental health care. She worked for 30 years in the adult eating disorders service at South London and Maudsley NHS Foundation Trust. As a dietician, her contribution to the team was in helping people towards recovery by developing an understanding of how to work with their own bodies in their own lives to achieve good nutrition and healthy eating for life. She also taught student dieticians at King's College London, and other universities. Kate has sought to understand the broad context of healthcare. Degrees in zoology and the history of medicine provided opportunities to learn about elements of that context. She has developed a particular interest in the relationships, which are often complicated and difficult, that people have with body weight and food, and has worked particularly on developing the application of psychological strategies for changing behaviour, especially in eating disorders and weight management.

Isis McLachlan, BSc

Isis is an occupational therapist in the eating disorders outpatient and day care team at the Maudsley Hospital. As Autism Champion in the PEACE Pathway she promotes assessments and adaptations specifically designed to inform and improve treatment for autistic people in the service.

Jake Copp-Thomas, BSc

Jake is an occupational therapist currently working in the eating disorder day care and outpatient services at the Maudsley Hospital. Jake joined the PEACE Pathway whilst he worked in the inpatient national eating disorder inpatient ward in South London and Maudsley NHS Foundation Trust. Jake has experience working in different mental health departments.

Elaine Smith, BSc, MSc Couns. Psych, Dip. Psychotherapy

Elaine is an accredited member of the British Association of Counsellors and Psychotherapists, British Psychological Society and ACAT. Elaine has worked with Eating Disorders outpatients for the South London and Maudsley NHS Foundation Trust for 18 years. Prior to working with eating disorders, she was Director for Alcohol Services in Bromley. Her interest in eating disorders began when many patients had a dual diagnosis of eating disorders and alcohol problems. Elaine developed an interest in autism spectrum disorders (ASD) when she began working with patients with diagnosed ASD and realized there were strong similarities with anorexia nervosa and recognized that some were undiagnosed ASD.

James Adamson, MSc, MBPsS

James is a clinical researcher and currently trainee clinical psychologist at UCL. He was involved in the PEACE Pathway project (as a project manager). James was a finalist for the National Institute for Health Research (NIHR) rising star award and has been the lead researcher on multiple funded studies within eating disorder settings. James holds an MSc in Mental Health Studies and is a member of the British Psychological Society.

Danielle Glennon MA, BSc, RMN, MBACP

Danielle is clinical lead and senior psychotherapist for outpatient and day care services in South London and Maudsley NHS Foundation Trust Eating Disorders Service and has her own private practice in Kings Langley, Hertfordshire. Danielle trained in humanistic psychotherapy and has since gone on to train as family therapy practitioner, and schema therapist. She works within various therapeutic models. She is an accredited member of the British Association of Counsellors and Psychotherapists, and the British Psychological Society, and a registered Psychiatric Nurse with the Nursing and Midwifery Council.

Dr Anna Burhouse, M.Psych.Obs., M.Psych. Psych., MSc, Leading for Improvement Health Foundation Improvement Fellow

Anna is Director of Quality Development at Northumbria Healthcare NHS Foundation Trust. She supports NHS teams across the UK to lead complex quality improvement work and to scale and spread innovations. Anna provides improvement coaching, training, board and executive development and leadership of improvement programmes. Anna is a Health Foundation Improvement Fellow, Ashridge Business School alumna in Leadership for Improvement and an Honorary Senior Research Fellow at the University of Bath Centre for Healthcare Innovation and Improvement and the University of West of England. Anna is chair of the Engagement and Involvement Advisory Board at THIS Institute at the University of Cambridge. Alongside her work in improvement Anna maintains her clinical practice as a Consultant Child and Adolescent Psychotherapist in the NHS where she has almost

30 years' experience of working with young people to innovate new approaches to health and social care. Anna is coach of the PEACE project helping the team to implement this work in real clinical setting and help to upscale this project nationally.

Subject Index

adapting the care
  after autism screening
    199–200, 204–5
  changing the
    environment
    111–2, 182–4,
    236–7, 247–8
  for patient-centred
    treatment 208
  vs. 'one size fits all'
    45–6, 182, 205,
    208, 246
adjusting to outside
  life 39–40
admissions
  clinical guidelines 20
  duration of 20, 185–6
  self-discharge from 83
  welcome pack 239,
    248–50
Adolescent/Adult Sensory
  Profile 164–5
anaemia 135–6
animal metaphors 99–101
anxiety
  common in ASD 245
  provoked by eating
    123–4
assessment
  in autism context
    240–2
  case study (Milly) 52–4
  feedback of results
    203–4
  routine autism
    199–200, 239

Assessment of Self-
  Regulation 166
Autism Diagnostic
  Observation
  Schedule (ADOS-2)
  52, 78, 202–3, 210
'Autism parents' (lack of
  support for) 21–2, 91
Autism Spectrum
  Quotient (AQ-10)
  78, 79, 200–1
autistic burnout 40–1
avoidant restrictive food
  intake disorder
  (ARFID) 161

Bell Curve 209, 216
'big picture' thinking
  79, 242
'Big Scary Chasm' 214
blame (felt by
  families) 112
bloating 142
Brixton Spatial
  Anticipation
  Test 53, 72
burnout 40–1

camouflaging
  (mimicking) 16,
  23, 192, 195, 203
Caregiver Questionnaire
  for Interoceptive
  Awareness 166

carers
  definition 97–8
  emotional over-
    involvement 94
  Expressed Emotion
    within family
    systems 90–1,
    94–5
  forum for 95–6
  guilt of 115, 117
  identity as 89
  lack of support for
    21–2, 91
  lowering Expressed
    Emotion of 95–6
  needs of 92–3, 98
  Pathway handbook
    102–5
  self-care 117
  workshop for 98–102
case formulation 55–7
case study (Milly)
  assessments 52–4
  case formulation 55–7
  cognitive behavioural
    therapy (CBT)
    63–7
  Cognitive remediation
    therapy (CRT)
    58–63
  complicating factors 68
  diagrammatic
    snapshot 55, 57
  dietetic feedback 54–5
  family history 51–2
  follow-up 68–70

personal history 51
presentation 50–1
sensory assessment 54
systemic family therapy
    69–70, 113–7
treatment implications
    72
what was learned 71–2
cause and effect
    (unpicking) 18, 19
change see quality
    improvement (QI)
choking (perceived
    risk of) 128
clinician fatigue 117–8
co-morbidity
    clinicians' approaches
        to 20–2
    denied by professional
        94
    highly complex 43–4
    prevalence of 18–9
    women 15–6, 192–4
cognitive analytic therapy
    (CAT) 196–7
cognitive behavioural
    therapy (CBT) 63–7
cognitive remediation
    and emotion skills
    training (CREST)
    81–3, 242–3
cognitive remediation
    therapy (CRT)
    58–63, 79–81, 84
communication
    conversations (on the
        ward) 251–7
    language use 187–8
    positive 188–9
'complex picture
    task' 79, 80
constipation 142
conversations (on the
    ward) 251–7

decluttering 237
decor 236–7, 247–8
dehydration 135

Detail and Flexibility
    Questionnaire
    (DFlex) 53, 72
diagnosis
    difficulty getting 198
    helpfulness of 16,
        23–4, 37
    late 204
diagrammatic
    snapshot 55, 57
dialectical behaviour
    therapy (DBT) 38
dissociative identity
    disorder 43
dual diagnosis see
    co-morbidity
duration of treatment
    20, 185–6

'early adopters' 216
Early Bird Programme 91
eating difficulties 18
Eating Disorder
    Examination
    Questionnaire
    (EDE-Q) 53, 72
electrolyte abnormalities
    135
emotion vocabulary 82
emotional expression 82
endings 63, 190
engagement with
    patient 185, 197
environment (making
    adjustments to)
    111–2, 182–4,
    236–7, 247–8
evidence into practice
    213–7
exhaustion (of
    families) 117
Experience Based
    Co-Design
    (EBCD) 224–5
Expressed Emotion (EE)
    overview 90–1
    strategies to lower 95–6

within family
    systems 94–5
    expression of emotion 82
    see also Expressed
        Emotion (EE)

failure as 'First Attempt
    in Learning' 227
familiarity (need for) 127
families
    ASD characteristics
        in 98, 194
    exhaustion of 117
    feeling blamed 112
    see also carers
feedback of assessment
    results 203–4
First episode Rapid Early
    intervention for
    Eating Disorders
    (FREED) 208
flexibility
    of care plans 45
    enhancing 59, 70,
        80–1, 172–4, 242
fluid intake 135, 141
food chaining 149–50
food variety 142–3,
    148–51
fullness (reduced
    sensitivity to) 128

gender differences
    AN 16–7
    ASD 16
genograms 112–5
goals
    setting 138, 139–40,
        172
    SMART 80
group therapy 38, 71
guilt (of carers) 115, 117
gut bacteria 129, 142

hearing (sensory
    sensitivity) 38,
    161, 182, 236

huddles 211–2, 232–3
hunger (reduced
    sensitivity to) 128
hypersensitivity 160,
    161–3, 169, 174–6
hyposensitivity 160

identity, self- 89
individual differences 205
interoception (sensory
    sensitivity)
    162, 166–7
Interoceptive Awareness
    Interview 166

labels
    care around
        additional 85
    helpfulness of 16,
        23–4, 37
language
    terminology 15,
        23, 110, 185
    use 187–8
late ASD diagnosis 204
leaflet (Carers'
    Pathway) 102–5
learning organizations
    218–9
logos 233

male presentation 78
masking 16, 23, 192,
    195, 203
meal patterns 143
medical stabilization
    anaemia 135–6
    electrolyte
        abnormalities 135
    fluid intake 135, 141
    goals for 139–41
    refeeding syndrome
        134–5, 140–1
meetings, team 212
menu (PEACE) 237–8
mimicking 16, 23,
    192, 195, 203

mind-maps 80–1
mini teams 211
modifying treatment see
    adapting the care
motivational ruler 54, 72

Narrative model 70
noise (sensory sensitivity)
    38, 161, 182, 236
nutritional recovery
    goals for 141–4
    overview of 136

obsessive-compulsive
    disorder (OCD) 76
occupational therapy
    171–7
odour (sensory
    sensitivity) 161, 183
'one size fits all'
    approach 45–6,
    182, 205, 208, 246
'optimal positive to
    negative emotions
    ratio task' 81
outcome statistics 207–8
overlapping
    difficulties 246

pathway see PEACE
    Pathway
patient-centred
    treatment 208
    see also adapting
        the care
PEACE menu 237–8
PEACE Pathway
    'buy in'/support
        for 210–1
    champions of
        209–10, 233
    embedding 209
    huddles 211–2, 232–3
    mini teams in 211
    overview of 240–3
    team meetings 212
    training 235

peer acceptance 44
physical discomfort (from
    eating) 129, 142
pink flamingo
    metaphor 100–1
Plan, Do, Study, Act
    (PDSA) cycle 225–6
portion size 143–4
positive communication
    188–9
positive thinking 189–90
'positive to negative
    emotions ratio
    task' 81
predictability (need
    for) 127
proprioception (sensory
    sensitivity) 163
psychotherapy file (in
    CAT) 196–7

qualitative interviews
    20–3
quality improvement (QI)
    agreeing purpose
        224–5
    definition 220
    'Developing People,
        Improving
        Care' 221
    failure as 'First Attempt
        in Learning' 227
    improvement
        groups 223–4
    measurement/
        evaluation
        of 226–7
    'Model of
        Improvement' 221
    national frameworks
        for 221
    overview of 217–21
    Plan, Do, Study,
        Act (PDSA)
        cycle 225–6
    relational components
        223

'Shared Commitment
to Quality' 221
six dimensions for
healthcare 219–20
sustainability of 227–8
tools 222
training in 222
questioning style 188

range of food (allowing
restricted) 38
rapport 185, 197
recovery
agreeing aims for 137–8
back-up meal plan 147
case example 145
consolidating 154–6
expectations of 40
pressure of concept
of 116
stages of 134–7
supporting changes
in eating 146–7
see also medical
stabilization;
nutritional
recovery;
social eating
redecoration 236–7,
247–8
refeeding syndrome
134–5, 140–1
referral pathway 105–6
regularity of time/
location 184
relapse 136–7, 155–6
restricted range of food
(allowing) 38
Rey-Osterrieth
Complex Figure
(ROCF) 53, 72
rigidity 172–4, 193
routine autism screening
199–200, 239
rules 130–1

screening for autism
Adam's story 78–9

Autism Diagnostic
Observation
Schedule (ADOS)
52, 78, 202–3, 210
Autism Quotient 200–1
routine 199–200, 239
Social Responsiveness
Scale (SRS-
2) 201–2
self-care 40–1, 84, 117
self-help strategies
248–50
self-identity 89
Self-Regulation,
Assessment of 166
sensory sensitivities
Adolescent/Adult
Sensory Profile
164–5
as a diagnostic
criterion 160
helpful strategies 161–3
hypersensitivity 160,
161–3, 169, 174–6
hyposensitivity 160
interoception 162,
166–7
noise 38, 161, 182, 236
overview of 159–60
sensory motor
preference
checklist 165–6
sensory summary
scales 167–70
smell 161, 183
taste 162
touch 162
vestibular 163
vision 162, 182
sequential oral sensory
approach 150
signs (used in systemic
family therapy)
115–6
similarities between
ASD and AN 17
SMART goals 80
smell (sensory sensitivity)
161, 183

social anxiety disorder
(SAD) 26–31
social eating
anxiety around 126
as goal of recovery 137
goals for 147–8
increasing variety
148–51
unacceptable
behaviours with
food 152–4
unexpected eating 152
in unfamiliar settings
150–1
social media 125
Social Responsiveness
Scale (SRS-2) 201–2
staff welcome pack 239
starvation (exacerbating
autism symptoms) 39
statistical process
control (SPC) 225
Structural model 70
substitutions (in
meals) 39
support
carers' forum 95–6
lack of for carers
21–2, 91
Swedish Eating
Assessment for
Autism Spectrum
Disorders 125
systemic family therapy
case study (Milly)
69–70, 113–7
genograms in 112–5
Narrative model 70
overview of 110–1
signs used in 115–6
'sparkling moments'
in 116
Structural model 70

tailoring treatment see
adapting the care
taste (sensory
sensitivity) 162

team meetings 212
terminology 15, 23,
    110, 185
thinking
    disordered 126, 130
    entrenched habits 125
timekeeping 39
timescale 20, 185–6
touch (sensory
    sensitivity) 162

training
    ASD assessment 234–5
    PEACE Pathway 235
    quality improvement
        (QI) 222

variety (expanding)
    142–3, 148–51
vestibular (sensory
    sensitivity) 163

vision (sensory
    sensitivity) 162, 182
visual representations
    186–7
vitamin/mineral
    supplements 136, 141

weight gain 144
welcome pack 239,
    248–50

Author Index

Adamson, J. 91, 92, 94, 199
Albury, D. 216
Alderwick, H. 217
Allison, C. 200
Amaral, S. 129
Amaresha, A.C. 91
American Psychiatric Association (APA) 26, 160
Andersen, T. 69
Anderson, H. 111
Ariely, D. 227
Ashton-Smith, J. 16
Aswathy, A. 128
Auyeung, B. 200

Baker, A. 219
Baker, L. 110
Balas, E. 214
Baron-Cohen, S. 16, 19, 54, 200
Batalden, P.B. 220
Bate, P. 216
Baum, S. 110
Bauman, L.J. 216
Beck, A. 50, 63
Beglin, S.J. 53, 72
Benson, J. 150
Bird, G. 159
Blainey, S.H. 30
Booth, T. 200
Boren, S. 214
Brewer, R. 159
Bromley, J. 98

Brownlow, C. 128
Buchholz, A. 27
Bulik, C.M. 27
Burgess, P.W. 53
Burr, V. 109
Burrell, L. 137

Cao, X. 129
Cardi, V. 27
Constantino, J.N. 201
Cook, R. 159
Cox, S. 150
Crane, A. 110

Davidoff, F. 220
Deming, W.E. 217

Eisler, I. 110
Emanuelli, F. 27
Epston, D. 70, 110, 114

Fairburn, C.G. 53, 72
Feigenbaum, A.V. 217
Fiene, L. 128
Fishbein, M. 113, 148, 150
Fishman, H.C. 110, 113
Fraker, C. 148, 150

Gast, F. 131
Gerson, R. 69, 112, 113
Godart, N.T. 27
Goddard, E. 27
Godfrey, J. 223

Goolishian, H. 111
Gould, J. 15
Grandin, T. 186
Grant, B.F. 26
Grant, J. 214
Green, L. 214
Greenhalgh, T. 215
Gruber, C.P. 201

Hadigan, C. 136
Halim, A.T. 28
Hardy, K.V. 112
Hare, D. 98
Harrison, A. 27, 189, 201
Hatem, S. 126
Hayley, J. 110
Helps, S. 111
Hinrichsen, H. 27
Hoekstra, R. 54
Holttum, S. 53
Horder, J. 123, 127
Horton, T. 215, 216, 221
Howarth, E. 216
Huas, C. 27
Hull, L. 23
Hummel, T. 54
Hunt, K. 17
Hus, V. 52, 78

Illingworth, J. 215
Institute of Healthcare 221
Ireys, H.T. 216
Ishikawa, K. 217

Jaquess, D. 137
Johnson, C. 124, 131
Jones, B. 221
Juran, J. 217

Karlsson, L. 125
Kaye, W.H. 27
Kerr-Gaffney, J. 27, 201
Kessler, R.C. 26
Kinnaird, E. 20, 49, 50,
    102, 125, 131, 160
Knightsmith, P. 31, 204
Kuipers, E. 94
Kyriacou, O. 98

Lai, M.-C. 16
Lam, D. 94
Lang, K. 53
Langley, G.J. 219, 222
Larsson, E. 199
Laszloffy, T.A. 112
Lázaro, L. 30
Le Grange, D. 110
Ledford, J. 131
Leff, J.P. 90, 94
Li, Q. 129
Linehan, M.M. 38
Lock, J. 110
Lopez, C. 73
Lord, C. 52, 78, 202
Lounes, N. 53
Lynggaard, H. 111

Macdonald, P. 99
McElhanon, B. 129
McGoldrick, M. 69,
    112, 113
Madanes, C. 110
Maddox, B.B. 28, 30
Magill-Evans, J. 124
Mandy, W. 23
Manoharan, A. 128
Manoharan, A. 128
Marí-Bauset, S. 131
Marlin, E. 112
Mason, B. 214
Mattar, L. 27

Minuchin, S. 70, 110, 113
Miyazaki, Y. 28
Mochon, D. 227
Montoya, P. 126
Moore, G.A. 214
Mueller, C. 54

Nadon, G. 124, 127, 128
NHS Improvement
    221, 225
NICE (National Institute
    for Health and Care
    Excellence) 20, 23, 29
Nicholls, D. 134
Norton, C. 20
Norton, M.I. 227

O'Connor, G. 134
Okuda, T. 242
Osterrieth, P.A. 53
Ostrovsky, N.W. 27

Panek, R. 186
Parracho, H. 129
Petrides, K.V. 23
Petry, S. 113
Pollatos, O. 128

Raisanen, U. 17
Rapee, R.M. 26
Råstam, M. 125
Rempel, G. 124
Richdale, A.L. 28
Riquelme, I. 126, 129
Roberts, M.E. 53
Rogers, E.M. 209, 216
Rogers, L. 124
Rosman, B.L. 110

Satir, V. 243
Sawaoka, T. 27
Schmidt, U. 50, 98, 99
Sedgewick, F. 52, 74, 203
Selvini, M.P. 70
Shallice, T. 53
Sharp, W. 137, 148

Sheffield, A. 27
Smith, G. 110
Spain, D. 27, 28, 30
Spek, A. 123
Spence, S.H. 26
Stahl, D. 73
Stein, R.E. 216
Steinhausen, H.C. 208
Stewart, C. 102
Strati, F. 129
Sundseth Ross, E.
    148, 150
Swinbourne, J. 27

Tavassoli, T. 54, 123, 127
Tchanturia, K. 20, 27, 49,
    50, 52, 53, 71, 73, 79,
    81, 102, 125, 186,
    189, 199, 200, 201
Tick, B. 98
Toomey, K.A. 148, 150
Treasure, J. 27, 50,
    98, 99, 110
Twachtman-Reilly, J. 128

Uljarević, M. 28

Vaillancourt, K. 30
van Gerko, K. 27
Vaughn, C. 90
Venkatasubrama-
    nian, G. 91

Walbert, L. 148, 150
Waller, G. 27
Warburton, W. 215, 221
Weber, S. 208
Wentz, E. 125
Westwood, H. 18
White, M. 69, 70, 110, 114
White, S.W. 28
Wiedemann, G. 95
Wittgenstein, L. 110
Wratschko, K. 214

Zebrowsli, P. 129